THE HOLY EPISTLE TO THE

Galatians

SERMONS ON A MESSIANIC JEWISH APPROACH

D. THOMAS LANCASTER

THE HOLY EPISTLE TO THE
Galatians

SERMONS ON A MESSIANIC JEWISH APPROACH

D. THOMAS LANCASTER

Second Edition 2014
Printed in the United States of America

ISBN Softcover: 978-1-892124-97-5

Cover Design: Joel Powell

Quantity discounts are available on bulk purchases of this book for educational, fundraising, or event purposes. Special versions or book excerpts to fit specific needs are available from First Fruits of Zion. For more information, contact www.ffoz.org/contact.

First Fruits of Zion

Israel / United States / Canada

PO Box 649, Marshfield, Missouri 65706–0649 USA
Phone (417) 468–2741, www.ffoz.org

Comments and questions: www.ffoz.org/contact

About the Cover

Rembrandt (Rembrandt Harmenszoon van Rijn), a famous seventeenth-century Dutch painter, was considered one of the greatest painters in European art history. Rembrandt was famous for portraits of his contemporaries, self-portraits, and illustrations of scenes from the Bible. His impressions for many of his works came from his observations of Amsterdam's Jewish population. Our cover is a replica of Rembrandt's "Apostle Paul" by Tigran Ghulyan (artmaestro.com). The original is in the National Gallery of Art in Washington, D.C.

To Maria

To Our Children

To Beth Immanuel

CONTENTS

INTRODUCTION

In the Holy Epistle to the Galatians, the Apostle Paul argues against Gentile believers in Yeshua (Jesus) of Nazareth undergoing conversion to become Jewish. Paul maintained that Gentile believers attained salvation and inherited the blessings promised to Abraham through faith, not conversion.

This book consists of a collection of sermons based on the Epistle to the Galatians. I originally prepared and delivered this series of sermons to my community of faith, Beth Immanuel, a Messianic Sabbath Fellowship in Hudson, Wisconsin, in the year 2008. In preparing for the sermons, I attempted to interface with some of the more recent Pauline scholarship on the epistle, but I did not do so in a systematic or exhaustive fashion. This book should not be considered a complete commentary on Galatians or an academic analysis of Pauline scholarship. This is merely a collection of sermons intended for Christians, Messianic Jews, and anyone curious about a Messianic Jewish perspective on Galatians.

The Apostle Peter said that the writings of "our beloved brother Paul" contain "some things hard to understand." If that was true in Peter's day, how much more so today. Paul was a prodigy educated in the most elite schools of Pharisaism. He wrote and thought from that Jewish background. Unfortunately, that makes several key passages of his work almost incomprehensible to readers unfamiliar with rabbinic literature. I invite Christians to use this book as an opportunity to study Paul's epistle to the Galatians from a Jewish perspective.

The Messianic Jewish movement still struggles with understanding Paul in relationship to the Torah and the Jewish people. Seeing Paul as the apostle to the Gentiles clarifies many problematic passages and reconciles Paul with Yeshua, the other apostles, and the rest of Judaism. I invite Messianic Jewish believers to use this book as an opportunity to come to terms with Paul and take hold of your own unique calling as Jewish believers.

This book will be especially pertinent to readers who identify themselves and their expression of faith somewhere between traditional Christianity and Messianic Judaism. Paul wrote his epistle to people whom we might today call "Messianic Gentiles." For those of you occupying that religious no-man's land, I invite you to use this study of Galatians as an opportunity to find your own unique and noble identity as children of Abraham by faith and to take hold of the Torah as it applies to the God-fearing Gentile believer.

The reader of Galatians (and the reader of these sermons) must always keep in mind that Paul's world is not our world, and if Paul were to write an epistle to us today, he would certainly address other concerns than those he addressed in Galatians. In Paul's day, the future of Gentile believers in Yeshua of Nazareth seemed tenuous and uncertain. The vast majority of people confessing faith in Yeshua as the Jewish Messiah were of course Jews. The Gentile believers in Paul's communities were an anomaly, not the norm. Many Jewish believers in Yeshua looked askance at the Gentiles, and others compelled them to undergo conversion. In those days, conversion did not require renouncing Yeshua. The Gentile believers could convert under the auspices of apostolic authority. Many did. Paul feared that his Gentile disciples were likely to vanish as they assimilated into the Jewish community.

Paul believed that the gospel message had universal implications for all human beings, but if all Gentile believers underwent conversion and became Jewish (albeit Jewish believers in Yeshua), no Gentile believers would remain to fulfill that universal destiny. As he saw Gentile believers receiving circumcision and undergoing conversion, he began to protect the Gentile believers as if they were an endangered species.

The situation today has dramatically reversed. Today Jewish disciples of Yeshua are the endangered species, not Gentile believers. If Paul wrote to us today, his letters would reflect that shift in demographics. His argument against conversion would not be so pronounced; he might not even bring it up at all.

The reader of Paul's epistles, and especially his epistle to the Galatians, must keep all of this in mind. Therefore, one should not read Galatians—or even this book about Galatians—and come to the conclusion that conversion to Judaism is anathema. In today's world, there are some compelling reasons why a Gentile disciple of Yeshua might want to undergo a conversion (albeit through Messianic Jewish authorities). For example, the Gentile spouse in an intermarried couple might consider conversion. Children of mixed marriages or people with mixed, Jewish ancestry might also want to undergo conversion to shore up their Jewish identity. People with concerns of this nature or similar questions about conversion may want to consult with a Messianic rabbi.

The reader of Paul's epistles should keep in mind that Paul was himself Jewish, as were all the apostles. The "Christianity" of Paul's day functioned as a subset of Judaism, not as a competing religion. Paul's seemingly anti-Jewish or anti-Law rhetoric needs to be understood as internal dialogue within Yeshua-believing Judaism of his day. More than that, the reader of Paul's epistles must keep in mind that Paul wrote like a rabbi, employing Jewish hermeneutics, rabbinic-type logic, and ideas current in Jewish tradition of his day. Hopefully, this book will assist Paul's readers by helping them understand Paul's words from within Judaism.

I want to extend my thanks to my colleagues Aaron Eby, Toby Janicki, and Boaz Michael for encouraging me to publish this collection of sermons, and I would like to thank the whole team at First Fruits of Zion for making that possible. I would also like to thank the community of Beth Immanuel for patiently enduring some thirty sermons from the book of Galatians. Thanks to my brother Steven Lancaster for providing me with feedback on the ideas. Special thanks to Pierre Porter for his comments and suggestions on the manuscript and to Robert Morris for the hard work of cleaning up sermon notes and transcribing audio recordings.

To every brother and sister in the Master who studies the Holy Epistle to the Galatians along with me, may you be blessed with grace and peace from God our Father and the Master Yeshua the Messiah who gave himself for our sins so that he might rescue us from this present evil age, according to the will of our God and Father, to whom be the glory forevermore.

THE WRITINGS OF OUR BELOVED BROTHER PAUL

Therefore, beloved, since you are waiting for these, be diligent to be found by him without spot or blemish, and at peace. And count the patience of our Lord as salvation, just as our beloved brother Paul also wrote to you according to the wisdom given him, as he does in all his letters when he speaks in them of these matters. There are some things in them that are hard to understand, which the ignorant and unstable twist to their own destruction, as they do the other Scriptures.

You therefore, beloved, knowing this beforehand, take care that you are not carried away with the error of lawless people and lose your own stability. But grow in the grace and knowledge of our Lord and Savior Jesus Christ. To him be the glory both now and to the day of eternity. Amen. (2 Peter 3:14–18)

Galatians

CHAPTER ONE

LETTER TO THE GOD-FEARERS
(GALATIANS 1:1–5)

An introduction of Paul's epistle to
the Galatians, identifying the author,
the addressees, and the situation that
occasioned its composition.

T he Apostle Peter says that Paul's letters contain some things
that are hard to understand, which lawless people twist, as
they do the rest of the Scriptures. The Holy Epistle of Paul to the
Galatians falls into this category.

Bible readers generally understand Galatians as Paul's disserta-
tion against the law and against Judaism. For that reason, Messianic
Jews often hear the question, "Have you read Galatians?" Well-
meaning Christian friends pose this question under the assumption
that, if a person had read Galatians, whether he be Jew or Gentile, he
certainly would not be attempting to keep the law or practice some
form of Judaism. The Epistle to the Galatians provides Christian
theology with its best argument against Torah.

For these reasons, the study of the Epistle to the Galatians
should be a major concern for those who practice Messianic Judaism, both Jewish believers and Gentiles as well. Our interpretation
of this epistle is critically important; more than any other book of
the New Testament, our understanding of Galatians defines the
line between Messianic Judaism and greater Christianity. Unfortunately, in my experience at least, the epistle has not received serious
attention in the Messianic movement, at least not on a popular

level. Worse yet, many Messianic believers with whom I discuss it have dismissive answers which oversimplify the message of Galatians. One hears them say, "Paul was only warning about legalism," or "It's just about the Oral Law," or "Paul was just arguing against the man-made tradition of ritual conversion." Others say, "I just don't understand Paul," and still others say, "I wish Galatians wasn't in the Bible." Statements like these reveal that Messianic believers have a serious problem with the Epistle to the Galatians.

Who, When, to Whom, and Why

Before we begin studying the Holy Epistle to the Galatians, we need to learn a little bit about the epistle's context. Every time we start to read a piece of biblical literature, we ought to understand who wrote it, when he wrote it, to whom he wrote it, and why he wrote it: who, when, to whom, and why.

The "who" and the "to whom" are simple because the salutation contains all of that information:

> Paul, an apostle—not from men nor through man, but through Jesus Christ and God the Father, who raised him from the dead—and all the brothers who are with me, to the churches of Galatia: Grace to you and peace from God our Father and the Lord Jesus Christ, who gave himself for our sins to deliver us from the present evil age, according to the will of our God and Father, to whom be the glory forever and ever. Amen. (Galatians 1:1–5)

Paul the Apostle to the Gentiles

Paul identifies himself as an apostle, not from men nor through man. The word "apostle" simply means "an agent sent to accomplish a task." In Hebrew, the word for "apostle" is *shaliach*, a "sent one." In Judaism, a man can send a *shaliach* out on a mission for him to represent him and accomplish a task on his behalf. For example, the Sanhedrin of the first century regularly sent out "apostles" on missions to the Jewish world living in the Diaspora. In those days, as today, more Jewish people lived outside the land of Israel than inside the land. Jewish communities were spread across the ancient world, widely dispersed, and this dispersion of Jews living outside of the land of Israel is what we mean by the word "Diaspora." Every major city in the Roman Empire, it seems, had a Jewish quarter with one or more synagogues—often several synagogues. The Roman government recognized Judaism as a legal religion, which means that Jews had state protection guaranteeing their freedom to practice their religion. Practically speaking, this meant that if you were Jewish, you were exempt from certain civic functions, such as worshipping in Roman temples. If you were not Jewish and refused to participate in the worship of the gods or the Roman emperor, you could potentially be arrested and tried for the crime of atheism. In those days, an "atheist" was someone who did not believe in the Roman pantheon.

Paul went as an apostle sent out to the Diaspora, but he did not go as one sent by the Sanhedrin or even by the other apostles. The risen Messiah himself, whom Paul had encountered in a series of mystical visions, sent him. Paul encountered him first on the road to Damascus and again later while praying in the Temple in Jerusalem when Yeshua appeared to him and said, "Go, I am sending you to the Gentiles."

For that reason Paul refers to himself as the apostle (the sent one) of Yeshua the Messiah to the Gentiles.

The Brothers at Antioch

Paul indicates in the salutation that this epistle comes from him and, he says, from "all the brothers with me." Who were the brothers with Paul? Paul based his operations in the city of Antioch, a large, ancient city with a substantial Jewish community and more than a dozen synagogues. In Antioch, the believers were first called *Christianoi* (Acts 11:26), which became the Greek name for the sect. "Christians" was not a pejorative name; rather, that was simply the Greek name of their particular sect of Judaism.

In those days each synagogue had a name like "Synagogue of the Hebrews," "Synagogue of the Freedmen," or something to denote their particular sect. Sociologist, historian, and scholar Magnus Zetterholm, in his book *The Formation of Christianity in Antioch*, suggests that originally our synagogue in Antioch was called the

Synagogue of the *Christianoi*, i.e., the Synagogue of the Christians—or to put it in our English, the Synagogue of the Messianics.[1]

The synagogue at which Paul worshipped in Antioch, perhaps a place called the "Synagogue of the Christians," served a congregation and community of both Jewish and Gentile believers. The book of Acts offers a quick glimpse of the community and the ordination of Paul and Barnabas for apostolic work:

> Now there were in the church at Antioch prophets and teachers, Barnabas, Simeon who was called Niger, Lucius of Cyrene, Manaen a member of the court of Herod the tetrarch, and Saul. While they were worshiping the Lord and fasting, the Holy Spirit said, "Set apart for me Barnabas and Saul for the work to which I have called them." Then after fasting and praying they laid their hands on them and sent them off. (Acts 13:1–3)

The men with Paul in Antioch included Barnabas (Yosef bar Naba), one of the apostles from the earliest days of the Yeshua movement; Manaen, once a member of Herod Antipas' court and someone who had perhaps known Yeshua personally; and also (according to a textual variant in Acts 11) Luke the physician, Paul's travelling companion and the author of the Gospel of Luke and Acts of the Apostles. These were a few of the men with Paul when he said "all the brothers who are with me."

Those brothers sent Paul and Barnabas off on *shlichut*, that is, they sent them out as apostles. If we were to follow Paul and Barnabas on their journey in Acts 13, we would leave Antioch with them and eventually end up in another important city, also named Antioch, in the territory known as Galatia. (For the sake of clarity, we refer to the Antioch in Galatia as Pisidian Antioch.)

---

[1] Magnus Zetterholm, *The Formation of Christianity in Antioch: A Social-Scientific Approach to the Separation Between Judaism and Christianity* (London: Routledge Tayor & Francis Group, 2005), 37–38; D. Thomas Lancaster, *Grafted In: Israel, Gentiles, and the Mystery of the Gospel* (Marshfield, MO: First Fruits of Zion, 2009), 149.

From Antioch to Antioch

> Now Paul and his companions set sail from Paphos and came to Perga in Pamphylia. And John left them and returned to Jerusalem. (Acts 13:13)

Paul, Barnabas, and young John Mark left Antioch on the eastern Mediterranean seaboard and spent some time ministering on the nearby island of Cyprus. We pick up the story just as they leave Cyprus. They set sail from Paphos and made for the mainland. Their ship entered the mouth of the Cestrus River, a generous and navigable river which flowed out of the Taurus Mountains. They sailed seven miles upstream to the river-harbor city of Perga, a beautiful Greek metropolis with all the amenities. The city of Perga sat atop a small, flat hill, nestled in a lush and well-watered valley in the territory of Pamphylia.

At Perga, John Mark left Paul and Barnabas. Some have suggested that the rigors of the journey were too much for him, but in truth, they had as yet not faced any great rigors. More likely, an interpersonal conflict between Paul and John Mark erupted. From reading Paul's epistles, one gets the impression that Paul might have been testy at times.

Paul and Barnabas set out north from Perga, following the Cestrus River into the Taurus Mountains. "They went on from Perga and came to Antioch in Pisidia" (Acts 13:14). They travelled nearly one hundred miles through the hills and mountains before arriving at the Galatian/Pisidian city of Pisidian Antioch. Though the book of Acts mentions nothing of the one-hundred-mile journey, Paul's own recollections suggest a long and arduous trek. Since ancient times, bandits and marauding tribes have haunted the routes through the Taurus Mountains. Although the Roman Peace (*Pax Romana*) had subdued the openly lawless tribes, the hills and the mountain passes along the Cestrus River remained treacherous. Regarding his adventures in passing through that territory, Paul said in 2 Corinthians 11:26, "I have been on frequent journeys, in danger from rivers, danger from robbers."

A debilitating illness further hindered Paul's journey through the mountains. Apparently when they arrived in Antioch in Pisidia-Galatia, Paul was sick and needed convalescence. In Galatians 4 he says, "You know it was because of a bodily ailment that I preached the gospel to you at first, and though my condition was a trial to you, you did not scorn or despise me, but received me as an angel of God, as Christ Jesus" (Galatians 4:13–14).

Three Types of Congregants

On the Sabbath, the two weary travelers found their way to the synagogue where they joined the congregation in the morning service. "They came to Antioch in Pisidia. And on the Sabbath day they went into the synagogue and sat down" (Acts 13:14). After the reading from the Torah and the *haftarah* (the reading from the Prophets), the elders of the synagogue encouraged the visitors to offer a few words of teaching, a *derashah*. "Brothers," they said, "If you have any word of encouragement for the people, say it" (Acts 13:15).

As Paul began his synopsis of the gospel, he said, "Brothers, sons of the family of Abraham, and those among you who fear God, to us has been sent the message of this salvation" (Acts 13:26). The threefold address refers to the three types of people one might find in any Diaspora synagogue of the first century. To make any sense at all out of Paul's epistle to the Galatians, one must differentiate between these three groups.[2]

1. **"Brothers" are Jews**: In the context of the Pisidian-Antioch synagogue, Paul's brothers are his fellow Jews. He means to refer to those who are legally Jewish, that is born Jewish as physical descendants of Abraham, Isaac, and Jacob through a Jewish mother.[3] In the first century, the term "Jew" did not specifically mean someone from the tribe of Judah. The term applied to all Israelites with legal standing in the Jewish community. Thus, Paul referred to himself as Jewish, though he was actually a Benjamite. Paul's brothers are the Jewish people.

---

[2] The following material also appears in Lancaster, *Grafted In: Israel, Gentiles, and the Mystery of the Gospel*, 17–20.

[3] Jewishness today is determined by maternal descent. Scholars are uncertain about whether or not the same standard applied in Paul's day.

2. **"Sons of Abraham" are Proselytes**: The second
type of congregant Paul found in the Pisidian-
Antioch synagogue was the proselyte. Proselytes
were those non-Jews who had, for one reason or
another, made a formal conversion to Judaism,
thus becoming legally Jewish. According to the
Jewish law, they were no longer regarded as
Gentiles, but through the rituals of circumcision
and immersion (and sacrifice when possible),
they had taken on the religious and legal status of
Israel. The Jewish community referred to them as
"sons and daughters of Abraham." This conversion
process was based upon biblical texts which speak
about the stranger who undergoes circumcision
as a member of Abraham's household (Genesis 17)
or as a sojourner who desires to eat of the Passover
sacrifice (Exodus 12). In the days of the apostles,
the biblical "stranger who dwells among you" was
understood by the Jewish world to refer primarily
(though not exclusively) to the formal, legal
proselyte to Judaism.

3. **"God-fearing Gentiles" are Non-Jews**: The third
type of congregant Paul addressed that day in the
Pisidian-Antioch synagogue was the God-fearing
Gentile. The term "God-fearing Gentiles" describes
non-Jews who, for some reason or another, were
attracted to Judaism. They worshipped in the
synagogue with Jewish people and proselytes, but
chose not to undergo the ritual of conversion. They
were not exactly pagans anymore, but they were
not Jews either. While the synagogue community
may have tolerated them and even appreciated
their financial contributions to the community (as
with the centurions in Luke 7 and Acts 10), they did
not regard them as Jewish. The God-Fearers did not
enjoy the rights and privileges of the Jewish people,
nor did they have responsibilities within Judaism.

As Paul discoursed on the gospel, he included all three groups of people in his address. The synagogue received his message enthusiastically and asked Paul and Barnabas to return and speak more the following Sabbath. "Many Jews (*Group One*) and devout converts to Judaism (*Group Two*) followed Paul and Barnabas, who, as they spoke with them, urged them to continue in the grace of God" (Acts 13:43). The next Sabbath, however, things did not go as well. "Almost the whole city gathered to hear the word of the Lord" (Acts 13:44). Apparently, the God-fearing Gentiles (*Group Three*) had invited their relatives, friends, and neighbors to attend. The large crowd of Gentiles in the synagogue irritated the Jewish community.

Provoked to Jealousy

Why was the Jewish community irritated by the presence of so many Gentiles? From the evangelical Christian point of view, a packed-out, standing-room-only church service sounds great. From the Jewish perspective, however, a Gentile majority in the synagogue creates a serious threat to the integrity of the community's identity. Jewish identity is precarious enough in the face of assimilation in the Diaspora. The mainstream culture is always chipping away at the particulars of Jewish monotheism and Torah observance. A Gentile presence almost certainly would accelerate the tendency toward assimilation.

Besides, it was annoying. Jews were, after all, the chosen people. It was *their* synagogue. Crowding practically every Gentile in the city into the synagogue created both a practical nuisance ("Hey, that guy's sitting in my seat!") and a theological conundrum ("If everyone is God's Chosen People, then being chosen loses its significance!").

Luke tells us, "They were filled with jealousy and began to contradict what was spoken by Paul, reviling him" (Acts 13:45). They were filled with jealousy. They were not jealous because they themselves had never been able to raise such large crowds. The synagogues were not about the business of trying to bring in big numbers. They were not "evangelical" as we would understand the term. They were not jealous that Paul and Barnabas had such appeal or that their message seemed to be so popular. They were jealous that the message of the gospel was compromising the particularity of Jewish identity. The message of the gospel seemed to be throwing the doors of Judaism wide open to the Gentile world. The religion that had previously been a fairly exclusive club was suddenly declared open to the public, no table reservations necessary.

The message of the gospel itself raised no objections from the Jewish community. On the contrary, the Jewish people of Galatia listened eagerly and wanted to hear more. The message of Messiah's death, burial, and resurrection, and the justification and salvation available through him, sounded good to their ears. They found no offense in the cross. Those were the days before Christian polemics had galvanized Jewish objection to the gospel.

They did not raise objections until they saw the Gentiles crowding into the synagogue. To the Galatian Jewish community of Pisidian Antioch, the offense of the cross was the inclusion of the Gentiles.

Paul and Barnabas shrugged off the concern and continued to teach the new believers. Paul cited Isaiah 49:6 as evidence that the salvation of the Gentiles had been the LORD's plan all along. In the prophecy, God addresses his chosen servant the Messiah and tells him to bring salvation to the nations:

> It is too light a thing that you should be my servant to raise
> up the tribes of Jacob and to bring back the preserved of
> Israel; I will make you as a light for the nations, that my
> salvation may reach to the end of the earth. (Isaiah 49:6)

Eventually, pressure from the Jewish community forced Paul and Barnabas out of Pisidian Antioch. Recovered enough to travel on deeper into Galatia, they set out for another Galatian city: Iconium. They shook the dust from their feet as they left.

Paul saw that pattern repeated over and over in city after city. Popular success at the synagogue was typically followed by the conversion of "a great many of the devout Greeks and not a few of the leading women. But the Jews were jealous" (Acts 17:4–5). Everywhere Paul went, Gentiles seemed to flock to the synagogue to hear him speak. All over Asia Minor, he found Gentiles eager to hear the message of the gospel and Jewish people eager to be rid of that same message, not because of theological objections about

Yeshua, but because they objected to the intrusion of Gentiles into their faith, religion, and synagogue.

That answers the "to whom" question. Paul and his colleagues in Antioch wrote the epistle of Galatians to the God-fearing Gentile believers whom they left behind in the territory of Galatia.

Reasons to Convert

The letter itself contains the "when" and the "why." Back in Antioch after completing that journey, Paul received word from the God-fearing believers whom he had left behind in Pisidian Antioch and Iconium. A large contingency of them had apparently succumbed to some type of pressure to go through conversion and become full proselytes and to achieve status as legal Jews. In other words, members from Group Three had decided to join Group Two.

They may have had several good reasons to do so. Jewish status granted them legal protection under Roman law. Jewish status granted them the right to intermarry with Jewish believers. Perhaps most importantly, Jewish status eliminated social ambiguity.

Roman law granted Jewish people the right to practice Judaism. It exempted them from the requisite emperor-worship and idolatry incumbent upon the rest of the population of the Roman Empire. Without Jewish status, the God-fearing Gentiles were vulnerable to arrest and prosecution for failure to participate in required civic and religious duties.

Being part of a community you cannot marry into does not work long. People tend to fall in love. The more taboo the match, the more attractive and inevitable. If a believing, God-fearing Gentile girl fell in love with a nice Jewish boy, and they married and had children, their children could not be considered Jewish by the community. They themselves might be ostracized by the synagogue.

The situation of God-fearing Gentiles in early Judaism, socially speaking, was not a long-term solution. The Gentile God-Fearers could not hope to sustain themselves long-term within a larger community that did not accept their membership or grant them full participation.

Moreover, it appears that the Galatian Gentiles had decided to undergo legal conversion to become Jewish because it had entered their heads that, unless they did, they would not obtain a share in the kingdom and the world to come. They had come to believe that only Israel proper, i.e., the Jewish people, could be saved. It did make some sense. After all, they were now looking to the Jewish God and the Jewish Messiah. If you are going to commit yourself to worshipping the Jewish God and following the Jewish Messiah, it seems only reasonable to become Jewish.

When Paul heard about this, he quickly composed the epistle to the congregations of believers in Galatia:

> Paul, an apostle—not from men nor through man, but through Jesus Christ and God the Father, who raised him from the dead—and all the brothers who are with me, to the churches of Galatia. (Galatians 1:1–2)

1. **Who**: Paul and his colleagues in Antioch

2. **To Whom**: The God-fearing Gentile believers in Galatia

3. **When:** After Paul received word of their intention to undergo legal conversion to become Jewish

4. **Why**: Because Paul believed that they had seriously erred, and he sought to bring correction

> Grace to you and peace from God our Father and the Lord Jesus Christ, who gave himself for our sins to deliver us from the present evil age, according to the will of our God and Father, to whom be the glory forever and ever. Amen. (Galatians 1:3–5)

SERMON TWO:
THE KING OF ADIABENE
(GALATIANS 1:6–10)

An introduction to the "influencers"
through a retelling of the conversion of
Izates, King of Adiabene.

S cholars tell us that the Holy Epistle to the Galatians is the
oldest document in the New Testament. Paul wrote it before
any of his other epistles. It is older than Mark, Matthew, Luke,
John, and the Acts of the Apostles. It almost certainly predates the
other epistles and the Revelation. Paul most likely composed the
epistle before 50 CE, less than twenty years after the resurrection.
Imagine that Paul wrote the book of Galatians today. To give you
a sense of perspective, that would mean that Jesus rose from the
dead in the 1990s—a fairly recent event.

Review and Recapitulation

Paul claims to send the epistle of Galatians from himself and the
brethren with him at Antioch, men like Barnabas and Luke. He
wrote the epistle to God-fearing Gentile believers living in the
province of Galatia, in the cities of Pisidian Antioch and Iconium.

God-Fearers were monotheists who worshipped the God of
Israel. They were neither Jewish by birth nor by conversion, but
they practiced Judaism, to some extent, as a Gentile. God-Fearers
were one of the three types of people that might be found in any
Diaspora synagogue:

1. Jews

2. Proselytes (Converts)

3. God-fearing Gentiles

God-Fearers are those Gentiles who had renounced idolatry and chosen to worship the God of Israel within the people of Israel, and even within the synagogues, but who had elected not to undergo a formal conversion in order to become halachically (legally) Jewish. Quite comfortable with being Galatians, they felt no need to become Israelites and undergo circumcision and conversion. They are the "to whom" that Paul wrote the epistle.

Paul wrote this epistle after he received word that some Galatian God-Fearers, under the influence of others, were undergoing, or planning to undergo, legal conversion to become proselytes. From Paul's perspective, the Galatian God-Fearers were looking toward conversion in order to merit God's favor and salvation. Paul saw this as a problem. He wrote his epistle to the Galatians to correct the underlying theology and to dissuade the Galatian Gentile believers from going through with their plan to become full proselytes.

The Influencers

> I am astonished that you are so quickly deserting him who called you in the grace of Christ and are turning to a different gospel—not that there is another one, but there are some who trouble you and want to distort the gospel of Christ. But even if we or an angel from heaven should preach to you a gospel contrary to the one we preached to you, let him be accursed. (Galatians 1:6–8)

Paul was disturbed to hear that the Galatian believers had accepted a "different gospel," i.e., a different "good news," which was really not good news at all. He said, "Not that there is another 'good news.'" This other gospel came from an outside influence. Paul said, "There are some who trouble you and want to distort the gospel of Messiah."

Who were these "troublers and distorters?" Christian expository preaching for centuries has referred to them as the "Judaizers." We will take a look at that terminology as we wrestle with this question in the ensuing material, but for now, we will adopt a term currently popular in Pauline studies and simply refer to them as the "influencers."[4] They are teachers within the Galatian communities who are influencing the God-fearing Gentiles to undergo conversion.

One quick observation about the "influencers:" They are most likely believers in Yeshua of Nazareth. This possibility is lost on many interpreters. They might be Jewish believers or believing proselytes to Judaism, but they are almost certainly believers.

How do we know? We will consider the evidence as we work through the epistle, but from the outset, Paul says that they "want to distort the gospel of Messiah." A non-believer does not want to distort the gospel; he wants to refute it and repudiate it. Only believers distort the gospel. Paul says that they preach "a gospel contrary to the one we preached to you," but they *are* preaching a gospel, they *are* teachers of the good news. For that reason we may deduce that they are believers in Yeshua of Nazareth. They believe in his birth, death, resurrection, and messiahship. They believe in the kingdom of heaven, and they are our brothers and sisters in the faith.

They are the influencers. They are believers, but Paul does not like their influence. And he says, "Let them be accursed."

> As we have said before, so now I say again: If anyone is preaching to you a gospel contrary to the one you received, let him be accursed. (Galatians 1:9)

When you are a leader and a teacher—a spiritual leader and a Bible teacher—there is nothing more devastating than the presence of "influencers" in your flock. Influencers always, always have a contrary agenda. They are always dissatisfied with the leadership; they always have a critical spirit; they are always trying to be leaders without leading, by spreading discontent and planting seeds of dissension.

---

4   E.g., Mark Nanos, *The Irony of Galatians: Paul's Letter in First Century Context* (Minneapolis, MN: Fortress Press, 2002).

According to Paul, the distorted gospel that the influencers spread in Galatia was hazardous to the soul, so dangerous that, even though the influencers were certainly his brothers in Messiah, Paul said, "Let them be accursed."

A Story from Adiabene

To help provide context for the Holy Epistle to the Galatians, it may be helpful to consider a story from about fifteen years earlier. The first-century Jewish historian Josephus tells a story that took place in the kingdom of Adiabene, shortly after the resurrection of the Master.

Some distance from Antioch or Galatia, straddling the highlands of what is today the Kurdish areas of Iraq, Armenia, and northern Iran, sat the kingdom of Adiabene with its capital at Arbela. Adiabene was part of the Assyrian province of the Parthian Empire.

Monobazus, the King of Adiabene, had many wives and many sons, but he loved his wife Helena the most. To her first son he gave the royal name Monobazus, making him the heir apparent. Helena conceived again. It is said that once while she was pregnant with her second son, Monobazus slept beside her with his hands on her stomach. A voice spoke to him in a dream telling him to remove his hands and to protect the child, for this one was chosen by God. Monobazus was a Zoroastrian. The voice so frightened him that he woke his wife Helena and told her what had he had heard. When the son was born, he named him Izates. Like Jacob with his son Joseph, Monobazus placed all of his affection on Izates, to the point that the other brothers hated the boy. For the protection of the young man, the king sent him away to be tutored and raised in the foreign court of King Abennerig of Charax-Spasini.

King Abennerig welcomed the young man into his court and even gave him the hand of one of his daughters in marriage. While Izates sojourned in the court of Charax-Spasini, some of the wives of King Abennerig encountered a certain Jew by the name of Chananiah. This happened around the time of the persecution that broke out in connection with the martyrdom of Stephen (Acts 8). Chananiah the Jew was a tradesman, perhaps selling his wares among the royalty and the women of court. Under his influence, the women became converts to Judaism and professed faith in the God of Israel.

The Conversion of Izates

The wives of Abennerig introduced their new son-in-law, Izates, to Chananiah, who in turn introduced the young prince to the God of Israel. Izates came to believe in the One God.

The conversion of Izates took place sometime between 30 and 36 CE, and it may have preceded that of Cornelius the centurion (Acts 10). When Izates did convert, he wanted to undergo circumcision as a sign of his conversion, but Chananiah discouraged him from doing so, telling him that he could still worship God without being circumcised, even though he resolved to follow the Jewish Torah entirely. Chananiah went on to say that keeping the commandments of the Torah was superior to circumcision.

The Fearers

Some years later, the Apostle Paul used the same argument with the Gentile converts in his congregations. In the story of Izates, however, Chananiah the Jew gave the same ruling ten years before Paul did. It may be that the particular brand of Judaism to which Izates originally converted was that of the believers, the disciples of Yeshua, but one cannot be dogmatic on that point. More likely, the type of advice Chananiah gave to Izates was common in first-century Judaism, and Paul drew his own theology from that common Jewish posture toward Gentiles. At any rate, Izates became a follower of Judaism, but not Jewish—not a proselyte either. He became a God-Fearer.

In the Persian language today, the word for "Christian" translates literally as "Fearer." Jewish scholar Shlomo Pines points out that, in at least three Iranian languages (Pahlavi, New Persian, and Sogdian), the name for Christians is derived from the Iranian root *tars*, which means "to fear."[5] Christians are called "*Tarsakan*," i.e., "Fearers," even to this day. These languages possess no other names

---

[5]   Shlomo Pines, "The Iranian Name for Christians and the 'God-Fearers,'" *Proceedings of the Israel Academy of Sciences and Humanities* 2 (1968):143–152.

for Christians except loan words borrowed from other languages. Izates became a "Fearer."

Ascent to the Throne

King Monobazus was near death. He desired to see his son again. He sent for Izates and bestowed upon him rulership of the country of Carrae (Armenia in eastern Turkey), a land that produced Amomum, a popular spice, and in addition a land famous among Jews as the resting place of Noah's Ark. Mount Ararat stood in Carrae, upon which (according to the first-century Jewish historian Josephus) the remains of the ark could still be seen on the mountain by anyone who desired to see them.[6]

Izates relocated then to Carrae, the land of Noah's Ark, and there he remained until his father's death.

When King Monobazus died, his wife Helena sent word to her son in Carrae. Then she went immediately to work securing the throne for him. She summoned all the political officers and told them how her husband Monozabus had wanted Izates to receive the throne. She said, "I believe you are aware that my husband wanted Izates to succeed him in the government and thought him worthy of the position. However, I await your decision; for happy is he who receives a kingdom, not from a single person only, but from the willing consent of the majority." And with such entreaties, she secured their loyalty.

Chananiah's Arrival

When he went to take his throne, Izates brought Chananiah the Jew with him to Adiabene. If he hoped that Chananiah might influence his mother to accept Judaism, he was too late. In his absence, his mother Helena had already embraced the religion of the Jews. What a surprise! Izates took this as a sign from Heaven, and he immediately sought full conversion to become Jewish. In the words of Josephus:

---

6   Josephus, *Antiquities of the Jews* 20:25. In the third century, the Church writers Hippolytus and Julius Africanus identified this as the land of Noah's Ark.

When he realized that his mother approved of Jewish practices, he was eager to convert, and to embrace them entirely. He supposed that he could not be completely Jewish until he underwent circumcision, therefore he was ready to have it done. When his mother realized what he was about to do, she tried to dissuade him from doing it. She told him that this thing would put him in [political] danger and that when his subjects came to realize that he, their king, was so fond of rites that were to them strange and foreign, they would find him odious. They would never submit to be ruled over by a Jew.[7]

Chananiah the Jew agreed with Queen Helena. He confirmed her words and comforted Izates, telling him that God would certainly forgive the omission of circumcision since it literally constituted a danger to his life. Izates consented to forego conversion and simply live as a God-Fearer.

Eleazar the Influencer

Sometime later, however, a certain Galilean Jew named Eleazar arrived in Adiabene. He was a sage and Torah scholar, and King Izates sought his teaching. When Eleazar entered the palace, he found Izates seated, reading the Torah of Moses. Eleazar had some sharp words for the uncircumcised king:

> Have you never considered, O King, that you unjustly violate the rule of those laws you are studying, and you are insulting to God himself, by omitting to be circumcised. For you ought not only to study the commandments, but primarily, you ought to do what they tell you to do. How long will you continue to be uncircumcised? But if you have not yet read the law about circumcision, and if you are unaware of how great an impiety you are guilty of by neglecting it, read it now.[8]

---

[7] *Antiquities of the Jews* 20:39.

[8] *Antiquities of the Jews* 20:44–45.

The king sent immediately for a surgeon. After circumcision, Izates and Helena completed their formal conversions to Judaism at Eleazar's behest and under his supervision. God protected and prospered Izates and strengthened him in his kingdom. Both he and Queen Helena became prominent characters in rabbinic lore from the end of the Second Temple era.

The story provides an insightful glimpse into the first century and illustrates the issues underlying Paul's ministry to the Gentiles. It seems that influencers like Eleazar of Galilee often followed Paul and refuted his teaching that the new Gentile converts need not undergo the ritual conversion (i.e., circumcision).

Pleasing Men or God?

Like Eleazar the Galilean in Adiabene, the influencers in Galatia wanted the God-fearing Gentiles to complete a legal conversion to become Jewish. They represented the position held by most other Jewish believers and the vast majority of the Yeshua movement, "many thousands ... among the Jews of those who have believed ... all zealous for the law" (Acts 21:20). Paul's Gentiles were something of an aberration in an otherwise primarily Jewish sect. The majority opinion among Jewish believers seems to have been that the Gentiles needed to convert sooner or later.

If Paul had delivered the same message as Eleazar of Galilee, teaching the Gentile believers to finish their conversion with circumcision, he could have earned favor with the other Jewish believers and with the greater Jewish community present in the synagogues in which he was teaching, such as the synagogues of Galatia. Within the Jewish context, that message would have been the more socially acceptable message: "Believe in Yeshua to be saved, but after that, you need to eventually accept upon yourself circumcision, conversion, and all of the obligations of Jewish life that legal Jewish status entails."

If Paul had been preaching that message, he might not have been forced out of the synagogue in Pisidian Antioch, run out of Iconium, or stoned in Lystra. He would not have had conflict with the other Jewish believers—the faction that he derisively refers to as "the Circumcision." To paraphrase, he explains in Galatians 1:10,

"I am not doing this to win friends. I am not preaching to please men. I am preaching the message that Messiah gave me to preach."

> For am I now seeking the approval of man, or of God? Or am I trying to please man? If I were still trying to please man, I would not be a servant of Christ. (Galatians 1:10)

PAUL'S GOSPEL
(GALATIANS 1:11–24)

A summary of Paul's autobiography, in which he describes his revelation from Heaven and his divine commission to preach the gospel to the Gentiles.

Prior to encountering Paul and the gospel, some, perhaps many, of the God-fearing Gentiles in Galatia had already begun a relationship with Judaism, Israel, and the God of the Bible. For example, in the previous sermon, we considered the case of King Izates of Adiabene who wanted to embrace the God of Israel but was counseled by his teacher Chananiah not to convert. Until undergoing circumcision, he remained a God-fearing Gentile, and to this day, Christians in that part of the world are called "Fearers."

Recap and Review: God-Fearers in the Synagogue

The God-Fearers had, to some degree or another, renounced paganism and found fellowship within the Jewish community. The synagogue did not regard them as Jewish; they were guests and visitors, contributors to the synagogue, and friends of the Jewish community. They had renounced idolatry to some extent but not completely. Roman law required them to participate in certain (mostly innocuous) ritual functions, something akin to saying the pledge of allegiance, except that it involved sacrificing to Roman gods. (By Roman law, Jews were exempt from those civic ritual duties. Instead, the Jewish nation offered a sacrifice in the Temple in Jerusalem every day on behalf of Caesar. That daily sacrifice exempted the Jewish community from emperor-worship and other civic duties involving idolatry.) To some degree, the God-Fearers kept the Sabbath, the festivals, and other matters of Torah along with the Jewish community, but they were not required to do so nor were they expected to do so. They participated to the extent that they were able.

From time to time, some of these God-Fearers might decide to become Jewish. These individuals then underwent a conversion ritual, which included circumcision for males. At the completion of the ritual, their legal status changed from Gentile God-Fearer to Jewish proselyte: fully Jewish with all the rights, responsibilities, obligations, and legal privileges and protection of a natural-born Jew, under both Roman law and Torah law. For example, in the previous sermon we considered how King Izates, under the instruction of a rabbi named Eleazar the Galilean, opted to become circumcised and legally Jewish—a proselyte.

Paul did not write his Galatian epistle to proselytes. He wrote to the God-fearing Gentiles in Galatia, synagogue-attendees who were not Jewish. When Paul came to Galatia, he introduced those Gentiles to the gospel and taught them that in Messiah, they had standing in the kingdom, a place among the people of Israel. As a result, he told them that they needed to completely break with idolatry because, in Messiah, they were part of the people of God. Then he left.

Sometime later he heard that the God-fearing Gentiles of Galatia were being influenced by other Galatian community members to "seal the deal," so to speak, and become Jewish. That irritated Paul. He viewed it as a twisting of the gospel, teaching a contrary gospel. So he wrote:

> I am astonished that you are so quickly deserting him who called you in the grace of Christ and are turning to a different gospel— not that there is another one, but there are some who trouble you and want to distort the gospel of Christ. But even if we or an angel from heaven should

preach to you a gospel contrary to the one we preached to you, let him be accursed. (Galatians 1:6–8)

Man's Gospel

As Paul began his epistle to the Galatians, he contrasted the gospel message he preached to what he called "man's gospel."

> For I would have you know, brothers, that the gospel that was preached by me is not man's gospel. For I did not receive it from any man, nor was I taught it, but I received it through a revelation of Jesus Christ. (Galatians 1:11–12)

What did Paul mean by "man's gospel"? He did not mean a false gospel, or corrupt gospel, or something fleshly and worldly. He meant to differentiate the way that he became a believer from the way that people ordinarily became believers in that day, and he wanted to differentiate between his gospel message and the one that other believers ordinarily proclaimed in his day.

In Paul's day, most of the people who became disciples of Yeshua of Nazareth were Jewish. All of the apostles were Jewish, and they told other Jewish people about Yeshua: his deeds, his words, his death, his resurrection, his ascension, his messianic claims, and his imminent return. That's how most people learned the gospel, and that is what Paul called "man's gospel." You heard the good news from someone, you believed it, and that's how you became a believer. It was a mostly Jewish phenomenon.

That was not how Paul became a believer. Instead, Paul once hated believers:

> For you have heard of my former life in Judaism, how I persecuted the church of God violently and tried to destroy it. And I was advancing in Judaism beyond many of my own age among my people, so extremely zealous was I for the traditions of my fathers. (Galatians 1:13–14)

At the time that Paul became a disciple of Yeshua of Nazareth, he hated all the disciples of Yeshua of Nazareth; he did not receive the gospel from men. Instead, he persecuted them and actually hunted them down. He described himself as advancing in Judaism beyond many of his own age among his people.

Paul the Prodigy

What does it mean to be "advancing in Judaism?" "I was," Paul explained, "extremely zealous for the traditions of my fathers."

The "traditions of the fathers" is the New Testament, apostolic-age term for what later came to be called the Oral Torah (i.e., the Mishnah, etc.) which, after several centuries, resulted in the voluminous literature of the Talmud. In those days, people did not call it the Oral Law (*Torah shebe-al Peh*); they called it "the traditions of the fathers," or sometimes just "the traditions." The religious party called the Pharisees adhered to those traditions and passed them on orally from teacher to disciple. When Paul said he was advancing in Judaism zealous for the traditions, he was not saying, "I used to be a legalistic, halachic, orthodox Jew, but after finding Jesus, I dumped all that." The Greek word translated as "advancing" is a term which originally meant "making headway at sea," but Josephus and contemporary literature used it to mean "making great progress in education."[9] Paul was saying, "I was an important disciple of an important sage (Rabban Gamliel the Elder), and I was zealous to learn the Oral Law, i.e., the traditions, and I was advancing fast to the top of the class. I was headed for a big seat on the Sanhedrin; I was going to be one of the top scholars because I was a prodigy."

But this prodigy had a mean streak, and he despised the believers. They irritated him badly, especially that guy Stephen who hung out in his synagogue and argued with all the other Greek-speaking Jews who attended there. After Stephen's stoning, Paul even went so far as to break his allegiance with his teacher Gamliel, defying his ruling regarding the believers (Acts 9:1–2). He went over to the Sadducees, to Caiphas the high priest, for legal permission to hunt down believers, drag them out of the synagogues and publically punish them by flogging, perhaps by excommunication as well.

---

[9] Richard Longenecker, *Galatians* (vol. 41 of Word Biblical Commentary; Dallas, TX: Word Books, 1990), 29.

He did not get the gospel from the believers or from the apostles. They were afraid of Paul.

Revelation from Heaven

While Paul was on the road to Damascus to find more believers and beat them up, he had a revelation from Heaven. No one witnessed to Paul. No one argued him into the conclusion that Yeshua of Nazareth was the Messiah. It was not as if he read all the prophecies in the Tanach, or saw Isaiah 53 and said, "Oh, I was wrong!" He did not read a tract or listen to a preacher on the radio. He did not attend a Billy Graham crusade. He did not receive the gospel from men; it was not man's gospel; it came direct from above. As Paul said, "I did not receive it from any man, nor was I taught it, but I received it through a revelation of Jesus Christ." It dropped from Heaven.

This type of thing happens. Not often, so far as we know, but it does happen. On some occasions, Yeshua of Nazareth, the expression of HaShem himself, appears to a person, reveals himself to a person, speaks to a person, and announces himself. I once met a Jewish believer who came to one of the Torah classes I was teaching, and he introduced himself and indicated that he had only recently become a disciple. I asked how it happened, and he said, "I was in downtown Minneapolis. I looked into a fountain, and he appeared to me and spoke to me." Sometimes it happens like that.

Paul's Gospel

Paul explained that he received the gospel through a revelation of Yeshua the Messiah. He claimed that the gospel message he preached to the Galatians was not man's gospel. It was not the normal gospel message. He received a different gospel. This is an important point—a critical point—for understanding Paul. The message of the gospel that Paul proclaimed was not precisely the same message of the gospel that the rest of the apostolic community proclaimed. In other places, Paul specifically refers to his unique gospel message as "my gospel."

[Gentile believers show that the work of the Torah] is written on their hearts, while their conscience also bears witness, and their conflicting thoughts accuse or even excuse them on that day when, according to *my gospel*, God judges the secrets of men by Christ Jesus. (Romans 2:15–16)

[God] is able to strengthen you according to *my gospel*. (Romans 16:25)

As preached in *my gospel*, for which I am suffering, bound with chains as a criminal. (2 Timothy 2:8–9)

This should be troubling to us. What makes Paul's gospel his gospel? How is this gospel that he received by special revelation different from what he calls man's gospel? How is his gospel message different from that of the rest of the apostolic community?

Paul's gospel differs because Paul taught that salvation in Messiah is efficacious for both Jews and Gentiles. The other apostles also included Gentiles, but they expected that once a Gentile received the good news about the king of the Jews, he would become Jewish. After all, it's not right to take the children's bread and throw it to the dogs (Matthew 15:26).

Scholars disagree about this point, but I believe there is ample evidence to prove that Paul wrote his epistle to the Galatians before the Jerusalem Council reported in Acts 15. Before that counsel, the question of Gentile participation had not yet been resolved. Other Jewish believers taught that Gentiles who embraced Messiah would, should, and eventually must convert and become Jewish.

Paul disagreed. His gospel was not just good news for Israel, but for all of humanity. This is what made Paul so radical and put him outside the Jerusalem circle.

What was Paul's gospel? One more time for the sake of redundancy: Paul's gospel taught that Gentiles can inherit eternal life, the kingdom of heaven, the resurrection of the dead, and standing among the people of God (i.e., Israel) without becoming Jewish—a radical idea.

Where did Paul get this information? Not from the teachings of Yeshua transmitted by his followers and disciples. Not from the teaching of Peter or John or James. Paul insisted, "I did not receive it from any man, nor was I taught it, but I received it through a revelation of Jesus Christ" (Galatians 1:12). He received it as "the revelation of the mystery that was kept secret for long ages, but has now been disclosed and through the prophetic writings has been made known to all nations, according to the command of the eternal God, to bring about the obedience of faith" (Romans 16:25–26).

Paul explicitly links the special revelation of the gospel message he received with his commission from Messiah to "preach him among the Gentiles" (Galatians 1:15).

> But when he who had set me apart before I was born, and who called me by his grace, was pleased to reveal his Son to me, in order that I might preach him among the Gentiles, I did not immediately consult with anyone; nor did I go up to Jerusalem to those who were apostles before me, but I went away into Arabia, and returned again to Damascus. (Galatians 1:15–17)

Paul in Damascus and Jerusalem

After receiving the revelation from heaven, Paul "went away into Arabia"—that is, the kingdom of the Nabataeans. Damascus was a large city within this Nabataean kingdom. When Paul wrote that he went away into Arabia, we should not imagine some monk-like retreat to Mount Sinai; rather, he was speaking of his sojourn in Damascus and that general area, a period of time well described in the book of Acts. When he first arrived in Damascus, he was blind and confused, fasting, praying, and seeking God. A disciple named Chananiah came to him and prayed over him and restored his sight. He underwent an immersion into Yeshua and remained among the disciples in Damascus.

Paul said he spent three years in Damascus and Arabia before returning to Jerusalem. He got in trouble in the synagogues of Damascus for preaching Messiah too boldly. Eventually, some enemies hatched a plot against him. His disciples had to lower him out of a window in the city wall, concealed in a basket. After that incident, he returned to Jerusalem and finally met the key apostles:

Then after three years I went up to Jerusalem to visit Cephas and remained with him fifteen days. But I saw none of the other apostles except James the Lord's brother. (In what I am writing to you, before God, I do not lie!) (Galatians 1:18–20)

When Paul first arrived in Jerusalem, the community and the apostles refused to welcome their persecutor; they did not trust him. They assumed he wanted to get inside information. Finally, Barnabas brought him before the apostles and vouched for his sincerity. He met James and Peter, and the community welcomed him. He ended up staying with Peter's family in Jerusalem for fifteen days, probably spending three Sabbaths together.

Why did Paul recount all of that for the Galatians? He wanted to emphasize that he did not get his unique gospel message from the apostles; he received it directly from the Master through a special revelation.

While with the apostles in Jerusalem, he received his commissioning. As he prayed in the Temple, he fell into a trance and saw a vision of the Master. Yeshua told him, "Go, for I will send you far away to the Gentiles" (Acts 22:21).

From Tarsus to Antioch

Then I went into the regions of Syria and Cilicia. And I was still unknown in person to the churches of Judea that are in Christ. They only were hearing it said, "He who used to persecute us is now preaching the faith he once tried to destroy." And they glorified God because of me. (Galatians 1:21–24)

Paul left Jerusalem and spent fourteen years in Syria and Cilicia. The first eight years or so he spent in his home town of Tarsus. He passed his time preaching Messiah (and the faith he once tried to destroy) in the synagogues there. He worked as a tent maker, a tailor. He spent his time studying, learning, trying to grasp the commission he heard in the vision: "Go, for I will send you far away to the Gentiles." He spent his time looking for confirmation in the prophets that this was indeed the word of the LORD—that the salvation of Messiah extended even to the Gentiles.

After about eight years, a remarkable thing happened. Joseph Barnabas, the disciple he knew from Damascus and Jerusalem, showed up in Tarsus looking for him. He explained, "Saul, the apostles in Jerusalem sent me to Antioch to see what's going on there. They heard a report from the synagogues in Antioch that large numbers of God-fearing Gentiles have joined the faith. I travelled to Antioch, and I saw the grace of God on the Gentiles, and I was glad, and I told them to remain faithful to the Master with steadfast purpose, and a great many of them have believed. That's why I've come looking for you. I need your help in Antioch." Barnabas must have also told Paul about Peter's experience with Cornelius (Acts 10), a story which would only confirm the revelation Paul had already received—the mystery of the gospel.

A Rule for All the Churches

That's how Paul ended up in Antioch for the next five years or so. He came to Antioch to help Barnabas, and he found Gentiles— God-Fearers—lots of them. His vision about the gospel going out to all nations was coming true. The only question was what to do with them.

The conventional plan, naturally, would be to teach them about Judaism and usher them along the path to full conversion until they became proselytes. Paul did not follow the conventional model. Instead, he taught the new believers to remain as Gentiles. This radical change of program became Paul's rule for all the communities of faith:

> *This is my rule in all the churches.* Was anyone at the time of his call already circumcised? Let him not seek to remove the marks of circumcision. Was anyone at the time of his call uncircumcised? Let him not seek circumcision. For neither circumcision counts for anything nor uncircumcision, but keeping the commandments of God. Each one should remain in the condition in which he was called. (1 Corinthians 7:17–20)

What's the Point?

Paul wanted the Galatian believers to know that his gospel (the gospel that teaches that Gentile believers are also a part of the kingdom, not as proselytes, but as real Gentiles) was something he received directly from God—a special revelation, a special commission, confirmed by his studies, yes, but straight from God.

That was important for his readers to know because "the influencers" exerting an influence on them were not teaching Paul's gospel. They were telling the Galatian believers that salvation and faith in Yeshua should naturally lead to becoming Jewish through conversion—the same message proclaimed by the rest of the apostolic community. Paul needed to clarify: "What I have been telling you is different than what everyone else is teaching. The reason that it is different is because I did not get this gospel message from the other apostles. I got it straight from Heaven."

Gentiles would not be present in the community of faith today, nor in any church, if not for that revelation from Heaven that God vouchsafed to his servant Paul. God set him apart before he was born, called him by his grace, and was pleased to reveal his Son to him, in order that he might preach Messiah among the Gentiles. As a Gentile myself, I have a great debt of gratitude to the Apostle Paul, the servant of Christ.

May his memory be for a blessing.

Galatians
CHAPTER TWO

FAMINE RELIEF
FOR JERUSALEM
(GALATIANS 2:1–2)

After an absence of more than a decade, Paul journeys to Jerusalem in the company of Barnabas and Titus with a collection for famine relief.

Paul did not receive the gospel from men in the ordinary way that men in his day did; that is, he did not receive it from the apostles or from the community of their followers. Instead, he received a personal revelation, a visitation from Heaven, while on the road to Damascus. And he made much out of how he did not receive the gospel from men and about how his gospel—Paul's gospel—differed from others. He said, "I would have you know, brothers, that the gospel that was preached by me is not man's gospel. For I did not receive it from any man, nor was I taught it, but I received it through a revelation of Jesus Christ" (Galatians 1:11–12).

Recap and Review:
The Believing-Gentile Movement

In the first chapter of the Epistle to the Galatians, Paul recounted the story of how he used to be a persecutor of the believers. He pursued them with zeal as if he were doing God a favor by afflicting them until he received the revelation of Yeshua on the road to Damascus. He spent three years in Damascus, and only after three years did he return to Jerusalem. The believers in Jerusalem did not want to receive him; they were afraid of him until Barnabas vouched for him. Then he met with James, the brother of the Master, and spent two weeks with Peter. At the end of those two weeks, he saw a vision of the Master while praying in the Temple. Yeshua told him, "Go, I will send you far away to the Gentiles." A plot had hatched against Paul, and he had to flee from Jerusalem for his own safety. The brothers in Jerusalem escorted him to Caesarea, and he left the Holy Land to go back to his native Tarsus.

While Paul sojourned in Tarsus, amazing things were happening. In the city of Caesarea, the Apostle Peter brought the gospel to the home of a Gentile named Cornelius. He was a God-Fearer, "a devout man who feared God with all his household" (Acts 10:2). He and his household believed. The Apostle Peter declared, "Truly I understand that God shows no partiality, but in every nation anyone who fears him and does what is right is acceptable to him" (Acts 10:34–35).

Not long after that, the gospel began to reach other God-fearing Gentiles. Believers from Jerusalem "traveled as far as Phoenicia and Cyprus and Antioch, speaking the word to no one except Jews" (Acts 11:19). They spoke the word to no one except Jews because the gospel was good news for the Jewish people. One would naturally assume that any Gentiles drawn into the kingdom of heaven movement would undergo conversion to become Jewish. Something else was afoot though. The book of Acts tells the story of how a large number of God-fearing Gentiles in Antioch came to faith:

> There were some of them, men of Cyprus and Cyrene, who on coming to Antioch spoke to the Hellenists also, preaching the Lord Jesus. And the hand of the Lord was with them, and a great number who believed turned to the Lord. The report of this came to the ears of the church in Jerusalem, and they sent Barnabas to Antioch. When he came and saw the grace of God, he was glad, and he exhorted them all to remain faithful to the Lord with steadfast purpose, for he was a good man, full of the Holy

Spirit and of faith. And a great many people were added
to the Lord. (Acts 11:20–24)

Barnabas left Antioch and headed for Tarsus to find his old
friend Paul. He needed Paul's help in overseeing the conversion of
all those Gentiles. He wanted someone with Paul's standing and
halachic credentials because this was not just a few, or a dozen,
but probably hundreds of Gentiles.

> When he had found him, he brought him to Antioch.
> For a whole year they met with the church and taught a
> great many people. And in Antioch the disciples were first
> called Christians. (Acts 11:26)

Paul spent a whole year in Antioch, teaching a great many
people there. He did not, however, conduct any conversions. This
is what made his gospel so radical. Instead of ushering the God-
fearing Gentiles along the path to conversion, he taught the Gentiles of Antioch to remain as Gentiles. He taught a risky, progressive
idea about Gentile inclusion in the kingdom, in the synagogue, and
even in Israel without conversion and without becoming Jewish.
This is what he called "my gospel."

That's where we left Paul in the previous sermon: in Antioch
among the Jewish believers teaching the God-fearing Gentiles who
had come to faith in Messiah.

Return to Jerusalem

In the second chapter of Galatians, Paul recounts a trip to Jerusalem. He wrote, "After fourteen years I went up again to Jerusalem
with Barnabas, taking Titus along with me" (Galatians 2:1). It had
been fourteen years since the Damascus road incident, or perhaps
it had been fourteen years since he had last been to Jerusalem.
The point is that after a long time, more than a decade, he finally
went back to Jerusalem.

Try to understand the significance of Jerusalem for the believers: They cherished it, not only as the Holy City, as the place of the
Temple, as the place of the Master's tomb, and as the place of the
future kingdom, but also as the place of the apostles. Jerusalem was
where the elders and the original disciples could be found. I do not

doubt that they had a synagogue of their own in Jerusalem. They had an academy of learning, I am sure. They had their own *beit din* (court of judgment), for certain. They had James (Yaakov) the Righteous, the brother of the Master.

Jerusalem was to the first-century believers what the Vatican is to Catholics. Jerusalem of that era is difficult for Protestants to understand because we have inherited disrespect for ecclesiastical authority, but Catholics will better understand the analogy. The first-century believers respected the authority of James the brother of the Master on par with the authority that the Roman Catholic Church accords to the pope. The apostles had the authority to bind and loose: according to the Master's word, whatever they bound on earth was bound in heaven, and whatever they loosed on earth was loosed in heaven. That is to say, they had the authority to make rulings and decisions for all believers everywhere.

After more than a decade, Paul went back up to Jerusalem. He took with him Barnabas, the man who vouched for him on his last visit, and he brought along Titus. Barnabas was a Jewish believer with good credentials among the apostles. Barnabas represented the original school of the Jerusalem-Yeshua movement; he was a veteran apostle and had belonged to the inner circle since the year of the Master's death and resurrection. Titus represented the opposite extreme: a God-fearing Gentile from Antioch, uncircumcised, who had not accepted conversion and did not seem to be planning on it. He was one of Paul's Gentile disciples.

The Revelation

Paul explained to the Galatians, "I went up [to Jerusalem] because of a revelation" (Galatians 2:2). A "revelation" is something revealed from Heaven. After that first encounter on the Damascus road, revelations like that directed Paul's life. The Master appeared to him in the Temple; the Spirit of Jesus prevented him from entering Bithynia; the LORD told him in a dream to remain in the city of Corinth; etc. Heavenly revelations, visions, and prophecies dictated Paul's comings and goings.

Acts 11 describes how some Jewish believers reputed to be prophets came to Antioch from Jerusalem while Paul and Barnabas were teaching there. The word of the LORD came to the prophet Chagavah (Agabus, a name that means "locust"). He predicted that a great famine was soon to come upon the Roman world:

> And one of them named Agabus stood up and foretold by the Spirit that there would be a great famine over all the world (this took place in the days of Claudius). So the disciples determined, everyone according to his ability, to send relief to the brothers living in Judea. And they did so, sending it to the elders by the hand of Barnabas and Saul. (Acts 11:28–30)

The communal believers in Jerusalem would be particularly hard-hit by such a famine. Sharing all things in common had taken its toll, and the impoverished community did not have the means to lay up provisions for themselves. In keeping with our Master's teachings about giving one's wealth to the poor, the early Jewish believers came to be known as *Evyonim*, i.e., "Ebionites." The Hebrew word *evyonim* means "poor ones." The early Church Fathers knew of the name. Centuries later they applied the name "Ebionite" to a particular sect of Jewish believers, but the name may have originated in the early days of the Yeshua movement in Jerusalem.

The *Evyonim* (the poor ones) stood to be the hardest hit by a coming famine. The prophets from Jerusalem saw that the result would be devastating if some measure was not set aside for the Jerusalem community. Following the Torah's example of Joseph's preparations for the seven-year famine, they requested a collection from the Antioch community. In the Jewish community, such collections were common. The Talmud preserves several anecdotes and incidents regarding similar collections for charity in the Diaspora.

The Antioch disciples collected funds for their brothers and sisters in Jerusalem and sent them back to the Holy City by way of Paul and Barnabas. The gift served a twofold purpose. On the one hand, it provided for the Jerusalem believers, much as the careful preparations of the patriarch Joseph in the Torah had provided for his brothers. On the other hand, the collection might buy the mixed-blood Antioch community a little bit of favor in the eyes of the Jewish Jerusalem assembly.

Famine Relief from Izates

The predicted famine came to Judea in about the year 44 and lasted three years. The Talmud refers to it as the "years of scarcity." The famine in Judea was severe, and not only in Judea, but also up the coast in Phoenicia as well. It stemmed from a great drought which lasted several years. Josephus reports that food was scarce, extremely expensive, and many people died for want. When King Izates of Adiabene heard from his mother about the famine in Judea, "he sent great sums of money to the principal men in Jerusalem."[10] In so doing, he emptied out the coffers of accumulated wealth that he had inherited from his fathers. The Talmud tells the story:

> It is related of King Monobaz [Izates] that he exhausted all his own treasures and the stores of his fathers during the years of scarcity. His brothers and his father's household brought a delegation before him and said to him, "Your father saved money and added to the treasures of his fathers, and you are wasting it." He replied, "'Truth springs from the earth, and [charity] looks down from heaven' (Psalm 85:11). My fathers stored their wealth in a place which is vulnerable to tampering, but I have stored my wealth in a place invulnerable to tampering, as it says, '[Charity] and judgment are the foundation of his throne' (Psalm 97:2). My fathers stored something which produces no fruits, but I have stored something which does produce fruits, as it is written, 'Tell the [charitable] that it shall be well with them, for they shall eat the fruit of their deeds' (Isaiah 3:10). My fathers gathered treasures of money, but I have gathered treasures of souls, as it is written, 'The fruit of [charity] is a tree of life, and whoever captures souls is wise' (Proverbs 11:30). My fathers gathered for others and I have gathered for myself, as it

---

[10] Josephus, *Antiquities of the Jews* 10:2.

says, 'It shall be [charity] for you' (Deuteronomy 24:13). My fathers gathered for this world, but I have gathered for the world to come, as it says, 'Your charity shall go before you'" (Isaiah 58:8). (b.*Bava Batra* 11a)

Izates' words sound like a midrashic expansion on the Master's own teaching and provide the closest Talmudic parallel to Yeshua's teaching about treasure in heaven: "Do not lay up for yourselves treasures on earth, where moth and rust destroy and where thieves break in and steal, but lay up for yourselves treasures in heaven, where neither moth nor rust destroys and where thieves do not break in and steal. For where your treasure is, there your heart will be also" (Matthew 6:19–21).

Izates sent his famine relief to Jerusalem after the famine was already severe. Paul, Barnabas, and Titus brought the Antioch collection up to Jerusalem before the famine had even begun.

SERMON FIVE:
RUNNING THE RACE IN VAIN
(GALATIANS 2:2)

Paul goes up to Jerusalem to submit
his gospel of Gentile inclusion to the
authority of the apostles.

After a fourteen-year absence, Paul went up to Jerusalem with the Apostle Barnabas and the God-fearing Gentile Titus. They carried a substantial sum of money with them—famine relief for a famine that had not yet begun. They may have arrived in Jerusalem around the time that Herod Agrippa put James the son of Zebedee to death, and shortly before the arrest of Peter.

While Paul and Barnabas were back in Jerusalem, they went to see the apostles. Paul told the Galatians, "I set before them (though privately before those who seemed influential) the gospel that I proclaim among the Gentiles, in order to make sure that I was not running or had run in vain" (Galatians 2:2).

Recap and Review: Paul's Controversial Gospel

The gospel that Paul proclaimed among the Gentiles was not "man's gospel." In the first chapter of his letter to the Galatians, Paul emphatically insisted that he did not receive it from the apostles but rather directly from God. Paul referred to his own version of the gospel as "my gospel."

The rest of the apostles preached the gospel as they had heard it from the mouth of the Master: "Repent, the kingdom of heaven is at hand." They declared the resurrection of Yeshua the Messiah, and they proclaimed repentance and forgiveness of sins in his name to Jews and Gentiles alike—so long as those Gentiles were willing to receive the message and become Jewish in order to serve the king of the Jews.

Paul presented a unique version of the gospel in that he included the Gentiles as Gentiles. Paul taught that Gentiles could be saved by faith and without any obligation to go through a legal conversion to become Jewish. He went so far as to discourage Gentiles from undergoing circumcision and taking on legal Jewish status. He had one simple rule for all congregations:

> This is my rule in all the churches ... Each one should remain in the condition in which he was called. (1 Corinthians 7:17–20)

Paul's approach made a radical departure from conventional proclamation of the good news. It was an unanticipated, new twist to the gospel. It came to Paul in a vision, but he found confirmation in the writings of the prophets. He found evidence that God intended salvation to be extended to all of humanity, not just to the tribes of Israel. Based upon this revelation, Paul taught that Gentiles could be saved in the name of Yeshua and obtain a share in the kingdom of heaven, the resurrection from the dead, the world to come, and inheritance among the people Israel. He also taught that Gentile believers received a spiritual adoption into the family of Israel through their repentance, confession of Messiah, and allegiance to him.

Paul's Sinking Feeling

Paul's controversial gospel message does not sound too controversial to Christians today, but Paul had a sinking feeling in his stomach as he and Barnabas and Titus approached Jerusalem. He knew that he was teaching a radical interpretation outside of the apostolic norm. Special revelations from Heaven are good, but Paul had not yet cleared this teaching with the authority in Jerusalem. He had never submitted it to the court of the apostles. Up until now, Paul had been operating as a "loose cannon," so to speak. He had been teaching on his own initiative, without authority and without sanction from those to whom our Master gave the power to bind and to loose and to govern the body.

The Authority of the Apostles

To Peter, Yeshua said, "I will give you the keys of the kingdom of heaven; and whatever you bind on earth shall have been bound in heaven, and whatever you loose on earth shall have been loosed in heaven" (Matthew 16:19). In saying this, he promoted Peter to the head over the Twelve, made him the chief disciple, and gave him, along with the other disciples, the legal authority to make Torah decisions regarding the community of believers (and all Israel). Rabbinic literature uses the terms "to bind" or "to loose" thousands of times to describe the rabbis' authority to interpret Torah, to set *halachah*, and to make legal decisions. The Roman Catholic Church understood that authority, from which it derived the tradition of papal authority. In essence, Yeshua set the apostles in the position of the Sanhedrin—not a replacement (not until the kingdom is revealed), but a higher authority with veto power if necessary.

The Torah instructs, "If any case arises requiring decision between one kind of homicide and another, one kind of legal right and another, or one kind of assault and another, any case within your towns that is too difficult for you, then you shall arise and go up to the place that the LORD your God will choose [i.e., Jerusalem]" to seek a ruling from the judges (Deuteronomy 17:8). In the late Second Temple era, the judges in Jerusalem were the Sanhedrin. Our Master, however, appointed a higher power above the Sanhedrin: the twelve thrones of the twelve disciples. He said they will sit upon twelve thrones judging over the twelve tribes. The twelve thrones should be understood as places of judicial authority immediately under the authority of the throne of David, i.e. the Messiah's throne.

In the absence of King Messiah, the authority over the throne of David passed on to a steward. Another from the same line and the same family, the next Davidic heir in line, took the position. In the days of the Apostle Paul, James the Righteous, the brother of the

Master, took the position. Not that James was the Messiah or the Messiah King, but he was the steward of that position of authority in Messiah's absence. The apocryphal Gospel of Thomas reports a tradition about James:

> The disciples said to Jesus, "We know that you will depart from us. Who is to be our leader?" Jesus said to them, "Wherever you are, you are to go to James the Righteous, for whose sake heaven and earth came into being." (*Gospel of Thomas* 12)

The expression "for whose sake heaven and earth came into being" may sound jarring to Christian ears, but it is a common hyperbole employed by the rabbis to praise a person's virtue. Over the Sanhedrin our Master appointed the twelve thrones, and above the twelve thrones he left the empty throne of David. In those days, temporarily occupying the throne of David on behalf of his older brother James, the brother of our Master, presided.

The Master said, "Wherever you are, you are to go to James the Righteous" as it says in the Torah, "If any case is too difficult for you to decide, between one kind of homicide or another, between one kind of lawsuit or another, and between one kind of assault or another, being cases of dispute in your courts, then *you shall arise and go up* to the place which the LORD your God chooses," i.e., to Jerusalem.

Hyper-Protestantism

American Protestants have a hard time with the notion of apostolic authority. We want to be more like Paul; we *are* more like Paul. Paul was not interested in that ecclesiastical authority. He received a private revelation from God, confirmed it in the Scriptures himself, and went with that. He had not bothered to check with the apostles above him. He boasted, "The gospel which was preached by me is not according to man. For I neither received it from man, nor was I taught it, but I received it through a revelation of Jesus Christ" (Galatians 1:11–12). He also boasted, "I did not immediately consult with anyone; nor did I go up to Jerusalem to those who were apostles before me" (Galatians 1:16).

I think that many of us can identify with Paul's sentiments. Who needs the rabbis, the sages, the Sanhedrin, all that Jewish tradition? Traditions and interpretations of men! And the same impulse says, "Who needs the twelve thrones? Who needs the interpretations of the apostles? Why do we need them to tell us what the Bible means?"

Spiritual authority grates against us, not because it is wrong, but because in this Western culture we resent authority. Protestants especially are trained and theologically inculcated with a distrust of spiritual authority, and that is why we tout the *sola scriptura* mantra. We cite the abuses. We point out the apostasies. We point to church history. In the past, men in authority over the church have twisted Scripture and abused authority and led us away from the truth. Therefore, we do not want to submit to apostolic authority. The *sola scriptura* Protestant says, "I can read the Torah myself and come to my own conclusions."

The defendant who represents himself in court has a fool for an attorney.

We need to consider our hearts. God's spirit works through authority structures. He instituted the authority structures. The LORD instituted priesthood, king, judge, the seventy judges, the Sanhedrin, the apostles, the twelve thrones, the court systems, the *beit din*, and even the eldership over the local body: heads over thousands, over hundreds, over tens.

What about when your leadership is wrong? Or what do you do if you disagree? A friend of mine told me an amusing story about Beth Immanuel. He informally polled the congregation about the authority of the elders. In every conversation, he asked, "Do you think we should submit to the authority of the elders?" In every conversation, the people answered, "Absolutely. The elders have the authority." Then he asked, "What if you disagreed with them on some matter?" And the answer was, "Well, in that case, then I would not submit." Some said, "I would leave." Others simply said, "I would not cooperate." The irony is that we have a mentality that believes in submission to authority so long as we agree with that authority. That's a dangerous mindset because if that is how we treat human authority, that is how we will treat God's authority. That will be the answer to Torah: I submit to the mitzvah so long as it makes sense to me and I agree with it. Likewise: I submit to the apostle's rulings so long as they make sense to me and I agree with them. That's not submission at all.

Running in Vain

I think that Paul had a sick feeling in his stomach as he went up to Jerusalem because he knew that he had not confirmed his calling, his ministry, or his gospel with the authorities. His message of salvation for Gentiles had not been confirmed with the Twelve, the elders at Jerusalem, or with James the brother of the Master.

He took advantage of the famine-relief trip to Jerusalem to seek a private audience with James, the brother of the Master, and with Peter, the first over the Twelve, and with John the son of Zebedee, the beloved disciple. He sought the counsel of those three pillars, and whoever of the Twelve might be available.

> I went up because of a revelation and set before them
> (though privately before those who seemed influential)
> the gospel that I proclaim among the Gentiles, in order
> to make sure I was not running or had not run in vain.
> (Galatians 2:2)

What does he mean by "I might be running, or had run, in vain?" He was talking about his gospel to the God-fearing Gentiles. Suppose Paul came to Jerusalem and said, "Shalom, I have good news. Lots of Gentiles have embraced the faith, and I told them that they don't even have to become Jewish to enter the kingdom of heaven, to merit the resurrection, the world to come, and a position within the people of God. In fact, I've been telling them they don't even need to be circumcised. Isn't that great?" And suppose that James and the apostles reply, "Paul, are you out of your mind? That's heretical and contradicts the teachings that Yeshua entrusted with us. You cannot teach that."

If they said that, Paul would have been running his race in vain. It's like a runner in a footrace who takes off from the starting line, running as hard as he can to win the race. He runs for miles. He sees no one around. He assumes he must be in the lead, but then someone tells him, "Hey, you are off the race route. You've been running in the wrong direction."

It has happened to me before.

No John Wayne

What does it profit a man if he expends his life proclaiming some other gospel? How do you know if you are off the path? Paul's teacher, Rabban Gamliel, used to say, "Do not rely on your own interpretation. Take upon yourself a teacher, and remove all doubt."[11]

Paul was no John Wayne or hyper-Protestant. He was a brilliant, spiritually gifted protégé, but he was also a man under authority. He turned to the authority, to the men of reputation regarded as the pillars of the assembly of Messiah:

> If any case arises ... that is too difficult for you, then you shall arise and go up to the place that the LORD your God will choose [i.e., Jerusalem]. (Deuteronomy 17:8)

> Wherever you are, you are to go to James the Righteous. (*Gospel of Thomas* 12)

> I went up because of a revelation and set before them (though privately before those who seemed influential) the gospel that I proclaim among the Gentiles, in order to make sure I was not running or had not run in vain. (Galatians 2:2)

Paul did not want to run his race in vain. He once wrote to the God-fearing Gentile believers in the city of Philippi, beseeching them to prove their faith and commitment to Messiah "so that in the day of Christ I may be proud that I did not run in vain or labor in vain" (Philippians 2:16). He regarded the Gentile believers as proof that he had not run or toiled in vain. They were the fruit of his unique gospel message. If the apostles in Jerusalem were to tell him that there was no such animal as a "God-fearing Gentile believer" and that a Gentile must be circumcised and become Jewish to be secure in the kingdom, then his efforts were in vain.

---

[11] m.*Avot* 1:16.

SERMON SIX:
THE BIG MEETING
(GALATIANS 2:3–5)

Paul brings Titus to a meeting with
the apostles to seek an apostolic
endorsement for his gospel to the
Gentiles.

In the early passages of his epistle to the Galatians, Paul provides
his readers with some background material and anecdotes from
his own spiritual journey to illustrate his experience with the message of the gospel as directed toward non-Jews. In the beginning
of the second chapter of Galatians, Paul describes his second trip
to Jerusalem after becoming a believer:

> I went up because of a revelation and set before them
> (though privately before those who seemed influential)
> the gospel that I proclaim among the Gentiles, in order
> to make sure I was not running or had not run in vain.
> (Galatians 2:2)

Recap and Review: Paul's Ulterior Motive

According to the narrative in the book of Acts, Paul and Barnabas went up to Jerusalem carrying a collection raised from the
Antioch community for the community of believers in Jerusalem.
They raised the collection and brought it to Jerusalem "because
of a revelation," a prophecy about coming years of scarcity and

a famine predicted by a prophet named Locust (Agabus). They wanted to fortify the *Evyonim* ("poor ones") against the famine. They brought along Titus, a God-fearing Gentile believer from Antioch.

Paul had an ulterior motive for this trip to Jerusalem. He intended to use the opportunity for a private meeting with the apostles, those reputed pillars of the assembly under James the Righteous, the brother of the Master. James presided over the assembly of Messiah as the steward of the throne of David, so to speak. Paul wanted to present his unique interpretation of the gospel to James and the apostles—namely the version of the gospel that he had been proclaiming in Antioch and among the Gentiles: that God-fearing Gentile believers need not become Jewish in order to inherit salvation, enter the kingdom of heaven, and obtain citizenship in the people of God; rather that faith in the Master was sufficient for even Gentiles.

Paul took that radical message to the council of the elders in Jerusalem. He met with James, Peter, John, and the elders present. They constituted the legal authority and high court over all believers and followers of Yeshua and, ultimately, the high court over all Israel. What they would bind on earth was bound in heaven and what they loosed on earth was loosed in heaven.

Paul went to them seeking an endorsement of his message "in order to make sure I was not running or had not run in vain." That is to say, they might have ruled: "Brother Saul, we commend you for your heart and your zeal, but you have gone astray and have led the Gentiles astray. It is needful for them to be circumcised and to become Jewish and submit to all the obligations incumbent upon Jewish people in order for them to inherit the kingdom of heaven." What if they had said that? Then Paul's gospel to the Gentiles would be invalid. As a man under authority, he would have had to go back to Antioch and to all those whom he had so misled and apologize to them and say to them, "I am sorry; I was wrong. You need to become Jewish now."

In the Principal's Office

Paul wanted to meet privately with "the pillars," those who were of reputation in the assembly of Messiah. James and the apostles in Jerusalem held positions of authority and could censure Paul if necessary, censor his message, and issue correction. That made the interview a dramatic moment for Paul. (He may have felt something like you do when you are fourteen or fifteen, in the ninth or tenth grade, and you are summoned to the principal's office for a meeting with your parents and the superintendent of the school to discuss your involvement in the crime of writing, reproducing, and distributing a subversive parody version of the student newspaper. I'm sure every kid has had that experience.)

Paul's gospel was controversial. It had huge implications for the public face of the believers and for the constitution of the synagogue—not just the believing congregations, but Jewish synagogues everywhere. Paul's gospel did not compel the God-fearing Gentile believers to become proselytes, i.e., "sons of Abraham." In that regard, Paul's gospel actually posed a threat to the constitution of the community of Israel.

Paul managed to secure a confidential meeting with the men at the top: James, the brother of the Master; with Simon Peter, the head over the twelve apostles; and with John the son of Zebedee, the beloved disciple. It's like scoring a meeting with the president, the vice president, and the secretary of state. It's like a meeting with the pope and his top two archbishops. (It's like a meeting with the superintendent of the school, the high school principal, and your dad.)

He submitted his gospel before them and presented his case. He said, "This is what I am teaching; this is what I am presenting; this is what I am telling the Gentiles. What do you think? Is it kosher?"

He also brought Titus with him to the meeting. If the meeting made Paul uncomfortable, think about how Titus must have felt. Why was Titus there? What did Titus have to do with it? Was Titus a guinea pig? Was he the token Gentile? Did Paul say, "Look, I brought a *goy*. What do you think? Shall we have him circumcised or not?"

Spies and False Brothers

Galatians 2:4 explains why Paul brought Titus along to the meeting. Titus was part of the discussion, Paul said, "because of false brothers secretly brought in—who slipped in to spy out our freedom that we have in Christ Jesus, so that they might bring us into slavery" (Galatians 2:4).

This verse requires some unpacking. It's hard to put the pieces back together. Who were these false brothers? In what sense were they false? In what sense had they been brought in? Into where did they slip? What was the freedom in Messiah Yeshua on which they spied? Who is the "we"? Who is it that they sought to subject to slavery? What did Paul mean by slavery? All of these questions need to be answered before we can make sense of Galatians 2:4, but unfortunately we cannot have definitive answers to all of these questions. We can only make a few halting guesses based upon some vague inferences.

In his book *The Irony of Galatians*, Jewish scholar Mark Nanos does not assume that the "false brothers" were believers in Yeshua. We have seen elsewhere that "brothers," in Pauline literature, can refer to the Jewish people in general. Nanos does not suggest that the "false brothers" are "false Jews," but that they are non-Yeshua-believing Jews. According to Nanos, Paul called them false brothers not to suggest that their brotherhood as Jews is false but rather their motives were false.

I disagree with Nanos. I think in this context, Paul used "brothers" to refer to fellow believers, and "false brothers" was Paul's way of dismissing their sincerity as believers. Nanos does raise an interesting suggestion on the passage though. Nanos retranslates the Greek word translated as "to spy out" in the phrase "who slipped in to spy our freedom," as "to investigate." So it is not that they were spies, so to speak, but rather, investigators, investigating what they considered to be a problem for Judaism.

Nanos suggests that they were investigating on behalf of some administrative authority. Suffice it to say that they had concerns about Paul, about his message, and about his work among the Gentiles.

Into where did they slip and do this investigating? We do not know. Nanos suggests they might have slipped into the meeting with the apostles. I would suggest that they slipped into the fellowship of the Antioch community. We have already seen traffic between the Jerusalem and the Antioch communities of believers, and when Gentiles first began joining the faith in Antioch, the apostles in Jerusalem sent Barnabas to "investigate."

Based on this information, I suggest that the so-called "false brothers" were actually believers sent from the Jerusalem community who had travelled to Antioch and become familiar with the situation there. They had gotten to know the people and the message that Paul was preaching. All the while, they were investigating the situation to report back to Jerusalem. Paul, Barnabas, and the other Antioch believers were unaware that the brothers from Jerusalem were there to investigate the Gentile phenomenon in Antioch—or as Paul puts it, the "freedom that we have in the Messiah Yeshua."

A Big Commandment

What was this freedom of which Paul spoke? It starts with circumcision and the concept that Gentiles, like Titus, were free from the mitzvah of circumcision. They did not need to become proselytes.

The Torah required a Jewish man to be circumcised and to circumcise his son on the eighth day:

> And God said to Abraham, "As for you, you shall keep my covenant, you and your offspring after you throughout their generations. This is my covenant, which you shall keep, between me and you and your offspring after you: Every male among you shall be circumcised." (Genesis 17:9–10)

One might have thought that this rule applied only to a baby eight days old and that an uncircumcised adult was not required to undergo circumcision so long as he circumcised his sons. That's why it says, "Every male among you." One might have thought that the law applied only to the physical descendants of Abraham, his literal, biological children. That's why it says, "Every male among you."

> You shall be circumcised in the flesh of your foreskins,
> and it shall be a sign of the covenant between me and
> you. (Genesis 17:11)

Circumcision is one of several commandments that the Torah identifies as a "sign." It was a sign of the covenant with Abraham. In the days of the apostles, Judaism did not consider the sign commandments as incumbent upon non-Jews because non-Jews were not part of the covenant. The Jewish people did not pressure the average Gentile to undergo circumcision. In the case of God-fearing Gentile believers, however, that was another matter entirely. Paul's Gentile believers claimed to have a position in the people of God and a share in God's covenants of promise. Therefore, logically they should also keep the sign commandments connected with those covenants.

That's how the logic goes. It is logical, but that was not what Paul taught. He taught that they need not keep the sign of circumcision.

According to the Torah, a man who neglected circumcision was liable for punishment. Genesis 17 requires circumcision of every male, whether born in Abraham's house (which would be Abraham's own sons and the sons of his servants and maidservants) or bought with money (which would be any foreigner brought into Abraham's household). This is a clear and certain rule. An uncircumcised male in Abraham's family or household was to be cut off from his people. The rabbis differentiate between being cut off by the hands of men and cut off by the hands of Heaven. Cut off by the hands of men means excision from the community or capital punishment, depending on the crime and situation. Cut off by Heaven means premature death—a death sentence from God.

The Torah presents an example of the latter in the case of Moses, who had not circumcised his son Gershon. The angel of the LORD appeared to him and his wife and was going to put Moses to death. The angel would have cut Moses off at the hands of Heaven if not for the quick intervention of Tzipporah, who circumcised the child. (Gershon was no longer eight days old, but the mitzvah to circumcise the child still stood.)

These texts indicate that the circumcision question was a serious matter, and it merited investigation. The so-called "false brothers" investigating in Antioch, I believe, were disturbed to see the "freedom in the Messiah Yeshua" that Paul proclaimed when they understood that it meant freedom from circumcision and free association between the circumcised and the uncircumcised.

Answering the Questions

Paul, Barnabas, and Titus arrived in Jerusalem. The so-called "false brothers" who had been in Antioch investigating were also there. They would have recognized Titus; they may have even approached the elders and placed the matter before them: "Paul and Barnabas have brought with them a fellow named Titus, a God-Fearer and Gentile from Antioch. Though they include him in the prayers, in the community, in our meals, in all of our fellowship and function, the fellow is neither circumcised, nor does he intend on being circumcised."

Assuming that this (or something similar) provides the context, let's see if we can answer the questions we posed regarding Galatians 2:4:

> False brothers secretly brought in—who slipped in to spy out our freedom that we have in Christ Jesus, so that they might bring us into slavery. (Galatians 2:4)

1. **Who are these false brothers?** Believing Jews from Jerusalem.

2. **In what sense are they false?** Either in the sense that Paul did not regard their allegiance to Messiah as sincere or in the sense that they did not disclose their motivations to him.

3. **In what sense had they been secretly brought in?** They had slipped into the fellowship of the community of believers in Antioch to investigate. They brought their complaint and concern against Titus (and the Gentile situation in Antioch) to the apostolic authorities in Jerusalem.

4. **What was the freedom in Messiah Yeshua on which they were spying?** They investigated reports of God-fearing Gentile believers neglecting the sign commandments, or at the very least, not taking on the sign of circumcision.

5. **Who is the "we" in Galatians 2:4?** Paul refers to himself and Barnabas and the message they proclaimed among the God-fearing believers in Antioch.

6. **Who is it that the "false brothers" sought to subject to slavery, and what does Paul mean by slavery?** They sought to require the Gentile believers to keep the sign commandments, at a minimum, the sign of circumcision, which entailed not just circumcision literally, but full, legal conversion to Judaism.

At some point, the false brothers had brought the results of their investigations in Antioch to the attention of the elders, the very men with whom Paul sought a private audience.

Results of the Meeting

Paul brought Titus with him to the meeting, and he presented his case for why he thought that Titus could remain as Titus the God-Fearer and did not need to take on the sign of the covenant with Abraham. The so-called "false brothers" may also have been present at that meeting because Paul says, "To them we did not yield in submission even for a moment, so that the truth of the gospel might be preserved for you" (Galatians 2:5).

Paul refused to yield "so that the truth of the gospel might be preserved" for the Galatians and for Gentile believers everywhere. When he says, "We did not yield in submission even for a moment," Mark Nanos suggests that the "we" includes James, Peter, John, and the rest of the apostles. They sided with Paul, and together they did not yield to the pressure regarding Titus. Paul announces the verdict in Galatians 2:3: "But even Titus, who was with me, was not forced to be circumcised, though he was a Greek."

That is to say, Paul learned that he had not run his race in vain. Instead, he received the apostolic endorsement that he had been seeking. They considered his case, listened to his presentation, weighed his argument, scrutinized his gospel, and they endorsed it. They gave Paul and his gospel the apostolic stamp of approval.

Paul's epistle to the Galatians is largely an explanation of the argument he presented at that meeting. It presents his gospel regarding Gentiles and their freedom in the Messiah.

REMEMBER THE POOR
(GALATIANS 2:6–10)

> The apostles in Jerusalem endorse Paul
> as an apostle to the Gentiles, and they
> endorse his gospel to the Gentiles with
> one caveat: that he remember the "poor
> ones."

After more than a decade, Paul went up to Jerusalem. He took along Barnabas and Titus. He "went up because of a revelation." According to the book of Acts, the revelation was a prophecy delivered by a prophet from Jerusalem by the name of Locust (Agabus), who predicted a famine that was to come upon the region. Like Joseph in Egypt preparing for the seven years of scarcity, Paul and Barnabas raised money for famine relief from the community in Antioch. They brought it to Jerusalem for the sustenance of the community of Jewish believers there.

Recap and Review: Paul's Big Meeting

The community of believers in Jerusalem needed the help. They had renounced personal property in order to live communally in the shadow of the Holy Temple. They assembled daily in the courts of the Temple to worship the LORD and to await the coming King Messiah. They were called the "poor ones," in Hebrew, *Evyonim* or, as the name passed into the early literature of the church fathers, "the Ebionites." (The apostolic community of *Evyonim* living in Jerusalem should not be confused with the Ebionite sect of later centuries who rejected the Temple and sacrificial system, became vegans, and also rejected the tradition of our Master's virgin birth and the writings of Paul.)

Their self-imposed poverty came from their radical dedication to our Master's teachings regarding selling one's possessions and giving to the poor. Their self-imposed poverty made the Jerusalem "poor ones" particularly vulnerable to the coming famine, so the believers in Antioch sent a financial contribution to the community to prepare for years of scarcity.

In addition, Paul had an ulterior motive for the trip to Jerusalem. He wanted to meet with the pillars, the elders of the apostles, to receive their endorsement for the radical gospel message he presented to Gentiles, namely that Gentiles could receive salvation and position in the covenants with Israel through the Messiah of Israel without being obligated to take on the sign commandments of the covenant. Paul's gospel exempted the Gentiles from the sign of circumcision, which represented a conversion to become Jewish.

Paul brought Titus, an uncircumcised, God-fearing, and believing Gentile from Antioch, to his meeting with the apostles as something of a test case. At the meeting, certain "false brothers" insisted that Titus should be compelled to undergo circumcision. The apostles, under James, the brother of the Master; Peter, the first among the Twelve; and John, the disciple whom the Master loved, refused to yield to that opinion. They defended Titus and his right to remain uncircumcised—thereby endorsing Paul's gospel, giving his message the seal of apostolic approval. As Paul said to the Galatians, this was "so that the truth of the Gospel might be preserved for you."

Paul's Dismissive Tone

Paul followed the story of how he received the apostolic endorsement with reference to the apostles with whom he met as "those who seemed to be influential." He claimed that "what they were makes no difference to me; God shows no partiality." He reported that "those who seemed influential added nothing to me" (Galatians 2:6).

By "those who seemed to be influential," Paul referred to James, Peter, John, and any other elders of the community who were present at the big meeting. It sounds like he dismissed their authority when referred to them as "those who seemed to be influential" and when he said "what they were makes no difference to me; God shows no partiality."

Despite the dismissive air, Paul submitted to their authority. He had already conceded that, if they had rejected his gospel of Gentile inclusion, he would have been running his race in vain. They had the power to utterly discredit the gospel message he had been presenting. Therefore, he certainly did respect their authority. But he seems less than reverentially respectful in Galatians 2:5.

In his commentary on Galatians, Richard Longenecker suggests that the influencers in Galatia based their appeal upon the practice of the elders in Jerusalem. That is, those teaching "some other gospel" to the Galatian Gentiles and compelling them to be circumcised did so in continuity with apostolic authority from Jerusalem, and they set that authority in antithesis to Paul. They pointed out to the Galatian God-Fearers that Peter and James received Gentiles into the faith as proselytes through circumcision and conversion. Therefore, Paul must be wrong. They may have asked, "Do you want to follow the real disciples of Yeshua—or Paul?"

As a result, Paul is a bit cheeky as he refers to their authority. This explains why he carefully taught in the first chapter of Galatians that he did not receive his gospel from the other apostles; he received it directly by divine revelation, confirmed by the Scriptures. Regarding the apostles in Jerusalem, he only sought validation, as a man under authority, but that authority was not the source of his gospel.

The people to whom Paul was writing (if Longenecker's suggestion is correct) had been told, "Yes, Paul says one thing, but the 'Pillars in Jerusalem,' James, Peter, and John, disagree with him." If so, Paul's point in retelling the whole story was to demonstrate that the charge is false. Remember, the entire Epistle to the Galatians predates the decision of the Jerusalem Council (Acts 15) which ruled on this issue in a definitive manner.

Paul's recitation of the story is consistent with Talmudic disputation. In the Talmud, when a halachic (legal) decision is in question, the sages relate anecdotes about their teachers or earlier generations as evidence to support their opinions. This is the situation here. "Not even Titus was compelled to be circumcised," Paul told the Galatians.

Apostle to the Gentiles

Paul's tone may sound dismissive, but he ultimately was not dismissive at all. Instead, he leaned heavily upon that apostolic endorsement as he declared, "Those, I say, who seemed influential added nothing to me" (Galatians 2:6).

What does it mean that they added nothing to him? Only this: that they did not add anything to his gospel. They did not correct him in any way. They did not say, "You must also teach the Gentile believers to keep the Sabbath and undergo circumcision." They added no further obligation than what Paul was already teaching to the Gentiles.

> On the contrary, when they saw that I had been entrusted with the gospel to the uncircumcised, just as Peter had been entrusted with the gospel to the circumcised (for he who worked through Peter for his apostolic ministry to the circumcised worked also through me for mine to the Gentiles), and when James and Cephas and John, who seemed to be pillars, perceived the grace that was given to me, they gave the right hand of fellowship to Barnabas and me, that we should go to the Gentiles and they to the circumcised. (Galatians 2:7–9)

The apostles in Jerusalem saw that Paul had been entrusted with the gospel to the uncircumcised, meaning that they acknowledged that Paul had been given a mission by God. They recognized that God had given Paul grace and favor to declare the message of the gospel to the Gentile world. They recognized his calling; they endorsed his message, and they endorsed his apostleship to the Gentile world. One might say, they ordained him.

Henceforth, Paul refers to himself as "the apostle to the Gentiles." For example, in Romans 11:13, Paul says, "Now I am speaking to you Gentiles. Inasmuch then as I am an apostle to the Gentiles ..." Again, in 1 Timothy 2:7, Paul declares: "For this I was appointed a preacher and an apostle (I am telling the truth, I am not lying), a teacher of the Gentiles in faith and truth."

This is not to say that Paul would never again declare the gospel of Yeshua to Jewish people. His first calling, mission, and goal, however, was to minister to the Gentile world, i.e., to call God-fearing Gentiles to faith in Yeshua.

Simon Peter, on the other hand, as head over the Twelve, worked primarily among the circumcised, that is, among Jewish people and proselytes to Judaism. His apostleship (and that of the Twelve) was first and foremost to the Jewish people. Not that Peter would never present the gospel to non-Jews. He certainly did, but he followed the Master's mission in seeking first the lost sheep of Israel, the sinners among the Jewish people, calling them to repent, turn back to the Torah, and believe in the risen Messiah for the forgiveness of sins.

The Tail Wags the Dog

For the last eighteen hundred years, the church has triumphantly declared that the gospel has cancelled the Torah and that Gentile Christians have replaced the Jewish people. Those dogmas stem from a failure to understand the distinction between Peter's ministry and Paul's ministry, between Peter's apostleship and Paul's apostleship. Christians quickly forgot that Paul was the apostle to the Gentiles and that his letters needed to be read as addressed primarily to God-fearing Gentile readers, not to Jewish readers. We forgot this detail. Since Gentiles were at the center of Paul's concern, we came to believe that Gentiles were at the center of the gospel's concern. We forgot that Paul's gospel was distinct from the gospel of the rest of the apostles and that his mission was an outgrowth of the mission of Messiah to redeem Israel.

We forgot that Galatians, Ephesians, 1 and 2 Thessalonians, Colossians, Philippians, Romans and 1 and 2 Corinthians—the whole batch of Paul's epistles—were written by the apostle *to the*

Gentiles. Therefore, when Paul speaks of not being "under the law" and free from the obligation of circumcision, having freedom in the Spirit, and all of that, he was speaking to Gentiles—not to Jewish believers. Christianity overlooked that important detail, and Christian theology became a Gentile theology positioned against Torah observance that taught (and still teaches today) that if a Jewish person becomes a believer, he should be compelled to set aside Torah and leave Judaism. What happened here? The theological tail of the New Testament has been wagging the dog.

Correcting this error has been at the heart of the teaching ministry of Beth Immanuel Sabbath Fellowship and the ministry of First Fruits of Zion. We are on a mission to correct the failure to distinguish between Paul's gospel to the Gentiles and the gospel to the Jewish people. We have been attempting to correct a nearly-fatal error in the transmission of the gospel. If faith in Yeshua means that Jewish people should be exempt from circumcision or the other sign commandments and distinctions enjoined upon them by the Torah, then faith in Yeshua, for a Jewish person, is a sin against God. According to the Bible's own testimony, Jesus must be castigated as a false prophet, and the gospel message should be rejected.

The God of Distinctions

We are one body, many parts. The foot is not the eye; the eye is not the foot. Oneness is not sameness. We can be one in the body but not have the same function and calling. Oneness is not sameness. There is one faith, one baptism, and one body, but that body has many parts.

Theologically, we run into trouble whenever we fail to make a distinction between one thing and another. Historically, in Christianity, we have obliterated distinctions between the Father and the Son, between the holy and the profane, between the seventh day and the six days, between Israel and the nations.

God is a God of distinction. He is called *HaMavdil*, "The One who separates." He formed the earth, separating light from dark, the waters above from the waters below, the sea from the dry ground, and the female from the male. At *havdalah*-time (end of the Sabbath), we say, "*HaMavdil*, he who separates between the holy and the profane, between light and dark, between the seventh day and the six days of labor, between Israel and the nations."

If there is no *havdalah*—no distinction—between Israel and the nations, then why did the apostles appoint one apostle to the nations and another to the Jewish people? If the end goal for the Gentiles was the same as that of the Jewish believers, why a distinct mission? Why appoint an apostle to the Gentiles with a gospel for the Gentiles distinct from the apostleship to the Jewish people?

You might ask, "But aren't we all one in Messiah?" Yes. But we are not the same.

We are swinging the pendulum back to correct the error of the last two thousand years that said Jewish Christians are one with Gentile Christians, so they should behave as if they are Gentiles. Some of us, however, have crossed the center and gone to the opposite extreme, now saying that Gentile Christians are the same as Jewish Christians so they should therefore be Jewish. It blurs the line of distinction, and ultimately it is the same mistake.

This does not mean that the God-fearing Gentile believers should not participate in commandments such as the Sabbath. As we will see later, there are good reasons for Gentile God-Fearers to do so, but they should not consider themselves as Gentile-Jews.

The Pillars

Paul referred to "James and Cephas and John, who seemed to be pillars" (Galatians 2:9). In early midrash, the rabbis referred to Abraham as "the Rock." God said, "Upon this Rock I will build my world." In the Yeshua movement, Peter is called the Rock, and the Master said, "Upon this rock I will build my assembly." In the *Midrash Rabbah*, Abraham, Isaac, and Jacob are also called the Pillars:

> When the patriarchs came and showed themselves righteous, God said, "On these will I establish My world; as it says [in 1 Samuel 2:8]: 'For the pillars of the earth are the LORD's, and on them He has set the world.'" (*Exodus Rabbah* 15:7)

In the Talmud, the disciples of Rabban Yochanan ben Zakkai referred to him as "the Pillar of the right hand," perhaps alluding to the right-hand pillar at the entrance to the Temple. Likewise, the body of believers referred to themselves as a living temple. Yeshua was the door. The primary apostles were the pillars.

Paul uses this language when he speaks of the whole body of Messiah as Jewish and Gentile believers being built into a spiritual house, i.e., a temple. Not every part of the temple is identical. It is one temple of the Holy Spirit, but it has different parts. So when Paul refers to James, Peter, and John as "those who seemed to be pillars," he speaks of their position of authority in the spiritual temple of the body of Messiah.

Remember the Evyonim

Paul said that James, Peter, and John, the reputed pillars, gave the right hand of fellowship to him and to Barnabas. They commissioned them to go to the Gentiles while they themselves continued to witness Messiah to the circumcised. Paul says, "Only, they asked us to remember the poor, the very thing I was eager to do" (Galatians 2:10).

I might have thought that the apostles laid upon the Gentile believers no greater obligation to Torah than the commandment of giving charity generously to the poor. In other words, they said to Paul, "We are fine with your message to the Gentiles and about their exemption from the covenant signs. In fact, they do not need to keep any of the commandments of the Torah, just so long as they give generously to the poor." Paul agrees, "That's exactly what I was thinking, too!"

I might have read it this way, but that's problematic. Paul already said that they added nothing to his gospel. It sounds like they are adding something here: "That's fine Paul, but have everyone remember to give charity to the poor." Out of the entire Torah, is that the only commandment that the apostles thought should apply to Gentiles?

Paul did not say, "Only they asked the Gentiles to give charity to the poor." He said, "Only they asked us to remember the poor." Look at this carefully. Who is the "us"? In this context, it must be Paul and

Barnabas. The apostles asked Paul and Barnabas to remember the poor. Why? What does that have to do with the entire question? "Paul, you be the apostle to the Gentiles, and we original apostles will take the message to the Jewish people, so long as you remember to give charity to the poor." That explanation does not work.

Why did they lay this one caveat on Paul's ministry? It does not even say that he should be generous with the poor or support the poor financially, just to remember them. In a Jewish context, to "remember" something can mean more than just remembering. For example, the Ten Commandments tell us to "remember the Sabbath day." The prophet says, "Remember the Torah of Moses." The LORD says, "Remember the covenant." In all of these contexts, to "remember" something is to be mindful of it and to remember one's obligations. It means to remember one's obligation to the thing remembered and to act upon that obligation.

I believe that the poor whom Paul and Barnabas are to remember are not just any poor. They are the *Evyonim*, the Poor Ones, i.e., the apostolic assembly of believers in Jerusalem: the pillars, the elders, the assembly of James and the apostles. In his commentary on Galatians, Richard Longenecker identifies "the Poor" in Galatians 2:10 as simply a shorthand abbreviation for the longer title that Paul gives them in Romans 15:26, where he refers to them as "the poor among the saints at Jerusalem."

In other words, the apostolic pillars at Jerusalem endorsed Paul's apostleship and his gospel message to the Gentiles. They put a *heksher* (kosher certification) on him and confirmed his message to the Gentiles with one caveat: "Remember the *Evyonim*," which is to say, "Remember us and our community in Jerusalem. Remember your obligation to us. Remember your position under our authority. Remember your obligations to this mother community, the Jerusalem community." Paul says that *this was the very thing that he was eager to do.*

This is the very thing that I am eager to do. I hope I can share with you my zeal to remember the authority of that community, to remember the *Evyonim*, the brothers of our Master, the original disciples of our Master, and the men in whom he invested his ministry. To them he gave the authority to bind and to loose and the keys to the kingdom of heaven. They preserved the gospel for us and transmitted it to us. They were the original mother of our faith, the pillars of the temple of the Holy Spirit, the assembly, the rock on which the assembly of Messiah is built, the men who endorsed Paul and to whom Paul submitted and to whom he was eager to submit. Let's not let the theological tail of the New Testament wag the dog any longer.

THE ANTIOCH INCIDENT

(GALATIANS 2:11–14)

Paul recounts how Peter, on his visit to
Antioch, separated from the God-fearing
Gentile believers and earned Paul's
sound rebuke.

Thus far in the epistle to the Galatians, we have noted that
Paul is arguing for his radical interpretation of the gospel
as it applies to non-Jews. He has just finished telling us that he
went to Jerusalem to discuss it with "the Pillars." He has happily
reported that the apostolic authorities sided with him, and they
did not even compel Titus to be circumcised. Until this point in
the epistle, Paul has cited only anecdotal testimony because all
of this took place prior to the Jerusalem Council's definitive legal
ruling in Acts 15.

The Antioch Incident

In Galatians 2:11, Paul relates a second anecdote to buttress his
contention that Gentiles need not keep the sign commandment of
circumcision. This is the famous (or infamous) Antioch Incident,
a conflict between Peter and Paul:

> But when Cephas came to Antioch, I opposed him to his
> face, because he stood condemned. For before certain
> men came from James, he was eating with the Gentiles;

but when they came he drew back and separated himself, fearing the circumcision party. And the rest of the Jews acted hypocritically along with him, so that even Barnabas was led astray by their hypocrisy. But when I saw that their conduct was not in step with the truth of the gospel, I said to Cephas before them all, "If you, though a Jew, live like a Gentile and not like a Jew, how can you force the Gentiles to live like Jews?" (Galatians 2:11–14)

The traditional Christian interpretation of this passage presupposes that Paul and the Jewish believers with him had given up Judaism and the practice of Torah. When Paul saw Peter waffling on this matter by practicing some aspects of Torah, such as returning to the Bible's dietary laws, he rebuked him for Judaizing—that is to say that Paul rebuked Peter for backsliding back to Torah and Judaism.

A Different Interpretation

Magnus Zetterholm of the Centre for Theology and Religious Studies in Sweden offers a different perspective in his book *Approaches to Paul*:

> Such a basic presupposition is far from self-evident—it is not at all certain that Paul's intention was that all Jews in the Jesus movement should stop observing the Torah. Furthermore, if the non-Jewish adherents of the Jesus movement were recruited from the group of non-Jews that already took part in the activities of the synagogue [i.e., God-Fearers], it is likely that they previously had adapted a Jewish lifestyle, especially with regard to food.[12]

> The problem in Antioch, then, was probably the degree of intimacy in social relations ... it probably did not affect the food they ate, but rather the ritual of community meals. Such matters as the seating at the table and how wine and food were handled may have indicated to some Jews (like James) who did not share Paul's ideology

---

[12] Magnus Zetterholm, *Approaches to Paul: A Student's Guide to Recent Scholarship* (Minneapolis, MN: Fortress Press, 2009), 25.

regarding the equal standing of the non-Jews before God that the Jewish identity of the community was threatened … the delegation from James—the circumcision faction that Peter feared—seems to have recommended that the status of the non-Jews should be altered. The reason for this may simply have been an effort to try to get the ethnic identity and the social intercourse to correspond. If Jews and non-Jews socialized as if they belonged to the same ethnic group, James's representatives may have thought it best to have the non-Jews turned into Jews, in spite of the earlier agreement from Jerusalem. This does not mean that James had changed his mind on the general principle that non-Jews could be saved without becoming Jews, only that he disagreed with Paul on the implications for social interaction resulting from this theology. According to James, non-Jews could very well be connected to the Jesus movement, but only if the distinction between Jew and non-Jew was manifest also in social relations.[13]

Peter in Antioch

Peter came to Antioch, the city in which Paul and Barnabas ministered among the Jewish community in the midst of the *Christianoi*, the Jewish believers, and specifically among those God-fearing Gentile believers like Titus. Simon Peter came to see the work there because Antioch had become the number-two city, after Jerusalem, for Jewish believers, and the number-one city for Gentile believers. In Antioch, the believers were first called Christians. They probably had a synagogue or two, perhaps several, which were Messianic, i.e., *Christianoi*. The believers in Antioch, no doubt, requested Peter to come and tell his stories and to teach them the Master's teachings. Can you imagine? They wanted to ask him, "What was it like to know him, to walk with him, to be with him? What was he like?"

In Antioch, Peter discovered an amazing community of believers where, in the midst of the believing Jewish community, God-fearing Gentile believers (the disciples of Paul and Barnabas)

---

[13] Ibid., 27.

mingled freely. They worshipped with the Jewish believers; they kept the Sabbath and the festivals along with the Jewish believers to the extent they were able; they fellowshipped with the Jewish believers; and they ate and drank with the Jewish believers at fellowship meals, at ritual meals, festival meals, and so forth—not as guests in the synagogue or second-class citizens, but as brothers and sisters in the Messiah.

Peter arrived in Antioch and saw this mix of Jewish and Gentile believers, and he had no objections. After all, it was through Peter that the revelation of the gospel for Gentiles had first come. It came, not through Paul, but through Peter when he had the vision of the sheet from heaven descending and a voice saying, "What God has made clean, let no man call unclean." Peter first crossed the line, tore down the metaphoric wall of partition, and went into a Gentile home. He was the first to preach the gospel to the God-fearing Gentile Cornelius and the God-Fearers in Caesarea. He saw them receive the Holy Spirit, and most importantly he ate and drank with them. The other apostles in Jerusalem expressed shock and dismay when they heard about Peter eating and drinking with Gentiles. When Peter returned to Jerusalem from Caesarea, they said to Peter, "You went to uncircumcised men and ate with them!" (Acts 11:3).

Eating with Gentiles

What's the problem with eating with uncircumcised men? Peter explained to Cornelius, "You yourselves know how unlawful it is for a Jew to associate with or to visit anyone of another nation, but God has shown me that I should not call any person common or unclean" (Acts 10:28).

Was it unlawful? According to *halachah* (Jewish law) of the first century, Jews were not supposed to eat food, even kosher food, that had been prepared by a Gentile. The possibility, indeed the likelihood, that the food might be contaminated by idols or by other Gentile defilements, prevented Jews from eating Gentile food. The Gentiles themselves were also ritually contaminated by idolatry, almost certainly. A Roman centurion, for example, had no choice but to participate in the Roman cult functions of his legion. From a first-century Jewish perspective, a clear and distinct wall of separation should have been maintained between Gentiles and observant Jews. Prior to the vision of the sheet, Peter considered it unlawful for a Jew to associate with or visit a Gentile, even a God-fearing Gentile, and the rest of the apostles were shocked that Peter went to a Gentile home and, most surprising of all, ate with them.

Years later, Peter visited Antioch. He saw how much things had changed since those days. In Antioch, Jewish believers and God-fearing Gentile believers freely mingled, ate together, and fellowshipped. Peter did the same. He mingled and ate with the God-fearing Gentile believers until some more guests from Jerusalem arrived.

> For before certain men came from James, he was eating with the Gentiles; but when they came he drew back and separated himself, fearing the circumcision party. And the rest of the Jews acted hypocritically along with him, so that even Barnabas was led astray by their hypocrisy. (Galatians 2:12–13)

Certain Men from James

Who were the certain men from James? Paul referred to them as "the circumcision party." By saying that they were certain men from James, Paul indicated that they were from the *Evyonim*, the Jerusalem community of Jewish believers. They must have been important people. Perhaps they were apostles themselves—certainly representatives of James, the brother of the Master, the head over the believers.

Why they came to Antioch, we are not told, but we do know that on arrival, they expressed their disapproval about the free intermingling of Jewish and Gentile believers. Paul refers to them as "the circumcision party," indicating that they were convinced that Gentile believers should undergo conversion; not for salvation, but, as Zetterholm has suggested, these men were only trying to bring the Gentiles to the obvious next step. If the Gentile believers were fellowshipping, worshipping, and eating within Jewish space, they should go the full distance and become Jewish. If they chose not to do so, they should be set aside from the Jewish community— quarantined, so to speak—so that the distinction remained perfectly clear.

We have this same issue in the Messianic Jewish movement all the time. This is always the issue, and it is always the question. When Gentiles start doing Jewish things, it blurs those neat lines of distinction. Our problems in Messianic Judaism are not new problems; they are ancient problems, biblical problems, the same problems with which the disciples of the apostles and the apostles themselves struggled.

Under their influence, Peter withdrew from table fellowship with the Gentile believers. Barnabas withdrew from table fellowship with the Gentile believers. The rest of the Jewish believers in Antioch followed suit. Paul saw where this was going. He saw that this could only result, ultimately, in two different faith communities, two different religions, and two different peoples: a Gentile *ekklesia* and a Jewish *ekklesia*, and he did not care for it.

He took a bold step; he even stepped out of line and rebuked Peter.

Halachah of the Gospel

Paul said that "their conduct was not in step with the truth of the gospel" (Galatians 2:14). We could understand it as "their conduct was not in keeping with the *halachah* of the truth of the gospel." The word *halachah* refers to the legal interpretation of Torah, but it literally means "walk." To be out of step with the truth of the gospel is to be outside the correct *halachah* of the gospel.

The *halachah* of the truth of the gospel of which Paul spoke was his belief that Gentile believers are part of the covenant and the greater commonwealth of Israel. They were no longer "Gentile sinners" and pagans. This new quasi-legal status enabled Jewish and non-Jewish believers to mingle freely, fellowship freely, worship together, and most importantly, eat together. The matter had already been established after Peter saw the sheet from heaven and after the Cornelius incident. It was already an accepted halachic practice of the apostolic community, so this new policy of segregation and separation that the circumcision party introduced in

Antioch ran contrary to the already-established halachic practice and norms of the believing community.

Judaizers

Paul rebuked Peter. He said to Peter, "If you, though a Jew, live like a Gentile and not like a Jew, how can you force the Gentiles to live like Jews?'" (Galatians 2:14). That is to say, "If you, though you are Jewish, have been, up until now, freely mixing with the Gentile believers, eating with them, fellowshipping and worshipping with them, unlike the common Jewish standard, i.e., you have been living 'like a Gentile and not like a Jew," how then can you now force the Gentiles to live like Jews?"

It does not mean that Peter was heretofore living as a Gentile in the sense of not keeping Torah, not keeping Sabbath, not keeping kosher, etc. It means that he was freely associating with the Gentiles and setting aside higher halachic concerns about food prepared by Gentiles and concerns about Gentile defilement. Consider the Young's Literal Translation on Galatians 2:14:

> If thou, being a Jew, in the manner of the nations dost live, and not in the manner of the Jews, how the nations dost thou compel to Judaize?

This is the passage from which we have inherited the appellation "Judaizers." In its original context, it refers to the ambitions of the Circumcision Party, namely the conversion of the Gentile believers. The Circumcision Party among the early Jewish believers sought to bring the God-fearing Gentiles "under the law" in the same manner as Jewish believers by requiring them to undergo conversion. The word is used this way in the LXX of Esther 8:17:

> And many of the people of the land became Jews; for the fear of the Jews fell upon them. (Esther 8:17, KJV)

> And many of the Gentiles were circumcised, and Judaized [became Jews], for fear of the Jews. (Esther 8:17, LXX)

So Paul said to Peter: "If you, though a Jew, live like a Gentile and not like a Jew, how can you force the Gentiles to Judaize, i.e., to become Jews?"

In later Christian use, the term came to mean "persuading Gentiles to live like Jews," that is, to keep the Sabbath in any measure, the Torah in any measure, attending synagogue or eating *matzah* at Passover, and so forth. The original context, however, and the goal of the Circumcision Party, was to compel the Gentile God-Fearers in Antioch to become Jewish. That is why this anecdote was relevant to the Galatians to whom Paul was writing. So Paul said, "If you, though a Jew, live like a Gentile in regard to fellowshipping with Gentiles, and not like a Jew who separates from them, how then can you force the Gentiles to become Jews?"

Rebuilding What You Tore Down

Paul went on to expand upon the rebuke by providing a theological argument:

> We ourselves are Jews by birth and not Gentile sinners; yet we know that a person is not justified by works of the law but through faith in Jesus Christ, so we also have believed in Christ Jesus, in order to be justified by faith in Christ and not by works of the law, because by works of the law no one will be justified. But if, in our endeavor to be justified in Christ, we too were found to be sinners, is Christ then a servant of sin? Certainly not! For if I rebuild what I tore down, I prove myself to be a transgressor. (Galatians 2:15–18)

We will study this passage in greater detail in the subsequent sermon. For now, allow me to add some clarifications in square brackets [like this]:

> We ourselves are Jews by birth and not Gentile sinners; yet we know that [whether Jewish nor Gentile] a person is not justified by works of the law [i.e., conversion, circumcision, etc.] but through faith in Jesus Christ, so we [the Jewish believers] also have believed in Christ Jesus, in order to be justified by faith in Christ and not by works of the law, because by works of the law no one will be justified. But if, in our endeavor to be justified in Christ, we too were found to be sinners [by eating and fellowship-

ping with Gentiles], is Christ then a servant of sin? [In other words, does becoming a believer mean we forsake Torah? Is eating and fellowshipping with Gentiles really a sin against Torah?] Certainly not! For if I rebuild what I tore down, I prove myself to be a transgressor. (Galatians 2:15–18)

That is to say to Peter, "If you of all people, Peter, rebuild a sharp division between Jew and Gentile by removing yourself from table fellowship with Gentiles, you are rebuilding the barrier that you originally tore down. If you refuse to eat and worship with them, you rebuild the barrier that you originally tore down. You yourself were the first of the apostles to tear that separation down. If now you are putting it back up, then you are admitting that you were wrong in the first place, and you are proving yourself to have been living in sin and transgression."

How did Peter receive this rebuke? How did he answer? We would like to hear the other side of this story. Ultimately, Paul was right, and ultimately Peter conceded. Several years later, at the Jerusalem Council in Acts 15, Peter offered an opinion, stating:

Brothers, you know that in the early days God made a choice among you, that by my mouth the Gentiles should hear the word of the gospel and believe. And God, who knows the heart, bore witness to them, by giving them the Holy Spirit just as he did to us, and he made no distinction between us and them, having cleansed their hearts by faith. Now, therefore, why are you putting God to the test by placing a yoke on the neck of the disciples that neither our fathers nor we have been able to bear? (Acts 15:7–10)

May God, who knows the heart, bear witness to us as well by giving us the Holy Spirit just as he did for them. And may he cleanse our hearts by faith so that we may serve him sincerely.

WORKS OF THE LAW

(GALATIANS 2:15–16)

An exploration of the terms
"justification," "works of the law," and
"faith in Jesus Christ."

In the previous sermon, we saw the Apostle Peter visiting the believing community in Antioch, the largest center of believers outside of Jerusalem. He found a community in which Jewish believers and God-fearing Gentile believers freely intermingled, worshipped together, and even ate together. Peter did the same until certain men from James arrived and applied pressure on the Jewish believers to separate from the God-fearing Gentiles. When Peter acquiesced to their pressure, Paul rebuked him.

Gentile Sinners

After retelling the Antioch Incident in which he rebuked Peter for returning to a segregationist policy of separating the Jewish and Gentile believers, Paul said in Galatians 2:15, "We ourselves are Jews by birth and not Gentile sinners." That sounds rather offensive. If you would like Paul to elaborate on what he means by "Gentile sinners," read the first chapter of Romans, and he will tell you exactly what he means by castigating the entire non-Jewish world as "Gentile sinners."

First-century Judaism divided the world into two main categories: Jews and Not-Jews. A "Not-Jew" could become a "Jew" by undergoing circumcision and legal conversion, so there was some crossover. Despite those few crossovers, there were two types of people in the world: Jews and Gentile sinners. Paul said to Peter:

> We ourselves are Jews by birth and not Gentile sinners; yet we know that [whether Jewish or Gentile] a person is not justified by works of the law but through faith in Jesus Christ, so we [the Jewish believers] also have believed in Christ Jesus, in order to be justified by faith in Christ and not by works of the law, because by works of the law no one will be justified. (Galatians 2:15–16)

Three terms from Galatians 2:16 need to be defined in order to make sense of the passage:

1. Justified
2. Works of the law
3. Faith in Jesus Christ

Justification

Justification always seems to me like a hopelessly slippery theological term, but if we examine its Hebrew equivalent, it helps nail down a concrete definition. For example, consider Deuteronomy 25:1:

> If there is a dispute between men and they come into court and the judges decide between them, *acquitting* the innocent and condemning the guilty, then it shall be if the wicked man deserves to be beaten, the judge shall then make him lie down and be beaten in his presence with the number of stripes according to his guilt. (Deuteronomy 25:1–2)

When judges decide a law case, they acquit the innocent and condemn the guilty. The English Standard Version of the Bible translates the Hebrew word *hitzdiku* as "acquitting." I might say, "legally exonerating." It is the opposite of "condemning." To be condemned is to be found guilty by a court of law and delivered for punishment. Here's an example from the gospels. Our Master says,

"For by your words you will be justified [acquitted, legally exonerated], and by your words you will be condemned" (Matthew 12:37). Likewise, in the parable of the Pharisee and the tax collector, Yeshua says, "I tell you, this man went to his house justified [acquitted, legally exonerated] rather than the other" (Luke 18:10–14).

In the sense that Paul employs the term, he uses it to refer to a verdict in the heavenly court of law. The antithesis of the term is "condemnation." When you go before a court of law, the judge will offer a verdict. He will either say "Innocent" or "Guilty."

As in our own court system, the judge in a Torah court of law offers his verdict only in the eyes of the law and the court. It is a legal ruling, that's all. If the judge declares a man innocent, that does not make him actually innocent nor does it mean that he did not actually commit the offense.

For example, imagine that you were seen murdering a man in ancient Israel. You were brought to court and the eyewitness testified against you, but no second corroborating witness appeared. The judge would be compelled to declare you innocent, "justified," even though you were guilty as sin. You could not be condemned for the crime because the Torah requires two eyewitnesses. That's what it means to be justified: to be declared innocent, even if you aren't. In that sense, the old adage works: "Justification means just-as-if-I never-sinned." Actually, you did sin, but you are going to get away with it.

The same justification applied to the tax collector in the Master's parable of the Pharisee and the tax collector. He was not innocent. He was a tax collector, collecting taxes for the evil empire of Rome. He left the Temple "justified," spared of condemnation in the eyes of God.

Justification does not make you sinless; it does not impart righteousness into your being and make you suddenly a more godly person. Instead, justification is a legal verdict of "not guilty" in the court of heaven, even though you are guilty. Justified means "not punishable." The justified person is reckoned righteous even if he is not.

Works of the Law

"Works of the law" is not a difficult term to understand. Works are deeds, so the term means "deeds of Torah." Among the Dead Sea Scrolls, one document has the title *Miksat Ma'asei HaTorah*, which I would translate as "Selection of the Works of the Law." The selection includes various purity measures, several of which are concerned with contamination by Gentiles. In 1994, Dead Sea Scroll scholar Martin Abegg published an article suggesting that when Paul spoke of the "works of the law," he was not speaking of keeping Torah in general, but rather of the type of rulings found in *Miksat Ma'asei HaTorah*.[14] Abegg does not suggest that Paul was referring specifically to that Qumran document. *Miksat Ma'asei HaTorah* was essentially a halachic discourse on a few matters of Torah which had no relevance for the situation in Galatia, or in Rome, or in any of Paul's communities (or anywhere outside of an Essene compound for that matter). Abegg suggests, nonetheless, that Paul might have had sectarian rulings of that type in view. It does seem possible, as Abegg suggests, that "works of the law" should be understood as a specific subset of the Torah's commandments. In other words, it's not a generic term for obeying the Torah; it refers to certain ceremonial matters of Torah.

Likewise, in his book *The New Perspective on Paul*, James Dunn suggests that "works of the law" should be understood more narrowly than just "deeds of Torah" in general.[15] Dunn claims that when Paul spoke of "works of the law," he was speaking of "the Torah's marks of Jewish identity." In that case, Paul had no problem with the Torah itself as a standard for righteousness for God-fearing Gentile believers. Instead, he took issue with imposing onto Gentiles the "works of the Torah" that marked Jewish identity: primarily the food laws, circumcision, the Sabbath, the calendar, and the sacrificial and Temple/Levitical obligations—specifically those things that define who is Jewish and exclude the non-Jew.

I think Dunn is right about this because, as we know from the context, at least the circumcision and Jewish-identity question is

---

[14] Martin Abegg, "Paul, 'Works of the law' and MMT," *Biblical Archaeology Review* 20:06 (November-December, 1994): 11–12.

[15] James Dunn, *The New Perspective on Paul: Revised Edition* (Peabody, MA: Eerdmans, 2008).

on the table in Galatians. At the very least, "works of the law" means keeping the commandments, and for Jewish people, the most characterizing works of the law were, as Dunn says, those identity markers: sacrifice, food laws, circumcision, Sabbath, and calendar. What are the "works of the law"? In the context of contrasting Jews and Gentiles, they are the markers of Jewish identity: circumcision, Sabbath, dietary laws, Levitical obligations, etc.

Faith in Jesus Christ

"Faith in Jesus Christ" seems easy enough to define. Faith in Jesus Christ means believing in Jesus Christ, right? It does miss something in translation though. The translation "faith in Jesus Christ" translates the specific Greek phrase *pisteos Yesou Christou* which, in a strictly grammatical sense, constitutes a genitive relation where two nouns stand next to each other and relate to one another somehow. It is similar to the Hebrew construct form or the English possessive case. It could be understood either as a subjective or objective genitive. Normally, it is translated as an objective genitive: "faith in Jesus Christ," but there is no Greek accusative here or anywhere that would cause Paul to use this term, i.e., there is no word "in." Rather, it is just "faith Jesus Christ." For that reason, in its plain and simple literal reading, the subjective genitive is to be preferred, similar to the Hebrew construct form.

Taken as a subjective genitive, the phrase could be translated not as "faith in Jesus Christ," but "faith of Jesus Christ," or better yet, "faithfulness of Jesus Christ." This is how Lloyd Gaston in his book *Paul and the Torah* translates the term.[16] So it is not primarily about you and your belief in Jesus Christ as much as it is about the faithfulness of Jesus Christ. This is literally what the Greek says. It requires a fairly radical concept that challenges a lot of conventional notions about faith, but it is consistent with a literal reading of the Greek.

---

[16] Lloyd Gaston, *Paul and the Torah* (Vancouver: University of British Columbia Press, 1987).

The "faithfulness of Jesus Christ" is his sinless obedience, his righteousness, his merit, and the favor (grace) that God found in him.

Rereading Galatians 2:15–16

Having defined our three terms, we are now ready to return to the text of Galatians:

- **Justification**: A legal verdict of exoneration (the opposite of condemnation) issued by a court of law or by God's court of law.
- **Works of the law**: The commandments of the Torah that identify a person as Jewish.
- **Faith in Jesus Christ**: The faithfulness of Jesus Christ.

Let's reread Galatians 2:15–16 with these definitions and see if it helps. I will mark the substituted definitions in square brackets [like this].

> We ourselves are Jews by birth and not Gentile sinners; yet we know that [whether Jewish or Gentile] a person is not [legally exonerated] by [the commandments of Torah that identify a person as Jewish] but through [the faithfulness of] Jesus Christ, so we [Jewish believers] also have believed in Christ Jesus, in order to be [legally exonerated] by the [faithfulness of Jesus Christ] and not by [the commandments of Torah that identify a person as Jewish], because by [the commandments of Torah that identify a person as Jewish] no one will be [legally exonerated].

According to that reading of the passage, Paul merely asked Peter, "Why would you require the Gentiles to take on the commandments of Torah that define a person as Jewish when even we Jews who keep those commandments know full well that those commandments do not exonerate us." If the faithfulness of Yeshua the Messiah is sufficient for Jews, it should be sufficient work for non-Jews. This is how Paul understands salvation. And he develops this concept in Romans.

"Works of the law" in Romans 3

We can apply the same term-substitution trick to an important parallel passage in Romans 3. It makes for tedious reading, but the clarity that it affords is worth the effort. Once again, I will indicate where I have substituted the text with these definitions and added clarifying language by setting those insertions and substitutions off from the text with square brackets [like this]:

> By [the commandments of Torah that define a person as Jewish] no human being will be [legally exonerated] in his sight; since through the [Torah] comes the knowledge of sin. But now the [legal exoneration] of God has been manifested apart from the [Torah], although the [Torah] and the Prophets bear witness to it—the righteousness of God through the [faithfulness of] Jesus Christ for all who believe. For there is no distinction [between Jew and Gentile, in this regard]; for all have sinned and fall short of the glory of God, and are [legally exonerated] by his grace as a gift through the redemption that is in Christ Jesus ... so that he might be just and the justifier [i.e., the one who legally exonerates] of the one who has [the faithfulness of] Jesus. Then what becomes of our boasting? It is excluded. By what kind of [Torah]? By [the commandments that identity a person as Jewish]? No, but by the [Torah] of faith.
>
> For we hold that one is [legally exonerated] by faith apart from [the commandments that identify a person as Jewish]. Or is God the God of Jews only? Is he not the God of Gentiles also? Yes, of Gentiles also, since God is one—who will [legally exonerate] the [Jewish people] by faith and the [non-Jewish people] through faith.
>
> Do we then overthrow the [Torah] by this faith? By no means! On the contrary, we uphold the [Torah]. (Romans 3:20–31)

Paul was not criticizing being Jewish or keeping the commandments, nor did he set those things in antithesis to faith. Instead, he maintained that becoming Jewish is not the mechanism of salvation. That's not how justification works.

This entire argument would be completely irrelevant if Paul expected the Gentiles to perform the same "works of the law" as the Jewish believers. Instead, Paul assumed the Gentile believers were not going to do that. He assumed that they were not obligated to the commandments that identify a person as Jewish. For Paul, those commandments are the ones that make a difference between Jews and Gentiles.

Don't misunderstand. He was not discouraging Gentile believers from keeping the Sabbath, participating in the biblical lifestyle, or eating kosher, or anything of that nature. He was not discouraging them from Torah observance, but he was making it clear that there is a difference between Jews and Gentiles and their obligation to the works of the Torah. In Paul's mind, Jews are beholden to the commandments that identify a person as Jewish because that is what it means to be Jewish, whereas Gentiles are not. This distinction is irrelevant when it comes to the question of justification because both Jew and Gentile are in need of the faithfulness of Yeshua the Messiah.

In practical terms this means that we are all saved by grace, not by works, lest any man should boast. It also implies that Paul had no anticipation of the Gentile believers coming into obligation to those commandments which he termed as "works of the law." Therefore, the attempt on the part of the "circumcision party," the men from James in Galatians 2, or the Influencers who were convincing the Galatians to undergo circumcision were misplaced and distorted the essence of Paul's gospel.

This should help us immensely in understanding not just the epistle to the Galatians but all of Paul's writings. Paul did not erase the distinction between Jews and Gentiles. He did not mean to say, "There is no difference between a Jewish believer and a Gentile believer." Instead, he was simply saying, "Being Jewish is not what justifies you." What justifies a person? The faithfulness of Yeshua the Messiah: his righteous life, his obedience, his propitiating sacrifice, his resurrection.

SERMON TEN:

THROUGH THE LAW
I DIED TO THE LAW
(GALATIANS 2:19–20)

A look at the mystical implications of
Paul's death to the law as a death to
relying on Jewish identity for salvation.

In the nineteenth verse of the second chapter of his epistle to
the Galatians, the holy Apostle Paul writes the cryptic words
"For through the Torah I died to the Torah, so that I might live to
God." How did he die to the Torah, and what does it mean to be
dead to the Torah? What does it mean to live to God? These kind
of Dr. Seuss riddles are the type of thing that makes reading Paul
frustrating:

> For through the law I died to the law, so that I might live
> to God. (Galatians 2:19)

Dead to the law

For most of Christendom, this saying holds little to no difficulty;
the meaning is self-evident. Paul simply distinguished between
his former life as a Jew and his new life as a Christian. Formerly,
he tried to live to Torah, for the Torah, and by keeping the Torah
in order to earn salvation, but ultimately he realized that he could
not earn salvation because his sin prevented him from meeting

the Torah's impossible standards. In that way he died to the Torah, became a Christian, quit trying to keep the Torah, and learned to simply live to God by grace through faith without practicing Judaism any longer—that religion of dead and lifeless works.

This is the conventional Christian interpretation of what it means to die to the law through the law and live to God. To put it more simply, Paul is saying, "I was a Jew, but now I'm a Christian." Or "I used to be under the law, but now I'm under grace."

That explanation will work for most of Christianity. It has worked for most of the nearly two thousand years that the book of Galatians has been read and revered by Christians. But it does not work for the Messianic Jewish movement.

The Ones with All the Problems

It does not work for Messianic Judaism because the Messianic Jewish perspective recognizes that Messiah did not cancel the Torah and that Paul walked faithfully according to the Torah all his life. By his own testimony, "Neither against the law of the Jews, nor against the temple, nor against Caesar have I committed any offense" (Acts 25:8). He went so far as to claim to have "done nothing against our people or the customs of our fathers" (Acts 28:17). Paul did not reject Torah or Judaism. According to the book of Acts, the testimony of James, the elders at Jerusalem, and according to Paul himself, he remained Torah-observant all his life: a Pharisee the son of a Pharisee, a Hebrew of Hebrews, a Jew, under the full obligation of the law, despite the fact that he considered himself an apostle to the Gentiles.

So it is not Christianity that has a problem with this verse or with most of the epistle of Galatians; it's those of us in Messianic Judaism. We are the ones with all the problems.

From a messianic perspective then, what did Paul mean when he said, "For through the law I died to the law, so that I might live to God"?

Antioch Context

Most of the time, the problem we have with Paul is our failure to recognize that he makes a distinction between Jewish and Gentile believers and their respective relationships to the Torah. For example, in the present case, when Paul says the law, or the Torah, we immediately are thinking about the scroll of Moses and keeping the commandments of Torah, whether the prohibition on adultery or the prohibition on pork.

But that's not what Paul was thinking about. He did not think of the Torah in a monolithic, one-size-fits-all sense. When Paul spoke of being "under the law," he meant halachically (legally) Jewish, and when he spoke of the "works of the law," he meant the commandments of the Torah that define and identify a person as Jewish. And it is in that same sense that he spoke of dying to the law through the law in our passage.

The troubling verse comes from the context of the Antioch Incident. It has to do with the anecdote about Peter and the men from James and their decision to withdraw from eating with the Gentile believers in Antioch. At that time, Paul rebuked Peter, pointing out that "If we rebuild the separation between Jew and Gentile that we originally tore down—that you yourself tore down—then we prove ourselves to be transgressors."

No Longer I Who Live

In the previous sermon, I provided amplifications and substitutions in square brackets [like this] for Galatians 2:15–16. We can continue the same method of reading the text with the same assigned values to unpack the meaning. We are not trifling with the text here or attempting to bend it to say something that it is not saying. Rather, we are attempting to bring clarity to an ancient document:

> But if, in our endeavor [as Jewish believers] to be [legally exonerated] in Christ, we too were found to be sinners, is Christ then a servant of sin? Certainly not! For if I rebuild what I tore down, [i.e., if I rebuild the exclusivity of Jewish segregation from Gentiles] I prove myself to be a trans-

gressor [because I as a Jew have already received and accepted Gentile believers and eaten and fellowshipped with them for years]. For through the law [that is to say, by virtue of relying on my Jewish status] I died to the law [which is to say, I realized that being Jewish is not sufficient for legal exoneration], so that I might live to God [by relying on the faithfulness of Messiah rather than on my Jewish status]. I have been crucified with Christ. It is no longer I who live, but Christ who lives in me. And the life I now live in the flesh I live by [the faithfulness of] the Son of God, who loved me and gave himself for me. I do not nullify the grace of God, for [if legal exoneration and salvation were the result of being Jewish], then Christ died for no purpose. (Galatians 2:17–21)

When Paul said that through the law he died to the law, he means that through being Jewish and relying on Jewish status for salvation, he realized his own inadequacy before God even as a Torah-keeping Jew. He learned he could not rely upon that status. It does not mean he ceased to be Jewish or keep the Torah.

Instead, it is as if he died with Messiah and was raised with Messiah. He learned to rely upon the Messiah for salvation, for justification, and for legal exoneration in the court of heaven. So he said, "I have been crucified with Christ. It is no longer I who live, but Christ who lives in me. And the life I now live in the flesh I live by faith in the Son of God, who loved me and gave himself for me" (Galatians 2:20).

Dogs, Evil Doers, and Mutilators

Paul expresses an almost identical sentiment in his epistle to the Philippians. Philippi was the Roman colony where Paul found Lydia and the other God-fearing women keeping the Sabbath in the absence of any Jews living in the city (Acts 16). They found no synagogue in the city; they met for Sabbath services by the river outside of town. Paul and Silas ended up in jail, and they sang through the night before their miraculous release. Paul addressed his epistle to the Philippians to that community:

Finally, my brothers, rejoice in the Lord. To write the same things to you is no trouble to me and is safe for you. Look out for the dogs, look out for the evildoers, look out for those who mutilate the flesh. (Philippians 3:1–2)

Notice here that Paul warned the God-fearing Philippian Gentiles to look out for three different types of people: dogs, evildoers, and mutilators of the flesh. These are not three descriptions of the same type of person, rather they are three different types of people.

Look out for the dogs!

In Jewish parlance, "dogs" are the heathen, the pagan world, the unbelieving Gentile world; as our Master said, "Do not cast pearls before swine or give what is sacred to dogs." Everyone to whom Paul wrote in Philippi was also a Gentile, so Paul redefined the term "dogs" to refer to idolaters. He contrasts them against the God-fearing believers of Philippi.

Look out for the evildoers!

Evildoers are evildoers. Philippi had a lot of evildoers, such as the men who used the python girl for fortunetelling and had Paul and Silas arrested and charged with the crime of being Jews.

Look out for those who mutilate the flesh!

Those who mutilate the flesh is a nasty, vitriolic way of referring to Paul's opponents among the Jewish believers who insisted on Gentile conversion to Judaism for the God-fearing Gentile believers. Since Paul's visit to Philippi, the God-fearing Gentile community he left behind had come into contact with both the larger Jewish world and other Jewish believers. They had experienced some of the same pressure to convert that the Galatian community did. Paul was not referring to circumcision as a mutilation of the flesh—except when it was pressed upon the Gentile believers under a theology of mandate. So Paul referred to them as "those who mutilate the flesh"—and no, Paul was not above being nasty with his opponents.

He went on to say, "For we are the circumcision, who worship by the Spirit of God and glory in Christ Jesus and put no confidence in the flesh" (Philippians 3:3). He referred specifically to himself and Timothy, the authors of the epistle, but the Philippians would have also remembered Silas and probably Luke the physician as well. He also referred to other Jewish believers in his camp, including the apostles in Jerusalem who endorsed his gospel to the Gentiles. He said that he and the Jewish believers in agreement with him "put no confidence in the flesh," i.e., they did not rely on being Jewish for justification.

Paul told the Philippians that if anyone should have confidence in Jewish identity, it was him. He boasted of being circumcised on the eighth day, meaning he was not a convert. He was of the people of Israel and of the tribe of Benjamin, meaning he was not a convert and not a descendant of converts. He described himself as a Hebrew of Hebrews and a member of the sect of the Pharisees. Regarding his zeal for God, he had so much zeal that he persecuted other believers for God's sake, and "as to righteousness under the law, blameless" (Philippians 3:6).

Since becoming a follower of the Messiah, however, Paul said, "Whatever gain I had, I counted as loss for the sake of Christ. Indeed, I count everything as loss because of the surpassing worth of knowing Christ Jesus my Lord. For his sake I have suffered the loss of all things and count them as rubbish in order that I may gain Christ" (Philippians 3:7–8). This does not in any way imply that after meeting the Messiah, Paul was no longer circumcised on the eighth day, or of the people of Israel, or of the tribe of Benjamin, or a Hebrew of Hebrews. It does not even mean that he no longer considered himself a Pharisee. (He did. See Acts 23:6.) It does not mean that he no longer lived blamelessly according to the righteousness under the law.

It does mean that he no longer relied on the status and prestige he once derived from those things for salvation or justification. He claimed to no longer seek legal exoneration of his own "that comes from the law," i.e., from being Jewish, "but that which comes through [the faithfulness of] Christ, the [legal exoneration] from God that depends on faith—that I may know him and the power of his resurrection, and may share his sufferings, becoming like him in his death, that by any means possible I may attain the resurrection from the dead" (Philippians 3:9–11).

Another way to say this: "Through the law, I died to the law, that I might live to God. I have been crucified with Christ. It is no longer I who live, but Christ who lives in me. And the life I now live in the flesh I live by faith in the Son of God, who loved me and gave himself for me" (Galatians 2:19–20).

A Different Perspective on Paul

When understood from this perspective of distinction between Jew and Gentile, Paul's letters become far more intelligible to Messianic believers in Yeshua. One is able to hear Paul's voice unfettered, unencumbered. His message is not that complex. It boils down to this: Gentiles can be saved, too. The faithfulness of Yeshua is adequate for Gentiles as well.

It turns out that Paul was not at all about denigrating the Torah or Torah observance. He was not starting a new religion. He was not advocating lawlessness or arguing against Judaism. He was not forsaking being Jewish. Instead, he was bringing the teachings of Judaism of his day, as they related to Gentiles, forward in his arguments against other Jewish believers who contended that Gentiles must be under the law.

The picture of Paul that emerges from this "new perspective" (as it is called in academic circles) is one of a faithful Jew. He lived his life faithfully in obedience to the Torah, but he no longer relied on that status for his place in the kingdom or the world to come. Instead, he relied solely upon the faithfulness of the Messiah, and he encouraged Gentiles to do the same.

Paul was also a mystic, always internalizing his theology. He did not speak only in legal categories; instead, he internalized his theology, saying in Galatians 2:20, "I have been crucified with Christ. It is no longer I who live, but Christ who lives in me. And the life I now live in the flesh [as a Jew and as a human being] I live by [the faithfulness of] the Son of God, who loved me and gave himself for me."

Three Christian Clichés

Consider the mysticism of that statement. It seems a little bit self-centered for Paul to claim that Messiah died for him. As far as we know, Yeshua of Nazareth and Paul of Tarsus never met one another during all the years that the Master lived in the flesh. It seems a little presumptuous for Paul to say that Yeshua died specifically for him. The Messiah died for everyone, right? At least for all Israel. But Paul said, "For me."

Have you ever heard this Christian cliché: "Even if I were the only person on earth, Messiah would have died for me"? Really? Paul says yes. It's no cliché; it's real. God has set his affection on you, and the height, the width, the breadth, the depth of God's love is unfathomable. Romans 5:8 says, "God shows his love for us in that while we were still sinners, Christ died for us." The Apostle John says, "In this the love of God was made manifest among us, that God sent his only Son into the world, so that we might live through him" (1 John 4:9).

Have you heard this cliché: "I have Jesus in my heart"? Paul said that he did. It's not a cliché. Paul internalized and personalized this theology of not just knowing about God and His Messiah, but of actually knowing God and knowing his Messiah on a personal level.

Have you heard this cliché: "Do you have a personal relationship with Jesus Christ?" The honest answer is "No." You do not know him personally, and neither did Paul. But the mystical answer is "yes." And it is not just a cliché or theological platitude; the believer knows him and is known by him. He is bound to him, and he to the believer. The believer must live to him. He lives through the believer.

This idea of being bound up with the Messiah so that the Messiah lives through us has parallels in Judaism. The evangelical Christian "clichés" of personal relationship with the Messiah are similar to expressions of Jewish mysticism.

Chassidic Judaism teaches the same kind of mystical internalization and personalization of relationship with God through an intermediary. The Chasid connects with God through his relationship with his rebbe, the *tzaddik*. For example, I once read an interview with some Lubavitch girls who were doing outreach to secular Jews, handing out Sabbath candles and inviting them to a

Shabbaton (Sabbath retreat). In the interview, they explained, "It wasn't us. It was the rebbe doing it through us." From their perspective, they had their rebbe in their heart. Likewise, Breslov Chassidim preface their prayers with a declaration, "I hereby attach myself to the soul of and in the merit of Rebbe Nachman."

The Christian life should be one of concentration on this inwardness. Every thought and action should be measured against this one intention: it is no longer I who live but Messiah who lives in me. This applies to every choice and decision in life, from the small things to the great things, from the choices we make in entertainment to the choices we make in employment and spouse. This mantra should be the thing that sets our alarm clocks and puts us to bed at night. A man should rise up in the morning like a lion because it is no longer he who lives, but Messiah who lives in him. We should take care of our bodies because they no longer belong to us, but to Messiah who lives in us. We should govern our passions because it is no longer about us and our desires, but Messiah who lives in us and through us. This is what Christian living is all about. It is the governing principle for the believer's life. Towards the goal that we may know him and the power of his resurrection, and may share his sufferings, becoming like him in his death, that by any means possible we may attain the resurrection from the dead. Not that we have already obtained this or are already perfect, but we press on to make it our own because our Master has made us his own.

"Through the law I died to the law, so that I might live to God" Paul says. All he means is, "It's not about being Jewish or not being Jewish. It is about the faithfulness of the Son of God, Messiah within you, the love of God lavished upon you."

Galatians
CHAPTER THREE

BEWITCHED
(GALATIANS 3:1–6)

A look at how Paul seemingly contrasts
the Spirit with the Torah in the first
verses of Galatians 3.

A t the top of the third chapter of his epistle to the Galatians,
the holy Apostle Paul lamented, "O foolish Galatians, who has
bewitched you?" (Galatians 3:1). That is a strong opening. In our
modern vernacular, he says, "Idiots, who has brainwashed you?"

Bewitched

Once there was a young man with a young family who served
as the worship leader in a fine church. He began listening to the
teachings of Messianic Judaism and became more and more certain that the Torah was relevant for believers today and that this
was the direction that he wanted to go with his family. He tried
to explain this to the pastor of the church where he led the worship. The pastor, in his genuine concern for the young man, kept
asking, "Who has bewitched you?"

Think of bewitched as simply meaning "put under a spell" or
"brainwashed" or "convinced."

A question: What is the folly of the Galatian God-fearing Gentiles that makes Paul say, "O foolish Galatians"?

Another question: In what sense have they been bewitched, put
under a spell, or brainwashed?

And one more question: "Who is the bewitcher?"

Those Dastardly Judaizers

Before answering these questions, consider the traditional Christian answer to them. In conventional Christian theology, the situation in Galatia is fairly straightforward.

In Paul's absence from Galatia, the Christians have fallen under the influence of "the Judaizers." The Judaizers have somehow persuaded the Christians (Jews and Gentiles both—it makes no difference; they are all Christians) that the law of Moses is not abolished. The Judaizers have managed to dupe the gullible Galatians into believing this absurdity with the result that some of the Galatians have been backsliding, so to speak, into legalism. Some of them have gone so far as to consider circumcision, and others might be keeping ritual observances such as the Sabbath and the biblical holy days; perhaps some are concerned even about the Bible's food laws.

To Paul, any keeping of the law is the opposite of what it means to be a Christian. He rebukes the Galatian Christians for being so gullible. He calls them foolish and says, "It was before your eyes that Jesus Christ was publicly portrayed as crucified. So how could you possibly be observing the law after this?" Then he rhetorically asks, "Who has bewitched you?" although he knows very well who has bewitched them: those dastardly Judaizers. That is the conventional Christian explanation regarding those unfortunate, bewitched fools in Galatia.

That explanation does not work for us in Messianic Judaism because we maintain that the gospel does not abrogate the Torah, that Christianity does not replace Judaism, and that Christians do not replace the Jewish people.

Christians in Galatia (Jews and God-fearing Galatians alike) were already a part of Judaism and had, in fact, never left Judaism. They worshipped on the Sabbath when Paul first found them and were doing so when he left them. They had never heard of a grace-versus-law dichotomy, nor had they heard of this Christianity-versus-Judaism dichotomy. Nor had Paul heard of these things. And they could not have considered themselves as a part of the Christian religion in antithesis to Judaism because that antithesis did not yet exist. The traditional Christian explanation of Galatians 3 is anachronistic; it does not fit the historical situation. If the Epistle to the Galatians had been written a century or two later, that explanation could work well. Of course that is how it has been read for most of Christian history, but that was not the situation when Paul wrote his epistle to the Galatians.

The Bewitchers

The bewitchers to whom Paul referred in Galatians 3:1 were the "influencers" of chapter one. The influencers might have been Jewish people within the synagogue, or they could have been people who came into the community from outside. In my opinion, most likely they were believers. I believe, however, that the influencers were not themselves born Jewish, but they were men and women who had become proselytes, either before or after becoming believers. They themselves used to be Gentiles. They had to jump through the conversion hoop to achieve Jewish status, and the new Pauline gospel irked them. Why should the God-fearing Gentiles be allowed to forego conversion? "Look, I had to do this; you should have to do this, too!"

They rose up against Paul and against his credentials and against his gospel. They conducted Bible studies in Galatia. They said, "Let's go over Genesis 17 again," and they studied the covenant with Abraham which introduces circumcision. They pointed out how every male in Abraham's house had to be circumcised. They preached hard on Exodus 12:49; they preached hard on Numbers 15:29. They convinced the God-Fearers in Galatia that salvation in Yeshua was a good starting point but not enough.

Now we can answer the questions about Galatians 3:1. The bewitchers were the influencers. They bewitched the God-fearing Galatians by convincing them of the validity of their argument—a position which may have been the majority opinion among believers in that day. The folly of the Galatians is that they fell under the influence of the influencers.

Publicly Portrayed as Crucified

Writing to Galatia, Paul reminded his readers, "It was before your eyes that Christ Jesus was portrayed as crucified" (Galatians 3:1).

How exactly was Christ portrayed as crucified before the eyes of the Galatians? It sounds like Paul arrived in Galatia, pulled out a projector and a screen, and showed them the "Jesus" film! How did he accomplish this public portrayal of Christ's crucifixion? The Greek word here for "publicly portrayed" is *prographo*—"graphically depicted." That makes it sound less like Campus Crusade's *Jesus* film and more like Mel Gibson's film *The Passion*.

When he publicly portrayed Christ Jesus crucified to them, he did not read the New Testament; it did not yet exist. He did not say, "Let's turn to the book of John." Instead, he said, "Let's turn to Psalm 22; let's look at Isaiah 53; let me show the suffering of the servant of the Lord." He showed them Scriptures; he publicly demonstrated in the *Tanach* that the Messiah had to suffer.

The Spirit and the Torah

Paul questioned his readers, "Let me ask you this one thing: Did you receive the Spirit by works of the law, or by hearing with faith?" (Galatians 3:2). It seems that Paul set the Holy Spirit and the Torah in opposition to one another, again creating an antithesis, a dichotomy:

> Holy Spirit = good
>
> Torah = bad

The conventional church perspective does explain the passage as an antithesis between the Spirit and the Torah. An evangelical or charismatic Christian perspective stereotypes the dichotomy. Prior to bewitchment under the Judaizers, the Christians in Galatia gathered together on Sunday mornings. They met together and took communion. That's as much ritual as they did. Then they sang a few praise choruses. There was a fellow with a guitar. They experienced manifestations of the Holy Spirit. Then the Judaizers came. They start shaking their legalism and Torah stuff around and quenched the Holy Spirit. That's the picture: Holy Spirit versus the Torah.

Paul was not saying this. Remember that "works of the law" refers to those specific signs that define Jewish identity. First and foremost, circumcision is the mark of legal conversion to become

Jewish, followed by full obligation to the other identity-marking commandments.

Paul's argument in Galatians 3:2 can be amplified as follows:

> When you believed on the Messiah and confessed the name of Yeshua, you received the Holy Spirit. There were signs; you saw miracles. And your spirit within you testified to a transformation. You experienced the intersecting of God's Spirit with your life, manifesting in your midst. All of this happened while you were still uncircumcised Gentile God-Fearers. If you received the Holy Spirit (the sign of the new covenant and the sign of your salvation) while you were still a God-fearing Gentile, then it should be obvious that your obligation to the commandments that identify a person as Jewish is not and cannot be a prerequisite to salvation.

Peter employed exactly the same logic when he saw the Holy Spirit poured out on the God-Fearer Cornelius and the people of his household. He said, "Who are we to deny them baptism?"— even though they were Gentiles. Paul was saying nothing more; he was not—God forbid—placing the Spirit of God and the keeping of Torah in antithesis to each other.

The prophets predicted the giving of the Spirit in the Messianic Era. God will pour out his Spirit to enable us to walk in his commandments. So it says in Ezekiel 36:27: "And I will put my Spirit within you and cause you to walk in my statutes and be careful to obey my rules." The Holy Spirit and the Torah work together, not against one another.

Paul asked the Galatians, "Are you so foolish? Having begun by the Spirit, are you now being perfected by the flesh? Did you suffer so many things in vain—if indeed it was in vain?" (Galatians 3:3–4). The "flesh" refers to the physical and the material. He asked, "Having begun with a spiritual transformation, are now looking for perfection through a physical transformation by becoming Jewish?"

The Things they Suffered

> Did you suffer so many things in vain—if indeed it was
> in vain? (Galatians 3:4)

What sort of things did the God-fearing Gentiles in Galatia suffer
in vain—if indeed it was in vain? I believe they suffered stigmatization in the synagogue where they worshipped and stigmatization
from the rest of the Jewish community when they bought meat and
interacted with them on a regular basis. Their belief in Yeshua the
Messiah was not the issue. Instead, their problem resulted from
what their belief meant for them.

Mark Nanos suggests that the stigmatization God-fearing Galatians felt from the rest of the Jewish community resulted from their
insistence that they were also covenant members, sons of Abraham,
heirs of the resurrection and the world to come. They claimed to
be of Israel but not Jewish—grafted in to the Jewish people, so to
speak, but not Jewish.

Let's take this out of Galatia and put it in Minneapolis. Suppose a Gentile Christian visits a synagogue in the local Orthodox
Jewish community. A Gentile can do that. He does not need to be
keeping a halachic Sabbath to do that. He can simply attend the
synagogue as a visitor and a guest. He does not need to be keeping
kosher. No one would give him any grief about that; they would not
ask him what he had for breakfast. Nobody would care because he
is a Gentile. The Jewish world does not expect him to be anything
but a Gentile. He can go to an Orthodox synagogue and say, "I'm a
Gentile; I'm a *ben Noach;* I keep the seven laws of the sons of Noah,"
and he would be welcome without further expectations. He would
be a modern God-Fearer.

But if he started to say, "… And I'm a son of Abraham, too; I
am a part of Israel, too; I have a share in the covenant, too," that
would be problematic. The rabbi might explain, "If you want to
be a son of Abraham and enjoy those privileges, there is a process
that you have to go through." And if he refuses to consent to that
process, and yet insists that he already owns the status on some
spiritual level, his convictions might affect his participation in that
community.

According to Mark Nanos, that's the suffering to which Paul referred. So Paul said, "If you're just going to go ahead and convert, then what was the point of all that stigmatization that you suffered in the first place?"

The Other Things They Suffered

They probably suffered acutely from the Gentile Roman community around them as well. Roman law required them to participate in idolatry, to worship the emperor, and to pay homage to the gods of Rome. Refusing to do so was a crime called "atheism." If you did not worship the emperor and the gods, you could be arrested as an atheist.

At the same time, Rome was liberal in its religious laws. The Romans allowed their subjects to worship whichever gods they preferred so long as they fulfilled their civic duty, showed up at the temple for the proper Roman feasts, and participated in a few perfunctory rituals. Roman subjects were only expected to bow down to the emperor once a year and bring a token sacrifice. You could even be a philosophical atheist or an agnostic and just go through the motions, so long as you submitted to the civic expectations. Strong expectations of social conformity governed and ordered Roman society. Rome was not like America where everyone does as he sees fit and lives out his personal convictions. Social caste and civic duty defined all of Roman life.

Failure to go through those motions of idolatry could bring persecution. It might get a person arrested, fined, or even imprisoned. At the very least, a person falling outside the normal social order would find himself ostracized by the larger society.

The only legal way to avoid worshipping idols, by Roman law, was by conversion to Judaism. Judaism was a legal religion. Jewish people were exempt from civic idolatry.

That option must have been extremely attractive to the God-fearing Gentiles who were suffering persecution on some level from the pagan world around them. Paul asked his readers, "What was the point of suffering as a Gentile God-Fearer if, after suffering for your convictions, you are just going to convert to become Jewish?

You should have converted long ago. Did you suffer so many things in vain—if indeed it was in vain?"

The Curious Place of the God-Fearer

As a Gentile God-Fearer practicing Messianic Judaism myself, I have a lot of sympathy for the precarious social position in which the Galatians found themselves. The Jewish world thinks we are out of line. The first thing a Jewish person (or even a Jewish believer) will ask when he finds out that I practice the Torah is, "Why? If you don't have to, why would you?"

We no longer live in the days of Paul and the apostles. We cannot go into a synagogue and expect the Jewish community to receive us.

At the same time, we are apt to get a similar reaction from our Christian friends, from our churches, and from our pastors: "Who has bewitched you? Why are you putting yourself under the law?"

Non-Jews in Messianic Judaism can identify with the Galatian Christians. They had assumed an identity which the religious establishments did not consider legitimate. In the eyes of both Judaism and paganism, the God-fearing Gentiles were nuts and oddballs. Far worse than open persecution—at least more corrosive to the human spirit—is social stigmatization where everyone looks at you like you are a cornball. It wears you down. Eventually, people tend to cave in to the social pressure and go one way or the other.

I don't know if there's any consolation for today's Messianic God-fearing Gentiles, but know this: If you find yourself in a category like that, being neither fish nor fowl, you are not the first to occupy a socially awkward position for the sake of the gospel. The Galatian people essentially suffered the same pressures and the same sorrows.

A Spiritual People

Paul drove his point home: "Does he who supplies the Spirit to you and works miracles among you do so by works of the law (i.e., by the commandments that identify a person as Jewish), or by hearing with faith?" (Galatians 3:5).

Paul expected the believer to experience the Spirit of God. God will supply us with his Spirit and will work miracles among us. We will know the Holy Spirit in our midst, experience him working miracles, wonders, and signs, and answering prayer. This is the regular result of an encounter with the supernatural. It was so self-evident to Paul that he uses it as the hinge of his argument.

We are supposed to be a spiritual people. We should be expecting the moving of the Holy Spirit in our midst—not at our behest, but as a natural part of what it means to be a Christian. Miracles are commonplace, matter-of-fact for us. God's Spirit is speaking to us, guiding us, helping us, revealing himself to us. We need to have eyes to see him, ears to hear his voice, and faith to experience those miracles in our lives.

FAITH VERSUS WORKS

(GALATIANS 3:6–7)

A resolution of the classic faith-versus-works debate through exploring Paul's theology of justification for the circumcised and the uncircumcised.

Have you ever heard of faith versus works? Another way to ask it, "Have you ever heard of grace versus law?"

The theological argument about whether God saves a person by grace alone or by a person's obedience and good works is old as the New Testament itself. We derive the argument from Paul's epistles. It does not come from the teachings of the Master. If we did not have Paul's epistles, we would all be a lot more "legalistic." For example, in the gospels, a young man comes to the Master and asks, "What must I do to inherit eternal life?" Yeshua tells him, "Keep the Torah. Keep the commandments."

This seems to flatly contradict the teachings of Paul. Paul says, "For by grace you have been saved through faith … not a result of works" (Ephesians 2:8–9).

Paul makes it sound like we do not have to be obedient to God at all. We probably should not be doing any good works or trying to achieve any merit with God because salvation comes from faith as a free gift, not of works. We can illustrate this theological supposition as follows:

Works = Bad
Faith = Good
Law = Bad
Grace = Good

The Epistle of James

Then comes the Epistle of James, the brother of the Master. James seems to completely contradict Paul. Remember, when James spoke, he spoke with authority, not only as the brother of the Master and one of the pillars of the apostolic assembly in Jerusalem but also as the steward of the throne of David, the head over the assembly of believers.

James declared that faith without works is dead. He insisted that faith must be demonstrated by deeds. He dismissed those who place their confidence in mere faith, reminding them that the demons also believe. Then he cited the same passages about Abraham that Paul used to make his faith-alone argument:

> Was not Abraham our father justified by works when he offered up his son Isaac on the altar? You see that faith was active along with his works, and faith was completed by his works; and the Scripture was fulfilled that says, "Abraham believed God, and it was counted to him as righteousness"—and he was called a friend of God. You see that a person is justified by works and not by faith alone. (James 2:21–24)

Consider the contradiction. Paul says, "Faith, not works; grace, not law." James says, "Faith without works is dead … A person is justified by works and not by faith alone."

I am setting two apostles opposite one another like two contenders in a theological boxing ring. In one corner we place Paul of Tarsus. He is saying, "We know that a person is not justified by works of the law but through faith in Jesus Christ … not by works of the law, because by works of the law no one will be justified" (Galatians 2:16). He is saying, "For by grace you have been saved through faith. And this is not your own doing; it is the gift of God, not a result of works, so that no one may boast" (Ephesians 2:8–9).

In the opposite corner we place the Apostle James the Righteous, the brother of the Master. He is saying, "You see that a person is justified by works and not by faith alone" (James 2:24).

- One apostle says, "Not justified by works."
- One apostle says, "Justified by works."

In this sermon on our study in Galatians, we will attempt to reconcile the faith-versus-works problem and the James-versus-Paul problem.

Abraham Believed God

Both James and Paul pointed to a common proof text. Genesis 15:6 is a cornerstone of Pauline theology. Paul used it as a proof text for his whole argument (Galatians 3:6). James quoted the same verse in what appears to be a contradiction to Paul's argument (James 2:23).

The passage appears in the context of the LORD's covenant with Abraham. In the story, the LORD appears to Abraham and promises him a great inheritance. Abraham objects, pointing out that this promise has little value to him because he has no son to whom he can pass on an inheritance. The LORD promises that he will have a son who will be his heir. He shows him the starry sky at night and says, "Look toward heaven, and number the stars, if you are able to number them. So shall your offspring be" (Genesis 15:5). Paul said:

> Does he who supplies the Spirit to you and works miracles among you do so by works of the law, or by hearing with faith—just as Abraham "believed God, and it was counted to him as righteousness"? (Galatians 3:5–6)

The Apostle Paul identified this single verse as a summary statement on the faith of Abraham. God made promises; Abraham believed the promises. God credited Abraham with righteousness because of his belief.

Paul wanted to know, "How does a human being find justification, legal spiritual exoneration, in the eyes of God?" In other words, "If everyone sins (and everyone does), then how can a person find acquittal for his sin?" Put in other words, "Only the righteous will inherit the kingdom and the world to come. So on what basis does God declare a sinner righteous?"

The influencers in Galatia and the circumcision party among the believers had the religious conviction that justification, whereby a person may inherit the kingdom and the world to come, was attainable primarily through covenant relationship with God. The Jewish people, the nation of Israel, are the only people in covenant with God; Gentiles are not. Therefore, Gentiles need to undergo conversion by taking on the "works of the law" to become part of the nation. By "works of the law," they did not mean just any deeds of Torah. They were not talking about, for example, the commandment to chase a mother bird away from the nest before taking its young or the commandment to honor one's father and mother. The "works of the law" are the particular commandments that define and identify a person as Jewish. When Paul used terms like "works," "works of the law," "circumcision", "under the law," or sometimes just "the law," he meant those commandments that identify a person as Jewish, commandments like circumcision.

Pauline terminology for the commandments that indicate Jewish status:

- Works
- Works of the law

Pauline terminology for halachic Jewish status:

- Under the law
- The law
- Circumcision

Like Paul, the rabbis used the word "circumcised" as a synonym for the Jewish people, and they applied the term "uncircumcised" to Gentiles, regardless of whether a Gentile was physically circumcised or not:

The word 'uncircumcised' is used only as name for Gentiles, as it is written [in Jeremiah 9:26], "for all these nations are uncircumcised." (m.*Nedarim* 3:11)

Paul's Big Insight

Paul had theological enemies. His opponents opposed his gospel which taught that Gentiles can be saved. They believed that being Jewish was a prerequisite for the kingdom of heaven and life in the world to come. One day, while reading through the scroll of Genesis, Paul had an insight. He read these words in the scroll of Genesis: "And he believed the LORD, and he counted it to him as righteousness."

Paul thought to himself, "Abraham was not even circumcised yet. He had not yet received the commandment of circumcision. The covenant in Genesis 15 takes place about fifteen years prior to the commandment of circumcision. So if circumcision is a prerequisite for salvation, for justification and righteousness, then how is it that the LORD reckoned Abraham as righteous prior to his circumcision?"

"Obviously," Paul thought to himself, "this implies that an uncircumcised person (that is to say, a Gentile, a non-Jewish person) can be saved without becoming Jewish."

Follow Paul's simple logic:

1. If Abraham was declared righteous on the basis of his faith in the promises of God prior to being circumcised, ...

2. ... then circumcision and Jewish status cannot be considered a prerequisite to salvation.

Based upon this big insight, Paul argued in his epistle to the Galatians that taking on "the works of the law," i.e., "circumcision," is not needed for salvation:

> Does he who supplies the Spirit to you and works miracles among you do so by works of the law [i.e., by those commandments that identify a person as Jewish, like circumcision], or by hearing with faith—just as Abraham "believed God, and it was counted to him as righteousness"? Know then that it is those of faith who are the sons of Abraham. (Galatians 3:5–7)

Sons of Abraham

When a Gentile undergoes conversion to become a legal proselyte, he receives a new identity as a Jew and a new last name: the patronymic *ben Avraham* (son of Abraham). A woman who undergoes conversion receives the name *bat Avraham* (daughter of Abraham). Therefore, proselytes are collectively called *benei Avraham* (children of Abraham). If a man was born as a Gentile and later converted to become Jewish, he henceforth belonged to this category of Jewish people.

This nomenclature explains Paul's statement in Galatians 3:7 where he concluded, "Know then that it is those of faith who are the sons of Abraham." This was a radical, counterintuitive statement. Paul claimed that those who do not convert and become Jewish achieve the status of "sons of Abraham" by exercising the faith of Abraham. With this language, he created a new category of people within Israel: the proselytes by faith.

Paul did not contrast "those who are of faith" against "those who are not of faith." He contrasted "those who are of faith" against "those who are of the flesh." In Paul's thinking, "those who are of faith" are those who have believed the good news of the gospel and rely on the faithfulness of Yeshua and the promises of God for justification. Those who are of the flesh are those who have placed their confidence in physical circumcision, flesh-level conversion, to become Jewish.

Test Drive in Romans 4

We can take all of this information and test drive it elsewhere in Paul's epistles to find corroboration. Several years after writing his epistle to the Galatians, Paul composed his epistle to the Romans. He returned to his central Galatians argument about the faith of Abraham as a justification for Gentile salvation, and he developed it further in Romans 4. Again, I offer my amplifications, paraphrases, and substitutions here and there, for the sake of clarification, in square brackets [like this].

> What then shall we say was gained by Abraham, our forefather according to the flesh? (Romans 4:1)

When the apostles use the term "the flesh", they do not mean sin or the evil inclination. The term "the flesh" means the physical body as opposed to the spirit (the *ruach/neshamah*), the divine soul. When you read the phrase "to (or of) the flesh" in the New Testament, think, "physically" or "bodily." Therefore, Romans 4:1 can read, "What then shall we say was gained by Abraham, our forefather according to the [physical body]?"

> For if Abraham was justified by works [i.e., the commandments that identify a person as Jewish, such as circumcision], he has something to boast about, but not before God. For what does the Scripture say? "Abraham believed God, and it was counted to him as righteousness." (Romans 4:2–3)

Abraham cannot boast that his Jewish status earned him legal exoneration before the LORD because God credited him with righteousness prior to his undergoing circumcision. He was not justified by "works." By the word "works," Paul only means the commandments that secure Jewish identity, such as circumcision.

> Now to the one who works, his wages are not counted as a gift but as his due. And to the one who does not work [i.e., does not take on Jewish identity or the commandments that identify a person as Jewish] but believes in him who [legally exonerates] the ungodly, his faith is counted as righteousness. (Romans 4:4–5)

Playing off the word "works," Paul pointed out that a laborer receives wages for works he performs, but if someone receives some compensation without having worked for it, then the compensation is not actually compensation; rather it is a gift. The "one who does not work" is not a godless or lawless person; he is a person who does not undertake the commandments of Torah that secure Jewish status. Although he does not undergo circumcision or take on the commandments that define Jewishness, he trusts in God, and God justifies him.

> Is this blessing then only for the circumcised [i.e., Jews and proselytes] or also for the uncircumcised [God-fearing Gentiles]? We say that faith was counted to Abraham

as righteousness. How then was it counted to him? Was it before or after he had been circumcised? It was not after, but before he was circumcised. (Romans 4:9–10)

As noted above, the term "circumcised" does not refer to a man's actual physical condition. In rabbinic language and in the language of the Apostle Paul, "circumcised" means either "a Jew" or "a proselyte to Judaism" who has undergone conversion. Quoting Psalm 32, Paul said, "Blessed are those whose lawless deeds are forgiven, and whose sins are covered; blessed is the man against whom the Lord will not count his sin" (Romans 4:7–8), and then he asked, "Is this blessing only for Jews and proselytes, or also for uncircumcised Gentiles?" He then argued that since God credited Abraham with righteousness before he underwent circumcision, this indicates that God can justify the uncircumcised as well as the circumcised.

This realization made Paul wonder what the point of circumcision is at all. He answered his unstated question as follows:

> He received the sign of circumcision as a seal of the righteousness that he had by faith while he was still uncircumcised. The purpose was to make him the father of all who believe without being circumcised, so that righteousness would be counted to them as well, and to make him the father of the circumcised [i.e., the Jewish people] who are not merely circumcised but who also walk in the footsteps of the faith that our father Abraham had before he was circumcised. (Romans 4:11–12)

In Paul's view, God credited Abraham with righteousness prior to his circumcision to demonstrate that Abraham is the spiritual father (by faith) of all who believe, whether Jewish or Gentile. Moreover, he received circumcision only after receiving the reward of faith in order to indicate that the Jewish people must also "walk in the footsteps of the faith" of Abraham and not merely rely on physical, national status.

> That is why it depends on faith, in order that the promise may rest on grace and be guaranteed to all his offspring—not only to the adherent of the Law [i.e., the Jewish people] but also to the one who shares the faith of

Abraham [i.e., the God-fearing Gentile], who is the father of us all, as it is written, "I have made you the father of many nations." (Romans 4:16–17)

Paul referred to Jewish people and proselytes to Judaism as those who are "adherent[s] of the law." The God-fearing Gentile who does not have Jewish status is "the one who shares the faith of Abraham." Paul viewed Jewish and Gentile believers as having differing relationships to the Torah. He called the Jewish believer in Yeshua an "adherent of the law," but he did not assign that same relationship to the Gentile believer. In any case, he reckoned both the adherent of the law and the Gentile God-Fearer as "sons of Abraham" because Abraham "is the father of us all."

The Faith of Abraham

Both the "adherent of the law" and the God-fearing Gentile believer must "walk in the footsteps of the faith that our father Abraham had before he was circumcised." What is it that Abraham believed? What was this saving faith that he had?

> [Abraham had faith] in the presence of the God in whom he believed, who gives life to the dead and calls into existence the things that do not exist. In hope he believed against hope, that he should become the father of many nations, as he had been told, "So shall your offspring be." (Romans 4:17–18)

In other words, Abraham believed in the promise about the stars. He believed God's promise from Genesis 15:5 when the LORD said, "Look toward heaven, and number the stars, if you are able to number them … So shall your offspring be." Paul explained that Abraham believed despite the fact that his body was as good as dead and Sarah was barren: "No distrust made him waver concerning the promise of God, but he grew strong in his faith as he gave glory to God, fully convinced that God was able to do what he had promised" (Romans 4:20–21). To be "of the faith of Abraham" means to be "fully convinced that God [is] able to do what he [has] promised."

That is why his faith was "counted to him as righteousness." But the words "it was counted to him" were not written for his sake alone, but for ours also. It will be counted to us [Jews, and Gentiles] who believe in him who raised from the dead Jesus our Lord, who was delivered up for our trespasses and raised for our justification [legal exoneration]. (Romans 4:22–25)

A Big Misunderstanding

Abraham was counted righteous prior to undergoing the "works" of circumcision; therefore, he is the father of faith both for Jewish believers and Gentile believers. This insight into Paul's theology provides the answer to the faith-versus-works question, the grace-versus-law problem, and the Paul-versus-James divide.

The entire argument about faith versus works and grace versus law is based upon wrong assumptions. When Paul spoke of "works," he was speaking only of circumcision and the other sign commandments and particulars that indicate Jewish status. He was not talking about obedience to God. He was talking about changing from being a Gentile and becoming Jewish. He also called it going under the law, circumcision, and so forth.

Very early on, however, believers misunderstood Paul's language and message. We know this from Acts 21 where the devout Jewish believers thought that Paul was dismissing Torah in general, even for Jewish people. James warned him about what people were saying. He told Paul, "[They think that] you teach all the Jews who are among the Gentiles to forsake Moses, telling them not to circumcise their children or walk according to our customs" (Acts 21:21).

James knew this was not so. He recognized that people had misunderstood Paul's message about "works." He realized that people in that day, like us, thought that "works" meant obedience to God's commandments in general and the performance of good deeds. In his epistle, James wrote to correct the error, but as he did, he did not adopt Paul's specialized use of the term "works." Instead, he used the term as it was being misunderstood and just as it is understood today. When James used the term "works," he meant obedience to

God in general, both obedience to the commandments and good deeds in general. He gave two examples: Abraham obeying God's commandments to sacrifice Isaac, and Rahab the Gentile saving the lives of the two spies.

There is No Difficulty Here

It comes down to a matter of terminology. When Paul, writing to Gentiles, said "works," he meant conversion, circumcision, and being Jewish. When James, writing to Jewish believers, said "works," he meant obedience to the Torah and doing good deeds. There is no contradiction.

> Paul: "Works" means conversion.

> James: "Works" means obedience.

There is no faith-versus-works or grace-versus-law in the Bible. That was not an issue for the apostles, nor was it a matter of controversy. The real faith-versus-works argument was over the question, "Can an uncircumcised Gentile be saved by *faith* or does he have to do the *works* of circumcision and become Jewish?" Likewise, the real grace-versus-law question was, "Can an uncircumcised Gentile be considered a son of Abraham and recipient of the *grace* Abraham received, or does he have to keep the *law* as a Jew to attain that status?"

So we can agree with Paul when he says: "A person is not justified by works of the law but through faith in Jesus Christ ... not by works of the law, because by works of the law no one will be justified" (Galatians 2:16).

And we can also agree with James when he says: "You see that a person is justified by works and not by faith alone" (James 2:24).

SERMON THIRTEEN:
ABRAHAM'S GOSPEL
(GALATIANS 3:8–9)

Understanding the textual basis for the
gospel preached beforehand to Abraham
as identical with Paul's gospel.

C hristians often wonder if the Old Testament saints are "saved."
Have you ever heard that question? It's problematic. Like most
of these questions, the person asking it usually does not know
what he means by it. What the person probably thinks he means
is this: "Did Noah, Abraham, Isaac, Jacob, David, and Isaiah, and
others go to heaven when they died?" What they are trying to ask
is this: "Did the divine souls of the men of faith who lived prior
to the atoning death of the Messiah find repose in paradise while
they await the resurrection? Will those men and women who did
not confess the name of Yeshua attain the resurrection?"

Were the Old Testament Saints Saved?

I have sometimes heard it taught that the answer is "Yes," the Old
Testament saints are saved by means of special revelation. That
is to say that God gave them a special revelation of the gospel, of
the name of Yeshua, and the mechanism of salvation, and they
therefore believed on the name of Yeshua and attained salvation.
Who can say this is not true? We have heard of such things happening before. One occasionally hears an anecdote about someone

who had no access to the gospel or knowledge of the gospel, but received a supernatural revelation or visitation.

But that theory does not seem credible. To be fair, God must have done so for all of his people for all of the years up until the death and resurrection of Yeshua. And if that is the case, why did he stop doing so in the generation of Messiah? When did he stop doing so? Another way of putting this: "In the Old Testament times, God had some different means of bringing people to salvation, and it worked up until the death of Messiah, at which point people now need to believe in Yeshua." If so, that makes the "good news" actually "bad news" because, prior to the coming of Messiah, Jews received a special revelation from God, but now God has cancelled that program and that is why Jewish people are not believers in Yeshua. That's a bad deal for Jews.

Nevertheless, one often hears the idea that God revealed the gospel beforehand, at least to certain individuals such as Abraham.

Abraham's Gospel

The Bible does display a pattern of progressive revelation. God did reveal more and more of his plan of redemption to his people as time went on, and he did grant earlier generations hints, clues, and glimpses of the future, just the same as he has granted such hints, clues, and glimpses to us. Abraham saw the day of Messiah through some revelation, and he rejoiced to see it (John 8:56).

The Bible does not give any indication that Abraham knew the name of the Master or the details of the gospel or the four spiritual laws or the sinner's prayer. To put it frankly, Abraham did not accept Jesus into his heart nor (if you prefer) did he participate in any sacraments of salvation. But if not, what does the Holy Epistle to the Galatians mean when it says that the Scripture preached the gospel beforehand to Abraham?

> And the Scripture, foreseeing that God would justify the Gentiles by faith, preached the gospel beforehand to Abraham, saying, "In you shall all the nations be blessed." (Galatians 3:8)

The word "gospel" means "good news." Paul had his own version of the gospel, a slightly different telling of the good news. Paul's good news declared that the kingdom and the world to come are open to Gentiles too. Paul's gospel included the Gentiles. According to Paul in Galatians 3:8, the good news that was proclaimed beforehand to Abraham consisted of just these seven words: "In you shall all the nations be blessed."

The Call of Abraham

The seven-word gospel proclamation preached to Abraham beforehand comes from the call of Abraham in Genesis 12. The LORD called Abram from his home in Ur, told him to leave his country and father's household and travel to Canaan. He promised to make Abram into a great nation, to bless him, and to make him into a blessing. He promised to bless those who bless him and to curse those who curse him. Then he added, "and in you all the families of the earth shall be blessed" (Genesis 12:3).

The call of Abram is remarkable in and of itself. It is remarkable that a small, ethnocentric, tribal religion would, from its very outset, have such universal ambitions as expressed in Genesis 12:1–3. The ancient Israelites believed that all nations on earth were destined to be blessed through their forefather Abraham. It was an amazing prediction. Four thousand years later, the God of Abraham is worshipped among all nations.

Blessed and Grafted

The LORD told Abraham, "In you all the families of the earth shall be blessed (*venivrechu*)" (Genesis 12:3). The Hebrew verb (*venivrechu*) translated as "shall be blessed" is in the *niphal* form, the passive form of the verb, and this is not the usual way that this verb appears.

When the Hebrew verb *barach* ("to bless") appears in the *niphal* form, it appears as *nivrach*, and in this case, as *nivrechu*. Apparently, this looks a lot like the Mishnaic Hebrew word *mavrich*, based on the same *barach* root, and it means to "graft" or "engraft" a vine or a shoot.

With that Apostolic Age reading of the Hebrew text, Genesis 12:3 could be translated to read: "In you all the families of the earth shall be engrafted."[17] The context of the passage makes this translation impossible. Clearly, the Torah intends us to read, "All peoples on earth will be blessed through you." The passage has nothing to do with the grafting of plants. Genesis 12 is not talking about horticulture. It is a passage about blessing and being blessed. A responsible translator would never translate the verse as, "In you all the families of the earth shall be engrafted." However, the sages are seldom accused of being responsible translators. And this is why we read in the Talmud, commenting on Genesis 12:3, as follows:

> Rabbi Elazar expounded, "What is meant by the verse, 'And all peoples on earth will be blessed through you'? The Holy One, blessed be he, said to Abraham, 'I have two goodly shoots (berachot) to engraft (lehivrich) on you: Ruth the Moabitess and Naamah the Ammonitess.' All the families of the earth, even the other families who live on the earth are blessed only for Israel's sake. All the nations of the earth, even the ships that go from Gaul to Spain are blessed only for Israel's sake." (b. Yevamot 63a)[18]

Rabbi Elazar uses the passage to explain how two Gentile women came to be regarded as part of Israel and even mothers of the Davidic kings. Ruth was a Moabite. Naamah was an Ammonite. The Torah specifically says, "No Ammonite or Moabite or any of his descendants may enter the assembly of the LORD, even down to the tenth generation" (Deuteronomy 23:3).

Ruth became the wife of Boaz, the mother of the Davidic line. Naamah became the wife of Solomon, mother of the Davidic line. How could a Moabite and an Ammonite be mothers of the kings of Israel? Rabbi Elazar says that the answer is that they were no longer to be considered Moabite and Ammonite. They had been grafted into Abraham through this blessing that God announced beforehand, "In you all the families of the earth shall be engrafted."

---

[17] Lancaster, *Grafted In*.

[18] שתי ברכות טובות יש לי להבריך בך

Paul and Romans 11

The rabbis imagined Abraham as actively involved in proselytizing the pagan world for monotheism.

In his efforts to turn the world to faith in God, Abraham could be likened unto a tree of faith. As people left idolatry to embrace the God of Abraham, they are likened to branches removed from trees of other faiths. They are cut from those trees and grafted into the tree of Abraham's faith—in a metaphorical sense, engrafted into Abraham. This engrafting process is a blessing to the peoples of the earth, for only in Abraham's faith can they find truth. Thus, we may read, "In you all the families of the earth shall be engrafted."

When Paul wrote to the believers in Rome, he addressed the Gentile God-Fearers in that community, "You were cut from what is by nature a wild olive tree, and grafted, contrary to nature, into a cultivated olive tree ... although a wild olive shoot, [you] were grafted in among the others and now share in the nourishing root of the olive tree" (Romans 11:17, 24).

The grafting parable is Paul's, but the concept that "all peoples on earth will be grafted into you" is not Paul's invention. Instead, it represents an intentional misreading of the Hebrew of Genesis 12:3. Paul and Rabbi Elazar were virtually contemporaries. They lived around the same time. Either Paul found the inspiration for his olive tree parable in the same misreading of Genesis 12:3, or both Paul and Rabbi Elazar shared a common source. At any rate, Rabbi Elazar's imagery is consistent with Paul's theology.

The verse that Rabbi Elazar intentionally misread in order to arrive at the engrafting metaphor is the same verse Paul quoted in Galatians 3:8, the same verse he referred to as "the gospel" that was announced "beforehand to Abraham."

And the Scripture, foreseeing that God would justify the Gentiles by faith, preached the gospel beforehand to Abraham, saying, "In you shall all the nations be blessed." (Galatians 3:8)

The gospel preached beforehand to Abraham was not the full revelation of how this promise will be fulfilled. It was not a special revelation of the death and resurrection of Yeshua in advance. According to Paul's theology, the gospel as it was preached to Abraham was: "In you shall all the families of the earth be blessed by being grafted into your faith." To Paul, the phrase, "All nations will be blessed through you," *is the gospel.* That was Paul's gospel.

> Abraham "believed God, and it was counted to him as righteousness"? Know then that it is those of faith who are the sons of Abraham. And the Scripture, foreseeing that God would justify the Gentiles by faith, preached the gospel beforehand to Abraham, saying, "In you shall all the nations be blessed." So then, those who are of faith are blessed along with Abraham, the man of faith. (Galatians 3:6–9)

CURSE OF THE LAW
(GALATIANS 3:10)

Paul invokes the Torah's curses for
covenant infidelity to dissuade the
Galatian God-Fearers from becoming
Jewish.

H as anyone ever warned you that you might be placing yourself
under a curse by keeping the Torah? It happens sometimes.
For example, if a Messianic Jew or Christian decides to keep the
Sabbath on the seventh day or to eat kosher, he might be warned
by a well-meaning brother in the Master, "Why would you place
yourself under the law? Don't you know that those who are of the
works of the law are under a curse?"

> For as many as are of the works of the law are under the
> curse: for it is written, Cursed is every one that continueth
> not in all things which are written in the book of the law
> to do them. (Galatians 3:10, KJV)

Curse of the law

One does not hear that sentiment as often nowadays as in the
past because, as biblical literacy wanes, people are less and less
aware of the basis for their own theology. In the past, one certainly
might have expected to hear such a statement in regard to any
form of "keeping the law." I wonder how many believers have been

scared off from the good things of the Torah such as the beauty, for example, of honoring the Sabbath or the festivals because they were afraid that by doing so they might be bringing themselves under a curse.

Moreover, I wonder to what extent Galatians 3:10 is responsible for the vilification of the Jewish people who, by common consent of the early church theologians, were an accursed race. The logic works quite naturally. If those who practice the works of the law are under a curse, then the Jewish people are an accursed, miserable people. When people are accursed, it is a lot easier to justify bigotry and brutality against them. In that regard, Galatians 3:10 is an important text for theological anti-Semitism, for anti-Judaism, and anti-Torah sentiment in general.

Under the Curse

Galatians 3:10 is yet another obscure, misread, misused, and problematic text. This is not a problem for most of Christian theology. From a traditional church perspective, the meaning is self-evident: Those who practice the Torah are under a curse.

That explanation does not work for us in the Messianic Jewish movement, and it does not work for explaining Paul either. We know, from Paul's own admission, that he himself kept the Torah as an observant Jew—a Pharisee, even. So in that case, Paul would be placing himself under a curse.

The King James Version of Galatians 3:10 is more literal than the English Standard Version. The ESV version says, "For all who *rely* on works of the law are under a curse." That is certainly a better thought-for-thought paraphrase which conveys the sense and the intention of the verse, but it is not what Paul literally wrote. The ESV translators supplied the word "rely", and they did well to do so. It brings a lot of clarity to Paul's intention, but when Paul wrote the Epistle to the Galatians, he did not say "who *rely* on works of the law," he said, "those who are of the works of the law." In the literal reading, it sounds like Paul is saying that those who keep the Torah are under a curse.

This is troubling because the logical implication is that in order to avoid this curse, one should do the exact opposite of everything that Torah says. Otherwise, he might fall into this obligation of keeping the Torah. If he does not continue to keep the whole Torah, he is under a curse. According to such interpretations, a person has only two options vis-à-vis the Torah: keep all of it flawlessly and without error or keep none of it whatsoever.

Recap and Review: "Works of the Law"

Paul said, "As many as are of the works of the law are under the curse." That raises a lot of questions. For example, if a man were to keep the commandment of the law that says "honor your father and mother," might he be placing himself under the curse of the Torah?

We have already learned in previous sermons that the term "works of the law" does not refer to just any of the commandments in the Torah. Instead, we learned that when Paul used the term "works of the law" he was referring specifically to those particular sign commandments and statutes which identify a person as Jewish, such as circumcision. Therefore, we are not just talking about obedience to God's commandments in general; we are talking about Jewish obedience—obedience to those commandments in the Torah which are specifically incumbent upon the Jewish people.

The "works of the law" are the commandments that defined Jewish status in first-century Judaism, beginning with circumcision as an act of legal conversion. When Paul used the phrase "as many as are of the works of the law," there were only two possible people groups he might be identifying: those born Jewish and those who had undergone a conversion to become a proselyte. Accordingly, people who are legally Jewish, whether by birth or conversion, fall under this troubling curse.

Curses and Blessings in the Torah

Only Israel-according-to-the-flesh, that is, "those who are of the works of the law," fall under the curse. The malediction Paul cites is not a New Testament imprecation. Paul quotes Deuteronomy 27:26, the conclusion of the covenant ceremony at Mount Gerizim and Ebal, where it says: "'Cursed be anyone who does not confirm the words of this law by doing them.' And all the people shall say, 'Amen.'"

> For it is written, "Cursed be everyone who does not abide by all things written in the Book of the law, and do them." (Galatians 3:10)

In the Torah, Deuteronomy 28 immediately follows with the full treatment of covenant blessings that Israel will attain for keeping the Torah and the withering curses that Israel will invoke for covenant infidelity and for breaking the Torah.

In that regard, Paul only reminded his readers of what the Torah has always said: there are terrible consequences for violating the covenant. The people of Israel receive consequences for violating the Torah. Moses himself said so. Here is a paraphrase of Galatians 3:10 in simple language:

> Every legally Jewish person who does not keep the Torah is under a curse because that is what the Torah says.

It certainly does not mean that a Messianic Jew should not keep the Torah or that if a God-fearing Gentile believer begins to honor the Sabbath or chooses to eat kosher, he places himself under a curse. It does not mean that Torah observance, as a simple act of obedience to God and conformity to his word, invokes his curse. That would create a bizarre theology.

Doctrine of the Influencers

But why would Paul state the obvious? If he is just reiterating what the Torah has always said about the consequences for breaking the covenant, then what is his point?

In previous sermons, we have learned about a group of people influencing the Galatian God-Fearers. The influencers have a theological assumption that only those who are legally Jewish (Israel proper) have standing in the kingdom of heaven and a guaranteed share in the world to come. Nevertheless, they are believers. More than that, they themselves are probably Gentile converts to Judaism who have taken on the so-called "works of the law." They have gone "under the law" and have become Jewish. The influencers, as I understand them, were themselves believing proselytes, and they pressured the believing, God-fearing Gentiles to also become proselytes.

They did not teach salvation through faith. Neither did they teach salvation by works. They taught salvation by Jewish status, a status which they attained by going through circumcision and taking on the commandments that identify a person as Jewish—the *works of the law.*

Many parallels exist within the Christian world. For example, traditionally, within the Roman Catholic confession, salvation is imparted through the sacraments, primarily the sacraments of baptism and the Eucharist. Through sacramental mechanism, a person attains recognized standing as a Christian. Without that standing as a Christian within the Catholic confession, one has no assurance of the world to come. Similar theologies exist in the other Christian confessions where one sacrament or another grants eligibility for heaven and the resurrection. In Evangelicalism, espousal of the proper theological belief system replaces the sacraments.

As with every human association, religion inevitably becomes an institution. When it does, those within the institution often assume that membership in their particular institution is a prerequisite to salvation. The Christian Fundamentalist does not anticipate encountering people from other denominations in heaven. In that mindset, doctrinal purity, the right confession, and the right set of beliefs defines a real Christian. Beyond achieving institutional membership, matters of obedience, personal devotion to God, commitment to his commands and directives, and so forth, are regarded as less consequential—certainly not inconsequential—but of less consequence. For example, consider the "cheap grace"—which Dietrich Bonhoeffer wrote against in *The Cost of Discipleship*—the idea that once a person is baptized, he is sealed for heaven regardless of his behavior.

The influencers in Galatia seem to have subscribed to a similar theological premise. They seem to have believed that, once a person goes though the conversion process and attains Jewish status, he is off the hook for the rest of the obligations. Once you are in Israel, you are in, and a Jew need not worry about the afterlife. This was not a theology of salvation by works. Neither was it salvation by grace. The influencers taught salvation by national identity and Jewish status within God's covenant with Israel.

One sees the same theological premises at work in the church. People often adopt the right rituals and say the right words, but then they live the rest of their lives in disregard for the demands of faith. Once in the club, they do not worry about the details and rules.

Sabbath Proselytes

Paul articulated his objection to this idea as he addressed the believers in Rome. In Romans 2, Paul addressed Gentiles who have already gone through the conversion ritual to become legally Jewish. They seem to be believing proselytes, not people from one of Paul's communities or the fruit of his gospel, but Gentile believers who had become proselytes, either before or after coming to know Messiah:

> If you call yourself a Jew and rely on the law and boast in God and know his will and approve what is excellent, because you are instructed from the law; and if you are sure that you yourself are a guide to the blind, a light to those who are in darkness, an instructor of the foolish, a teacher of children, having in the law the embodiment of knowledge and truth—you then who teach others, do you not teach yourself? While you preach against stealing, do you steal? You who say that one must not commit adultery, do you commit adultery? (Romans 2:17–22).

Paul warned the proselytes that being "Jewish" means nothing if one does not live according to the obligations of Torah. He said, "Circumcision indeed is of value if you obey the law, but if you break the law, your circumcision becomes uncircumcision" (Romans 2:25). He made the same charge against the influencers in Galatia:

> For even those who are circumcised do not themselves keep the Torah, but they desire to have you circumcised that they may boast in your flesh. (Galatians 6:13)

"Those who are circumcised" refers to those who had gone through the proselyte conversion ritual and now are confirmed, so to speak. They felt that they had attained the status needed for their salvation, and therefore they did not need to worry about the particulars of obedience to Torah beyond those commandments which identified them as Jewish. Of course they keep the "works of the law" that identify them as Jewish, but the Torah contains more than just circumcision, Sabbaths, holy days, dietary laws, *tzitzit*, *tefillin*, and *mezuzah*.

This can be compared to the churchgoer who dutifully attends church, receives baptism, confirmation, affirms the confessions, and whatever other minimal hoops he needs to jump through to become part of the club and maintain his member status, but he never lets faith in God, his relationship with God, or the demands of God impact his real life in a significant way. When I was young, we used to call them "Sunday Christians." In Galatia, we could call them "Sabbath Proselytes."

Real Religion

If I am correct in this assessment, I think we can make better sense of Galatians 3:10, where Paul said, "For as many as are of the works of the law are under the curse: for it is written, Cursed is every one that continueth not in all things which are written in the book of the law to do them." In other words, if you accept this covenant membership of conversion to become Jewish, you must also accept all of its national, covenantal obligations, including the imprecations for covenant infidelity. In other words, if you become Jewish, you are liable for the full weight of punishment spelled out by Torah if you do not keep the Torah. It's not a free ticket to heaven.

Real religion and real faith in God cannot be institutionalized or reduced to the level of membership status. True godliness transcends one's affiliation. Real religion and real relationship with God must be a fulltime endeavor. One cannot punch in and punch out from faith any more than one could punch out of marriage. No decent person thinks of their marriage that way—as if you are married at home, but when you leave the home, you are a single person with all of the romantic potential of a single person on the dating scene. Such a spouse would be sick in the head: an adulterer.

Instead, real religion requires a life of faith and faithfulness—an ever-present sense of the fear of God, the conviction that he is real, that he punishes sin and rewards righteousness, that there is "an eye that sees, and ear that hears, and all your deeds are recorded in a book" (m.*Avot* 2:1). Real faith is the practical outworking of the conviction that God is present with us and holding us accountable, even when we are not in church, even when we are not in the synagogue, even when no one is watching.

The influencers, however, taught confidence in ritual, institutional status. They neglected the weighty obligations of Torah and focused on the external boundary markers. Paul said, 'They do not themselves keep the Torah, and now they are trying to get you to join their members-only club.' He warned, 'Don't you realize that there are serious biblical consequences to that decision?' He said in Galatians 5:3, "I testify again to every man who accepts circumcision that he is obligated to keep the whole law." That is to say, if you become Jewish, you will be obligated to keep the whole Torah, not just the "works of the law."

What is the Curse of the law?

In this interpretation, the curse of the law is not something new. It refers to the maledictions against the people of Israel for violation of the Torah's commandments. Deuteronomy 28 spells out those curses.

Paul warned the God-fearing Galatian Gentiles that becoming Jewish brings serious responsibilities. As a Jew himself, Paul understood himself to also be included under the same curses for covenant disobedience as the rest of his people. One cannot take the blessings and leave the curses; they come in tandem.

The God-fearing Gentiles of Galatia, however, stood outside of the legal, national covenantal identity of Israel-proper. The litany of curses in the Torah did not apply to them in the national sense as they applied to the Jewish people. If, however, they chose to take on Jewish identity, they needed to also take on the full weight of Jewish responsibility.

THE TORAH IS NOT OF FAITH
(GALATIANS 3:11–12)

Paul quotes Leviticus 18:5 and Habakkuk
2:4 in a manner consistent with rabbinic
interpretation to establish that it is not
the hearers of the Torah who will be
declared righteous but the doers of the
Torah.

When Paul said "the law is not of faith," he seemed to imply that a great chasm lies between those who have faith unto salvation and those who practice the law. Anyone reading the Epistle to the Galatians might conclude that a person who practices the law is not a person of faith. That idea has prevailed for most of the history of church interpretation. Consider Galatians 3:11–12:

> Now it is evident that no one is justified before God by
> the law, for "The righteous shall live by faith." But the law
> is not of faith, rather "The one who does them shall live
> by them."

The Torah Is Not of Faith

Christian interpreters typically understand this passage to demonstrate the difference between Christianity and Judaism, the difference between a Christian and a Jew, and the difference between faith and works. The Apostle Paul flatly stated, "The Torah is not of faith." He seemed to contrast "those who keep the Torah" against "those who live by faith." A Jewish person, therefore, is not a person of faith if he practices the law, for the law is not of faith. If you want to have faith, the one thing you cannot do is keep the Torah. This is the conventional interpretation of the passage and seemingly the plain meaning.

When Messianic believers tell their friends in the mainstream church that they have decided to begin to keep the Sabbath or to eat a biblically clean diet, their friends often react with alarm and concern. Any perceived observance of the law is cause for alarm because the "Torah is not of faith."

The Christian church has maintained this standard even for Jewish believers in Yeshua. When a Jewish person became a believer, he quickly learned that he must no longer practice Judaism or keep the Torah. Christian confessions often considered renouncing Torah Judaism as a prerequisite to the life of faith for Jewish believers because the "Torah is not of faith." Throughout Christian history, churchmen castigated Jewish Christians who kept the Torah in some fashion (for example, kept the Sabbath on the seventh day or refused to eat unclean meats). Churchmen considered such Jews insincere converts, backsliders, and not of true faith. The church often made abandonment of Torah the litmus test for Jewish believers, a test by which they had to prove the authenticity of their commitment to Christ and Christianity. As David Stern said in his book *Messianic Judaism*, "Now that you are a Christian, you are free from the law. Have a ham sandwich!"[19] That litmus test remains the standard for most of Christianity even to this day.

(Sadly, the same is true for much of what is called Messianic Judaism as well. In light of this unfortunate theological history, we should not be surprised whatsoever when we find that Jewish "Christians" are often resistant to the idea of Torah observance and Jewish practice. They have been taught that the Torah is the opposite of faith. That makes it difficult to find observant Jewish believers, even in the Messianic Jewish movement. Ironically, we see far

---

[19] David Stern, *Messianic Judaism: A Modern Movement with an Ancient Past* (Clarksville, MD: Messianic Jewish Resources International, 2007), 144.

more Gentiles eager to take on the full yoke of the commandments than Jewish believers.)

When Paul said that "the Torah is not of faith," historical Christianity understood it to mean that Torah observance and faith are incompatible. That's what it means for much of the body of Messiah to this very day, but that interpretation does not work for Messianic Judaism.

Life and Death

Life and death are a big deal. Those two words cover the whole of human existence. Everything a human is or ever will be can be expressed in two words: life and death. It starts out with you alive, and then you are not. Death comes, most often uninvited, an unwelcome, rude intruder, an antithesis to being. Death is not our friend; death is our enemy—the last enemy to be defeated. The prophets tell us that one day death will be defeated. We can be sure of this hope because we have seen it happen in the resurrection of Yeshua of Nazareth. The empty tomb he left behind bears testimony. He is the one who is alive forever more. Death holds no sway over him, for he holds the keys of death and Hades.

Yet these both remain: life and death. The Torah commands us, "Choose life." God says, "I have set before you life and death, blessing and curse. Therefore choose life" (Deuteronomy 30:19).

Paul did not use the words "life" and "death," "live" and "die" in a strictly literal sense. Instead, he often invested the terms with more meaning. For Paul, "to live" is to attain the resurrection, eternal life, and the world to come. "To die" is to die without hope of the world to come, with only the dread of the final judgment.

> **To live:** What some Christians call "saved," to live means to attain the right to resurrection and eternal life in the kingdom and in the world to come.
>
> **To die:** What some Christians call "unsaved" or "lost," to die means to face death without hope and with only dread of the final judgment.

Paul used the terms life and death to indicate eternal destinies. He did not create these post-mortem definitions himself. His broader definitions reflect a terminology and method of interpretation which he learned as a Pharisee. The rabbis spoke like this and interpreted the Scriptures in the same manner. They often spoke of life and death not merely as literal life and death but also as eternal destinies.

The Pharisees may have adopted this method of biblical exegesis as part of their ongoing argument with the Sadducees. The Sadducees claimed that the Torah did not teach about an afterlife or resurrection; the Pharisees claimed that it did. It all depended on how you interpreted the words life and death.

Eternal Life

The apostles followed Pharisaic interpretation. Paul was not the only apostle to use the terms life and death this way. All of the apostles used the same terminology, and so did our Master. For example, Yeshua said, "I am the resurrection and the life. Whoever believes in me, though he die, yet shall he live, and everyone who lives and believes in me shall never die" (John 11:25–26).

The same specialized used of the terminology is at work in Galatians 3:11–12, where Paul quotes two passages, one from the prophet Habakkuk and one from the Torah.

> Now it is evident that no one is justified before God by the law, for "The righteous shall *live* by faith." But the law is not of faith, rather "The one who does them shall *live* by them." (Galatians 3:11–12)

> But the righteous shall live by his faith. (Habakkuk 2:4)

> You shall therefore keep my statutes and my rules; if a person does them, he shall live by them. (Leviticus 18:5)

Both of Paul's proof texts and his interpretation of both of the proof texts are represented in early Jewish teaching.

Leviticus 18:5

In Pharisaic and apostolic interpretation, the words "he shall live by them" in Leviticus 18:5 mean "a man may attain the resurrection from the dead and eternal life if he does them." Rashi explains, "'Live by them' refers to life in the world to come, for if you should say that our verse refers to life in this present world, is it not man's destiny to die?" The Aramaic *targumim* paraphrase the passage as follows:

> And you shall keep my statutes and my judgments, which if a man do he shall live by them and have everlasting life. (Leviticus 18:5, *Targum Onkelos*)

> And you shall keep my statutes and the order of my judgments, which if a man do he shall live in them, in the life of eternity, and his position shall be with the just. (Leviticus 18:5, *Targum Yonatan*)

Paul stayed in line with the mainstream of Jewish interpretation by explaining Leviticus 18:5 as saying that if a person keeps the commandments, he will attain eternal life by them. Yeshua himself quoted the same passage to the same effect in Luke 10:28.

Rabbi Meir, who lived about two generations after Paul, also quoted Leviticus 18:5 to prove that a Gentile can attain eternal life.

> Rabbi Meir used to say, "How do we know that even a Gentile who studies the Torah is equivalent to the High Priest?" From Leviticus 18:5, where it says, "You shall therefore keep my statutes and my rules; if a person does them, he shall live by them." Meir says, "It does not say if a priest, a Levite, or an Israelite does them, he shall live by them. It says "if a person" does them. You learn here that even a non-Jew who studies the Torah is equivalent to a High Priest. (b.*Sanhedrin* 59a)

Meir interpreted this verse to mean that a person can attain life through obedience, whether or not he is Jewish. Both Jew and Gentile can attain life by obedience to God. The immediate relevance to non-Jews is that Leviticus 18 contains prohibitions on sexual immorality and idolatry, for the violation of which God punished the Gentile Canaanites. Therefore, the sages deduced from this passage that Gentiles are required to keep the Torah's prohibitions on idolatry and sexual immorality.

Habakkuk 2:4

After quoting Leviticus 18:5, which seems to imply that eternal life can be attained by keeping the commandments, Paul brings a seemingly contradictory verse from Habakkuk 2:4, which says that "the righteous shall live by faith." So Paul was saying, "On the one hand, the one who does the commandments will live by them. On the other hand, the righteous will live by faith."

Habakkuk 2:4 receives prominent attention in a famous passage in the Talmud. In that passage, the sages begin by stating that God gave Israel 613 commandments by which they could attain eternal life. If a man does them, he will live by them. But since 613 is far too many commandments and far too difficult (who can remember 613 commandments?), King David simplified it, summarizing the 613 in eleven principles expressed in Psalm 15. Eleven is still a lot. That's still too much. So Isaiah simplified it, summarizing it in six principles in Isaiah 33:13–14. Six is still a lot to remember. So Micah simplified it to three in Micah 6:8, where he says, "He has told you, O man, what is good; and what does the LORD require of you but to 1) do justice, and to 2) love kindness, and to 3) walk humbly with your God?" But even three things are a bit imposing, so Isaiah again simplified it, summarizing the whole Torah in two principles. In Isaiah 56:1, he says, "Keep justice, and do righteousness." That's concise enough, but the Talmud goes on to say, "Then came Habakkuk, and reduced and simplified the whole Torah into one principle, saying, 'The righteous shall live by his faith'" (b.*Makkot* 24a). By the word "live," the Talmud means "live in the world to come."

The sages and rabbis also used this Habakkuk text as a Messianic passage. The righteous who live by faith are those who have faith in the coming of the Messiah. This is the passage from which Maimonides derived his twelfth article of the Jewish faith: "I believe with a complete faith in the coming of the Messiah, though he may tarry, yet I will await him every day."

> For still the vision awaits its appointed time; it hastens to the end—it will not lie. If it seems slow, wait for it; it will surely come; it will not delay ... the righteous shall live by his faith. (Habakkuk 2:3–4)

Pauline Terminology

The above provides us an overview of how Judaism interpreted the two passages. What did Paul mean by quoting them in Galatians? Was Paul contrasting them against one another to demonstrate that faith and keeping Torah are opposites, since the Torah is not of faith?

According to most interpretations, he set the two passages in antithesis, one against another, pitting faith against Torah as competing paths to eternal life. In the past, I have always understood it that way as well, but I am no longer certain that Paul intended to place the two passages in contradiction to one another.

When Paul used the phrases "the works of the law," going "under the law," and even just "the law," he ordinarily was not speaking of the Torah in a generalized sense as God's instruction, the commandments, or even the five books of Moses. Instead, he used that terminology in a very narrow sense to refer to being Jewish (and/or converting to become legally Jewish) and therefore bound to the observance of certain identity markers, i.e., specific commandments that define Jewish identity, such as circumcision.

Previously in this study, we have also learned that the words "justify," "justification," "righteous," and "righteousness" are all different forms of the same word in both Hebrew and Greek. We have been translating them as "exoneration," i.e., a "not-guilty" verdict in the heavenly court before God. To be "justified" is to be declared "not guilty" by the court.

We can take all of this specialized Pauline terminology and apply it to Galatians 3:11–12. Again, I will offer glosses, paraphrases, and substitutions in square brackets [like this]:

> Now it is evident that no one is [exonerated as righteous] before God by [attaining Jewish status through the works of the] Torah, because "The righteous shall live [in the world to come] by faith." And [attaining Jewish status by the works of the] Torah is not of faith; instead, "The one who does [the commandments] shall live [in the world to come] by them." (Galatians 3:11–12)

"And" or "But"

Ordinarily, we understand Paul's two proof texts as set in opposition to one another, as if Paul used one to refute the other. On the one hand, "The righteous will inherit eternal life by faith," but on the other hand, "The one who does the commandments will inherit eternal life." I suggest that Paul did not contrast the two verses. The Greek conjunction *de* between the two verses need not be translated in the adversative. I am translating it as "and" instead of "but".

> "The righteous shall live by faith." ~~But~~ *And* the law is not of faith, rather "The one who does them shall live by them." (Galatians 3:11–12)

In that case, Paul simply presented two proof texts to prove the same thing. "The righteous will live by faith" is the same as "He who does them will live by them." "He who does them" is the righteous man, living by faith.

The real opposites that Paul contrasted was "living by faith" and "the works of the Torah," that is, "having Jewish status." He called Jewish status "the law" as a shorthand reference for "works of the law," the term he used in the previous verse.

Again, Paul countered the theology of the "influencers" who taught that, once a person becomes Jewish, he need not worry about keeping the commandments except for those works of the law that identify him within the nation and covenant. The influencers taught an approach to faith and practice like the churchgoer who does not worry about living a Christian life after he has been baptized, confirmed, said the sinner's prayer, or whatever religious ritual he felt he needed to do to earn salvation. Paul countered that cheap-grace theology in Galatians 3:10, and he continued to argue against it in Galatians 3:11–12.

Corroborating Evidence

Paul makes a verbal analogy (*gezerah shavah*) based upon a common term shared by the two passages. The common term is "will live." The first passage says, "The righteous *will live* by faith." The second passage says, "The one who does them *shall live* by them." The rabbis quoted verbal analogies between two passages in precisely the same manner, not to contrast them but to link them together or to use one to define the other. According to that type of rabbinic interpretation, the righteous one who *lives* by faith in Habakkuk 2:4 is the same person as the fellow who does the commandments in Leviticus 18:5. He is not the one who converts to take on Jewish status under the works of the law. Converting to become Jewish is not of faith. Keeping the commandments is of faith.

This interpretation has the advantage of solving the otherwise hopelessly cryptic statement, "The law is not of faith." Paul only means that "converting to become Jewish by the works of the law is not of faith." This is essentially the same point that Rabbi Meir made in the Talmud when he used Leviticus 18:5 to prove that even a Gentile who studies and practices the Torah is equivalent to the high priest in the eyes of God. As demonstrated above, this interpretation also finds corroboration in the early *targumim,* in the Talmud in Tractate *Makkot,* and in the interpretations of Rashi. Finally, we can find further corroboration elsewhere in the writings of Paul:

> For God shows no partiality. For all who have sinned without the law [Gentiles] will also perish without the law, and all who have sinned under the law [Jews] will be judged by the law. For it is not the hearers of the law who are righteous before God, but *the doers of the law who will be justified.* (Romans 2:11–13)

If I am understanding Paul correctly, what he is saying is the exact opposite of what we usually think he is saying. He is not pitting "faith" against the keeping of the Torah. Instead, he says that the righteous man who lives by faith is the man who does the commandments and lives by them. Faith and faithfulness are two sides of the same coin: faith and obedience.

Paul contrasted the man who lives by faith and shows his faith by his obedience to God's commandments (as they apply to him, whether Jew or Gentile) opposite the man who believes that salvation is achieved simply by being under the Torah, i.e., simply by attaining and maintaining Jewish status through a few works of the law, such as circumcision.

Paul was not saying that keeping God's commandments is the opposite of faith. I suggest that he was saying that keeping God's commandments is part of what it means to be a man of faith. It is this man of faith who is reckoned righteous because "it is not the hearers of the law who are righteous before God, but the doers of the law who will be justified."

SERMON SIXTEEN:
TALUI
(GALATIANS 3:13–14)

Paul reinvents a popular anti-Yeshua taunt derived from Deuteronomy 21:22–23 to argue that the Messiah's suffering and death releases those who rely upon him from the curse of the law.

Within Judaism, Yeshua of Nazareth has been often known by the name *Talui*, or *haTalui*, which literally translated means "the Hanged One," or contextually, "the Crucified One." In old anti-Christian writings, the pejorative is sometimes combined with other unflattering descriptions, but in general *Talui* means Jesus, the crucified one.

The Asham Talui

Ironically, the word *talui* is also a Talmudic-era Hebrew term, still in use today, for uncertainty. Because it means "hanging," it is used to express a matter hanging in doubt. For example, in English we sometimes speak of a "hung jury." Something hanging swings back and forth, so hanging can mean uncertainty. In the days of the apostles, Jewish people offered a special kind of a sacrifice in the Temple called an *asham talui*, which literally means "a guilt offering hanging," but idiomatically "a guilt offering of uncertainty." One who was in doubt as to whether he had committed a transgression or not brought a guilt offering of uncertainty. The Talmud says that Bava ben Buta brought an *asham talui* to the Temple every day because he thought, "Perhaps I have transgressed and did not realize it."

Our Master is contemptuously called *Talui*, meaning the crucified one, but ironically the name also implies uncertainty: Might he not be the promised Messiah? What if his claims are true? Even more ironic, Isaiah 53:10 predicts that the Messiah will suffer on behalf of the nation "when his soul makes an offering for guilt (*asham*)." Yeshua, the crucified one (*talui*), went to the cross as an *asham talui*, so to speak.

Our Master's detractors called him *Talui* as a pejorative, but God meant the name for good. It comes from the Torah:

> And if a man has committed a crime punishable by death and he is put to death, and you hang (*talita*) him on a tree, his body shall not remain all night on the tree, but you shall bury him the same day, for a hanged man (*talui*) is cursed by God. You shall not defile your land that the LORD your God is giving you for an inheritance. (Deuteronomy 21:22–23)

Hung upon a Tree

The Torah says that if a corpse is hung upon a tree, it is not to be left hanging overnight. Instead, the corpse must be taken down and buried that same day. This passage is relevant to the Master's death. However, the Torah is not speaking of crucifixion. In Tractate *Sanhedrin* (46b), the Talmud points out that the man hung on a tree in Deuteronomy 21:22 was not crucified. He was already dead prior to being hung on the tree.

In the ancient world, authorities sometimes hung the corpse of an executed man as a public warning to others. Hopefully, those who saw the executed man's body on display would resolve not to commit the same crimes. The Torah does not actually prescribe such a grisly method of dissuasion. Instead, the Torah's legislation aims to ensure the dignity of the corpse by requiring a timely burial.

Hanging on a tree is not a Torah-prescribed means of delivering a death sentence. Crucifixion was never a Jewish mode of execution and would itself be a violation of Jewish law. In Roman law, however, a person could be crucified for piracy, highway robbery, assassination, forgery, false testimony, mutiny, sedition, or rebellion. The Romans also crucified soldiers who deserted to the enemy and slaves who denounced their masters.

The Romans used crosses of different shapes. Some were in the form of a capital T. Others were shaped like the letter X, while still others were in the traditional shape that Christian iconography identifies with the Master's cross.

According to Christian tradition, several of the Master's disciples also died by crucifixion in Roman cities. According to church legend, the Romans crucified Peter. He did not deem himself worthy to be crucified in the same manner as his Master, so he begged them to crucify him upside down. The Romans accommodated the request.

A cross could be a tree or simply a post embedded in the ground. The condemned carried the crossbeam to the place of execution with the *titulus* (an inscription identifying his crime) hanging from his neck. The executioners might have used ropes and pulleys to raise the executed man, nailed to the crossbeam, up into position. The Romans stripped the man to be executed and crucified him naked. Typically, a crucified man agonized at least twelve hours, and in some cases languished for up to three days on the cross. This explains why it was necessary on the day of the Master's death to break the legs, so that the men would die quicker from asphyxiation. Normally, outside of Judea and in the greater Roman world, the bodies were not taken down. Instead, they remained on the cross, food for birds of prey until they rotted or were cast before wild beasts.

Rome introduced this cruel means of execution in Judea as a way of punishing zealot rebels. Routine crucifixions had been going on for as long as three decades before the birth of the Master. Thousands of Jewish men died by crucifixion. Josephus claims that by the end of the Jewish revolt, the Romans had cut down all the trees of Judea for crosses.

The Romans did not observe Deuteronomy 21:22–23. The bodies of the crucified might be left hanging indefinitely. In the case of the Master's execution, however, the Jewish authorities entreated Pilate "that the bodies would not remain on the cross on the Sabbath" (John 19:31). Since the Sabbath was about to begin, they wanted the men dead and removed. When the soldiers came to break the legs of the crucified men, they found that Yeshua was already dead. Joseph of Arimathea, one of the sages of the Sanhedrin, "took courage and went to Pilate and asked for the body of Jesus" (Mark 15:43). In taking his body down from the cross, Joseph kept the commandment of not leaving the body hanging overnight. In *Targum Pseudo-Yonatan*'s translation of Deuteronomy 21:23, it says, "you shall bury him at the going down of the sun." According to Luke 23:54, Joseph of Arimathea closed the tomb of the Master right at the going down of the sun, as it says, "and the Sabbath was beginning."

Regarding the commandment of taking down the body and not letting it hang overnight, Rabbi Meir brings a parable in the Talmud.

> Rabbi Meir said, "There is a parable about this matter. To what can it be compared? It can be compared to two identical twin brothers. Both lived in a certain city. One was appointed king, and the other became a bandit. At the king's command they hanged the bandit. But everyone who saw him hanging there said, 'The king has been hung!' Therefore the king issued a command and he was taken down." (b.*Sanhedrin* 46b)

In other words because the human body is made in the image of God, it would be a sacrilege against God to leave a corpse hanging overnight. Like the identical twin in the story, Yeshua is the "image of the invisible God" (Colossians 1:15) and "the radiance of the glory of God and the exact imprint of his nature" (Hebrews 1:3). As the parable says, "Everyone who saw him hanging there said, 'The king has been hung!'" Yeshua is the king. The sign above his cross said, "King of the Jews."

Accursed of God

> But you shall surely bury him on the same day (for *talui* is accursed of God), so that you do not defile your land which the Lord your God gives you as an inheritance. (Deuteronomy 21:22–23)

Deuteronomy 21:23 says, "He who is hanged is accursed of God." This passage explains why the name *Talui*, the Crucified One, the Hung One, became a common title for Yeshua in Judaism. As the Jewish people struggled under the polemics and persecutions of the church, the *Talui* moniker provided an inside joke. Who is Yeshua? He is *Talui*, the Crucified One. And what does the Torah say? "*Talui* is accursed of God."

Anti-missionaries still use the passage today, and I suspect that this joke goes all the way back to the earliest years of the Yeshua movement. As the apostles proclaimed "Christ crucified" within the Jewish community, the early detractors who resisted their message probably responded with this passage: "*Talui* is accursed of God. The Crucified One is Accursed of God."

Opponents of the early believers used this passage to argue that Yeshua could not be the Messiah, just as anti-missionaries do today. They probably said, "You see, he could not be Messiah because he was hung on a tree, and everyone hung on a tree is accursed of God. Surely the real Messiah is not accursed of God."

The most learned and most vicious anti-missionary whom the believers ever faced was Paul of Tarsus. Paul knew this passage. He used it in his debates against the early believers in contempt of Yeshua *haTalui*, the Crucified One.

Reflecting on this matter, Paul wrote to the Corinthians, "I make known to you that no one speaking by the Spirit of God says, 'Jesus is accursed'; and no one can say, 'Jesus is Lord,' except in the Holy Spirit" (1 Corinthians 12:3). He also brought it up in the book of Galatians.

Under the Curse

In Galatians 3, Paul returned to his old anti-Yeshua, *Talui*-polemic and cited Deuteronomy 21:22–23 in reference to Yeshua again. That passage was always popular with the anti-Yeshua crowd, but in Galatians 3, Paul put a new spin on it.

> Christ redeemed us from the curse of the law by becoming a curse for us—for it is written, [in Deuteronomy 21:23] "Cursed is everyone who is hanged on a tree"— so that in Christ Jesus the blessing of Abraham might come

to the Gentiles, so that we might receive the promised Spirit through faith. (Galatians 3:13–14)

Previously, Paul declared that "all who rely on works of the law are under a curse; for it is written, 'Cursed be everyone who does not abide by all things written in the Book of the law, and do them'" (Galatians 3:10). Those who are "of the works of the law" are those who are already Jewish or becoming Jewish through legal conversion. Paul said that everyone who is Jewish or a proselyte falls under the curse when they do not keep the Torah and walk in obedience to the covenant obligations stipulated in the Torah as explained in Deuteronomy 28. Therefore, Paul wanted to warn the God-fearing Gentiles along these lines: "Do not suppose that becoming Jewish is the easy ticket to salvation. In fact, it's just the opposite. If you become Jewish, the standard goes up. You place yourself under responsibility to the whole Torah, and under a curse if you fail to meet that responsibility."

This argument, however, seems to imply two different paths of salvation. Jewish people must keep the Torah to earn life in the world to come, but Gentile believers need only faith. On the contrary, Paul goes on to demonstrate that both Jew and Gentile must rely upon Messiah.

A Blessing and a Curse

According to Paul's view, the curse for failing to keep the Torah was not just a run of bad luck; it extended beyond this world and into the next. He said, "The righteous man will live by faith," that is to say, live in the world to come; and he said, "The one who does the commandments will live by them." In that respect, to fall under the curse for disobedience is to forfeit the resurrection and the world to come. Like Moses, Paul sets before his readers a choice of blessing and curse.

> **Blessing**: Those who are of faith are blessed along with Abraham, the man of faith. (Galatians 3:9)

> **Curse**: For all who rely on works of the law are under a curse; for it is written, "Cursed be everyone who does not

abide by all things written in the Book of the law, and do them." (Galatians 3:10)

According to Paul, the final curse of the Torah is condemnation in the eternal court of judgment. Elsewhere, he points out that "the [Torah] brings wrath" (Romans 4:15). It does so because it defines sin. He said, "the [Torah] came in to increase the trespass" (Romans 5:20). In other words, one of the functions of the Torah is that man might be made more aware of his sin. Because the Torah—in its broad, ethical sense—defines sin and condemns sin, Paul identified one role of the Torah as "the ministry of condemnation" (2 Corinthians 3:9). When Paul spoke of the "curse of the [Torah]" in Galatians 3:13, he referred to the Torah's condemnation of sin. Yet for those who rely on the faithfulness of Messiah, whether they be Jewish or Gentile, there is no longer any condemnation:

> There is therefore now no condemnation for those who are in Christ Jesus. For the law of the Spirit of life has set you free in Christ Jesus from the law of sin and death. For God has done what the [Torah], weakened by the flesh, could not do. By sending his own Son in the likeness of sinful flesh and for sin, he condemned sin in the flesh, in order that the righteous requirement of the law might be fulfilled in us, who walk not according to the flesh but according to the Spirit. (Romans 8:1–4)

When Messiah came, he accomplished what the Torah could not accomplish. Paul reasoned that since Messiah was completely righteous, he had not earned the condemnation (curse) of the Torah. Yet the Torah clearly says: "If a man has committed a crime punishable by death and he is put to death, and you hang him on a tree ..." Despite the fact that in his innocence, he had committed no crime or sin, much less a crime punishable by death, the Master was put to death and hung upon a tree. He who is hanged (*talui*) is accursed of God.

The Accursedness upon Messiah

If Yeshua was accursed of God and yet had not earned that curse through his own transgressions, from where did he acquire the curse of being hung on a tree? Paul believed he took the Torah's condemnation for the sins of others upon himself. He took upon himself the curse due to Jewish believers, who were previously included under the curse of the law, and he also opened the Abrahamic blessing to Gentiles:

> Christ redeemed us [i.e., the Jewish believers] from the curse of the law by becoming a curse for us—for it is written, "Cursed is everyone who is hanged on a tree"—so that in Christ Jesus the blessing of Abraham might come to the Gentiles, so that we [all believers] might receive the promised Spirit through faith. (Galatians 3:13–14)

Paul took an old taunt, a taunt that he himself had probably used against believers in *Talui*, and turned it around. Our Master became, so to speak, accursed, in that he took upon himself the accursedness of his people and suffered on behalf of all those under the curse of the law—and not only for the Jewish people, but for all who will believe in him and rely upon his faithfulness.

PASSOVER AND THE SEED OF ABRAHAM
(GALATIANS 3:13–14)

Paul employs a rabbinic tradition about the duration of Israel's sojourn in Egypt, interprets the "seed of Abraham" as a reference to the Messiah, and compares the Torah to a competing inheritance document.

Before proceeding further in the text of the book of Galatians, we need to do some homework in the Torah. I never have cared for homework, and I was especially poor at mathematics, but further progress in Galatians requires some math homework in the Torah.

Four Hundred and Thirty Years

In the Torah's story of Israel's sojourn in Egypt, the children of Israel remained in Egypt 430 years before their departure. "The time that the people of Israel *lived in Egypt was 430 years. At the end of 430 years, on that very day,* all the hosts of the LORD went out from the land of Egypt" (Exodus 12:40–41).

Notice that "they lived in Egypt 430 years," and at the end of 430 years, "to the very day," they departed. To what very day? The Torah never indicates the "very day" that they began to live in Egypt. Of which "very day" is the Torah speaking?

Question One: On which "very day" did Israel enter Egypt?

The 430-year sojourn of the children of Israel in Egypt raises a problem. According to Genesis 46:11, Kohath the son of Levi entered Egypt with Jacob in the days of Joseph. Kohath had a son named Amram, who in turn had a son named Moses. Moses was 80 years old at the time of the Exodus. The math does not work out. Subtract the 80 years of Moses from the total 430-year sojourn in Egypt, and that leaves 350 years between Moses' birth and the year his grandfather Kohath entered Egypt. It's too long.

Question Two: How do we account for 430 years in Egypt over only three generations: Kohath, Amram, and Moses?

These are not really matters of critical concern. One should hold these sorts of details loosely and not demand too much of the biblical text. The biblical text was neither designed nor written to bear the weight of such critical literalism. The rabbis, however, can never leave well enough alone. The rabbis looked at this text, and they said, "This is a difficulty!"

To solve the difficulty, they factored in another text about the duration of Israel's sojourn in Egypt. In Genesis 15:13, the LORD predicted that Abraham's "seed" would sojourn for four hundred years.

Abraham's Seed

In Genesis 15, the LORD made a covenant with Abraham. He promised to give Abraham a "seed." The Hebrew word is *zera,* which literally means "seed." English translators try to do us a favor when they translate *zera* as "descendants." For example:

> And he brought him outside and said, "Look toward heaven, and number the stars, if you are able to number them." Then he said to him, "So shall your descendants [*zera*] be." And he believed the LORD, and he counted it to him as righteousness. (Genesis 15:5–6)

Likewise, all of the other Abrahamic promises, including the promise that all nations would be blessed in him, were also given to his *seed*. For example, after the binding of Isaac, the LORD tells Abraham:

> Because you have done this and have not withheld your son, your only son, I will surely bless you, and I will surely multiply your [seed] as the stars of heaven and as the sand that is on the seashore. And your [seed] shall possess the gate of his enemies, and in your [seed] shall all the nations of the earth be blessed, because you have obeyed my voice. (Genesis 22:16–18)

The funny thing about a word like "seed" is that it is a singular noun that might also be plural, both in Hebrew and in English. For example, you might say, "I needed to get seed for the field this spring, so I went to the seed store and bought some new seed." Those are all plural applications of the word "seed," but the word appears as a singular form. Other English words have the same plural/singular ambiguity. For example, a person may count one sheep or two sheep but not two sheeps. A person might see a moose or a whole herd of moose but not a herd of mooses. The Hebrew word *zera* ("seed") works exactly the same way. It might be singular, or it might be plural. Abraham's *zera* can refer to one person, as in the case of his son Isaac, or it can refer to all of his descendants.

Four Hundred Years

In Genesis 15, the LORD told Abraham, "Look toward the heaven, number the stars, so shall your [seed] be." Then the LORD made a covenant with Abraham. He told him to slaughter some animals and separate their parts. As the sun set that day, Abraham fell into a deep sleep, and a dreadful darkness fell upon him.

> Then the LORD said to Abram, "Know for certain that your [seed] will be sojourners in a land that is not theirs and will be servants there, and they will be afflicted for four hundred years. But I will bring judgment on the nation that they serve, and afterward they shall come out with great possessions." (Genesis 15:13–14)

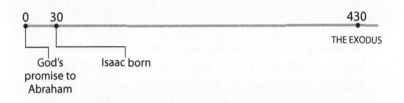

The "430-year" Problem and Abraham

Four hundred years? Another problem! God told Abraham that the exile *in Egypt would last 400 years,* but in Exodus 12, it said the children of Israel *lived in Egypt 430 years.* How can this be reconciled? Was God just giving Abraham an estimate?

- 430-year sojourn in Egypt (Exodus 12:40)
- 400-year sojourn in Egypt (Genesis 15:14)

A Rabbinic Solution

The rabbis looked at this thirty-year discrepancy and proposed a solution:

> "Your seed will be sojourners in a land that is not theirs and will be servants there, and they will be afflicted for four hundred years." This means that they will remain there until four hundred years have passed after seed shall be granted to you. Rabbi Yudan said, "The condition of being strangers, in servitude, and afflicted in a land not theirs was to last four hundred years, which was their decreed term." (*Genesis Rabbah* 44:18)

The rabbinic interpretation of the passage explains that God promised Abraham that his seed (plural) would inherit the land of Canaan four hundred years after he had borne a seed (singular), namely Isaac. In other words, his seed, the children of Israel, will come out from oppression and inherit Canaan four hundred years after the birth of his seed Isaac. The counting of the four hundred years will not start until the birth of Abraham's seed Isaac.

The oppression of Abraham's seed would not happen only in Egypt; rather, it is "the condition of being strangers and afflicted in a land not theirs which was to last four hundred years." This refers to Canaan. Isaac was a stranger in a land that did not belong to him, the land of Canaan. His descendants (seed) went down into Egypt where they were enslaved and oppressed until four hundred years had passed since the birth of Isaac, at which time they came out with many possessions. That's what the rabbis say.

That ambiguity of the word "seed" allowed the sages to account for the thirty-year discrepancy between the two passages. The rabbis simply said, "God made the promise to Abraham thirty years before Isaac was born. Therefore, the Exodus from Egypt took place exactly four hundred years after Isaac was born, but 430 years after God made the covenant with Abraham."

This also explains the meaning of the term "on that very day" in Exodus 12:41. The Exodus from Egypt took place 430 years, to the very day, from the day that God made the covenant with Abraham. Therefore, God made the covenant with Abraham on Passover, and thirty years later Isaac was born on Passover.

The Sojourn in Egypt

This explanation also solves the problem about the duration of the sojourn in Egypt. Isaac was born 30 years after God made the covenant promise to Abraham. Sixty years later, Isaac's wife gave birth to Jacob. Jacob was 130 years old when he and his sons entered Egypt:

$$30 + 60 + 130 = 220$$

Subtract the 220 years from the 430 reported in Exodus 12:41, and it leaves 210 years for the total sojourn in Egypt. Subtract the 80 years of Moses' life, and that leaves only 130 years between Moses and his grandfather Kohath, still a large number, but far more reasonable than 350 years.

The Math

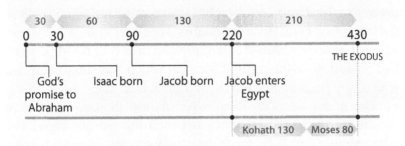

To clarify, the sages overturned the literal meaning of the 430 years found in Exodus 12 and the 400 years in Egypt predicted in Genesis 15 in favor of 430 years from the day God made the covenant with Abraham and 400 years from the birth of Isaac, Abraham's singular seed. This is not what the Torah literally says, but this is how the rabbis interpreted it. One can only arrive at this solution through rabbinic tradition and interpretation.

The Blessing of Abraham

Paul encouraged the Galatian God-Fearers to take hold of the blessing available to them through faith. He described how the Messiah had suffered to free Jewish people from the curse of condemnation so that "in Christ Jesus the blessing of Abraham might come to the Gentiles" (Galatians 3:14).

Paul quoted the LORD telling Abraham in Genesis 12:3, "In you shall all the nations be blessed" (Galatians 3:8). God repeated that same promise in Genesis 22 when he said to Abraham, "In your seed shall all the nations of the earth be blessed." Paul described this "blessing in Abraham" as the faith of Abraham. Abraham believed in the promise; God credited it to him as righteousness.

Paul taught that through the Messiah, this blessing in Abraham has come also to the Gentiles, so that both Jew and Gentile might receive the promised Spirit through faith:

> That in Christ Jesus the blessing of Abraham might come to the Gentiles, so that we might receive the promised Spirit through faith. (Galatians 3:14)

That's getting pretty abstract. A concrete example might help.

The Diatheke

The rabbis often used what they called a parable of "flesh and blood" to illustrate an abstract, spiritual point about the Holy One, blessed be he. Paul did the same. He said, "To give a human example, brothers: even with a man-made covenant, no one annuls it or adds to it once it has been ratified" (Galatians 3:15). The Greek word *diatheke*, translated here as "covenant," can also mean a person's last will and testament. The Greek version of the Hebrew Scriptures (LXX) consistently uses the word *diatheke* to translate the Hebrew word for covenant (*brit*). But the larger Greco-Roman society of Paul's day used the word *diatheke* to mean the last will and testament by which a person left instructions assigning the inheritance of his possessions.

Paul said, "Even with a man-made covenant—a *diatheke*—no one annuls it or adds to it once it has been ratified." In Greco-Roman society, however, a person could certainly add to or modify his *diatheke*, his last will and testament, up until the day of his death.

In Jewish society, the rabbis had strict rules regarding inheritance law. An entire tractate of the Talmud (*Bava Batra*) deals with inheritance law. In the Mishnaic Hebrew of the Talmud, the rabbis referred to a person's last will and testament as a *deyateke*, obviously a loan word from Greek, meaning exactly the same thing.

The Talmud's Tractate *Bava Batra* explains the rules. A person's *deyateke* cannot contradict the Torah's inheritance laws. For example, if a man has a son and daughter and he wants to split the inheritance between them and says so in his *deyateke*, the rabbis declare the document invalid because it contradicts the Torah's law that only sons inherit. Likewise, if a man wants to give a double portion to a different son than his firstborn and he says so in his *deyateke*, the rabbis declared the document invalid.

Contrary to what Paul said in Galatians 3:15, the rabbis did allow a man to change or add to his *deyateke* right up until his death. At the point of death, a man's *deyateke* became final, and no one could further add to it or change it—so long as it did not contradict the Torah.

On the other hand, the rabbis did allow for an alternative route—a legal loophole—around the whole matter. They allowed a man to give away his property before he died. This gift required a different kind of document called a *mattanah*, i.e., a "gift document." If a man gave away his property before he died, the gift was permanent and could not be reversed at his death, even if it did not meet the Torah's expectations for inheritance laws. In that case, a man could split his property between his son and his daughter or give it to anyone he wanted, so long as he did it before he died. The Talmud explains the difference between the two types of documents:

> Which type of document is called a *deyateke*? Any in which it is written, "This shall be valid and enduring upon my death." And which type of document is a *mattanah*? Any in which it is written, "From today on and also after my death." (b.*Bava Batra* 135b)

The *deyateke* was inalterable after death. The *mattanah* was inalterable from the day it was issued.

"This is What I Mean"

All of the above information provides the background for Galatians 3:15–17:

> To give a human example, brothers: even with a man-made covenant, no one annuls it or adds to it once it has been ratified [i.e., becomes legally binding]. Now the promises were made to Abraham and to his [seed]. It does not say, "And to [seeds]," referring to many, but referring to one, "And to your [seed]," who is Christ. This is what I mean: the [Torah], which came 430 years afterward, does not annul a covenant previously ratified by God, so as to make the promise void.

Notice how Paul played with the singular/plural discrepancy with the word "seed," much as the sages did. The rabbis used that ambiguity to apply the 400-year-promise in Genesis 15 to the birth of Isaac, the singular seed of Abraham. Paul said that all nations will be blessed in Messiah, the singular seed of Abraham. According to Paul's rabbinic-style reading of the Torah, God made the promises to Abraham and to his seed, i.e., the Messiah. That is not literally what the Torah means, but Paul makes a midrash on the text, just like the sages did with Isaac as Abraham's seed. In Paul's interpretation, Yeshua is the Seed of Abraham.

Also notice that Paul stated that the Torah came 430 years after God made the covenant with Abraham in Genesis 15. Paul followed the rabbinic interpretation of Exodus 12:41 that we learned above, not the literal reading of the passage.

Finally, he pointed out that the giving of the Torah, which defined Jewish identity and the nation of Israel, cannot annul a covenant (*deyateke*) previously ratified by God:

> This is what I mean: the [Torah], which came 430 years afterward, does not annul a covenant previously ratified by God, so as to make the promise void. For if the inheritance comes by the [Torah], it no longer comes by promise; but God gave it to Abraham by a promise. (Galatians 3:17–18)

The Torah defines Jewish identity, and it defines who is part of the nation and who is not. But the Torah came 430 years after the promise that all nations would find blessing in Abraham's seed.

Working through the Maze

The entire passage is a complex, rabbinic-style parable invoking Torah, inheritance law, midrash, and messianic interpretations. Working through Paul's illustration feels something like groping blindfolded through a twisting maze. To help illustrate the illustration, I have composed the following parable:

> To what can it be compared? It can be compared to a man of flesh and blood who had two wives, and sons by both. He left a *deyateke* for his descendants, designating the disposition of his possessions among his sons. After the man died, the sons of the one wife rose up and said,

"We have written a new *deyateke* which says only the sons of our mother may inherit." The sons of the second wife said, "No one may annul or add to the original *deyateke* after our father's death." In a similar way, God made covenant (*deyateke*) promises to Abraham that *all* nations would be blessed in him and in his seed, the Messiah. Four hundred and thirty years later, Abraham's sons, the children of Israel, received the Torah, and they said, "This new *deyateke* is ours alone; no other nation can inherit Abraham's blessing." But a later covenant cannot overturn an earlier one, and the Torah given at Sinai cannot cancel God's promises to Abraham.

Paul says that the commandments of the Torah which define Jewish status came 430 years after God had already promised to bless all nations in Abraham's seed, the Messiah. Therefore, the Gentile nations need not come under the obligations of Jewish identity, "under the law," in order to receive the promised blessing in Abraham's seed, the Messiah.

This simple logic also reveals a corollary truth: Just as the Sinai covenant cannot overturn or nullify the Abrahamic covenant, neither can the new covenant overturn or nullify the Sinai Covenant. Instead, one covenant builds on another; they must all work together.

Passover

Paul followed the standard rabbinic interpretation when it came to explaining Israel's 430-year sojourn. He explained it as 430 years from the day God gave the covenant to Abraham in Genesis 15 until the Exodus from Egypt; as it said in Exodus 12:41: "At the end of 430 years, on that very day, all the hosts of the LORD went out from the land of Egypt." That is four hundred years from the birth of Isaac to the Exodus. Thanks to Paul, these rabbinic explanations are no longer just rabbinic opinions. Now they are apostolic opinions, and that has important implications.

That interpretation makes Passover the birthday of Isaac, as it says in Genesis 21:2: "And Sarah conceived and bore Abraham a son in his old age at the time (*mo'ed*) of which God had spoken to him." The Hebrew word *mo'ed* means "appointed time." The Torah uses the same word in Leviticus 23 to mean a biblical festival. The festivals are God's appointed times: "These are the appointed times (*mo'adim*) of the LORD" (Leviticus 23:2). The Talmud (b.*Rosh Hashana* 11a) concurs with this conclusion: "On Passover Isaac was born."

The same interpretation also makes Passover the anniversary of the covenant between God and Abraham. Four hundred and thirty years before the first Passover, Abraham slaughtered the animals for his covenant on the fourteenth of Nissan. Then he waited. He drove off the birds. He waited for the LORD. The sun went down, darkness fell, and the fifteenth of Nissan began, which is the first day of the week of Passover. God appeared in the form of the blazing torch and made the covenant with Abraham. Four hundred and thirty years later, to the very day, Israel came out of Egypt.

This implies that on the anniversary of the day on which Abraham slaughtered the animals in order to make the covenant between the parts with the LORD—that very same day, the fourteenth of Nissan—the children of Israel slaughtered their Passover lambs in Egypt. According to the Gospel of John, our Master suffered and died on the anniversary of that same day. On the same day Abraham sacrificed the animals to make his covenant with the LORD, our Master died as the sacrifice of the new covenant. On that same day, he said to his disciples, "This is the cup of the new covenant." The day of Passover draws a line of connection from Abraham's covenant to his singular, promised seed, the Messiah.

The Torah says, "As the sun was going down, a deep sleep fell on Abram. And behold, dreadful and great darkness fell upon him" (Genesis 15:12). Out of the darkness, the LORD appeared to Abraham in the light of a flaming torch and passed between the sacrificial portions of the covenant. The LORD spoke to Abraham and made covenant promises to him about the birth of a seed and about his seed returning and possessing the land of Canaan. On the anniversary of that night, the angel of death slew Egypt's firstborn. On the anniversary of that night, as the sun set, they closed the Master's tomb—dreadful and great darkness, but out of the darkness, a light blazed forth.

SERMON EIGHTEEN:

THE PEDAGOGUE
(GALATIANS 3:19–26)

Paul compares the Torah and Jewish
status to a *paidagogos*, a guardian-slave
entrusted with the care and supervision
of a child.

The majority of traditional church thought holds that the Torah
remained in effect only until the coming of Messiah and was
cancelled at his death. For Messianic believers, this is troubling
because it seems to contradict the words of our Master, who says
that we are not to think that he came to abolish the Torah. Moreover, it contradicts numerous passages of Scripture which speak
of the Torah as eternal and enduring, and it seems to suggest a
contradiction in the character of God himself.

From where did this concept arise? Yeshua did not teach it. I
believe that one place from which it arose is Galatians 3:19, where
Paul says, "The Torah was added because of transgressions, *until*
the offspring should come to whom the promise had been made."
Now that the promised seed (i.e., the Messiah) has come, the Torah
must no longer be "added"; instead, it is subtracted from the equation.

Moreover, if you have been around the church, you have probably heard the teaching that "the law was only a guardian until faith
in Messiah came, but now that Messiah is here, we are no longer
under it, therefore, the Torah has been done away with."

Is that what Paul meant? If he meant that the Messiah has cancelled the Torah, then Paul disqualified himself as a teacher and an apostle because his conclusion is blasphemous and contradicts the clear teaching of our Master. That cannot be what Paul meant. Our task is to try to get a better handle on what he meant.

Recap and Review: Galatians 3:18

In the previous discussion, we concluded with Galatians 3:18: "For if the inheritance comes by the law, it no longer comes by promise; but God gave it to Abraham by a promise." The inheritance is the good news proclaimed to Abraham as a promise that all nations would be blessed in his seed and that he would become the father of many nations. This blessing came to the nations through Abraham's seed—his singular seed—the Messiah. So to paraphrase what Paul said in Galatians 3:18: "If the blessing that God promised we would receive in Abraham's seed comes only to those who are legally Jewish, then it is no longer a promise about all nations."

Here is a second attempt at a meaningful paraphrase of Galatians 3:18:

> For if salvation comes only to those who come under the full obligation of the Torah by converting to be Jewish, it no longer comes by promise to all nations; but God gave it to Abraham by a promise.

Why then the law?

Paul has demonstrated that one need not be Jewish to receive the blessing in Messiah, but this begs the question: Why should anyone be Jewish? Paul asks it this way: "Why then the Torah?" What's the point of being Jewish, of being circumcised and under the Torah?

If salvation is available to those who are not under the law, then what is the point of anyone ever being under the law? Why have the Torah at all?

Paul did not really have Jewish people like himself, the Hebrew descendants of Abraham, Isaac, and Jacob, in mind. His mind was on the God-fearing Gentiles in Galatia and all over the world. He was asking, "If salvation comes by a promise and not by convert-ing and coming under the law, then what is the point of anyone ever converting to come under the law?" That was his question. Paul spread the answer to this question over the rest of the third chapter of Galatians.

> Why then the law? It was added because of transgres-sions, until the offspring should come to whom the promise had been made, and it was put in place through angels by an intermediary. Now an intermediary implies more than one, but God is one. (Galatians 3:19–20)

Paul taught that the Torah "was added because of transgres-sions." To what was it added? He referred back to the promise of all nations being blessed in the seed of Abraham. God made a prom-ise to Abraham that all nations will be blessed in his seed, some-time in the future. To this promise, he added the Torah. Why? Paul explained: "because of transgressions." God added the Torah to condemn sin, to identify sin, to define sin, and to reveal the righ-teous standard until the coming of the Messiah. Paul presented something similar in Romans 5:20, where he wrote, "The law came in to increase the trespass," i.e., to define sin.

Paul said angels put the Torah in place by an intermediary, which is Moses. The martyr Stephen made a similar statement in Acts 7:53 where he spoke of "the law as delivered by angels." The angel of the LORD delivered the Torah into the hands of Moses, the intermediary, who delivered it to the nation of Israel, Abraham's children. God added the Torah to the promise that he had already made to Abraham to define, forbid, and convict sin—until the "seed" should come to whom the promise had been made: that all nations would be blessed in him.

Allow me to paraphrase the gist of what Paul wrote in Galatians 3:17–20:

> If salvation comes by being Jewish (under the law), then it is no longer a promise that all nations will be blessed in Abraham. But the promise that God made to Abra-ham was for all nations. If so, what was the purpose of the Torah? He added the Torah to the promise to define sin. He delivered it by angels through the hand of Moses,

the intermediary, until the Messiah comes, the promised seed through whom God promised to bless all nations. And Moses, as the intermediary, delivered it from the one God to Israel.

Paul said, "Now an intermediary implies more than one, but God is one" (Galatians 3:20). The words "God is one" allude to the *Shema* (Deuteronomy 6:4) to remind the reader that, despite the fact that the Torah was given to Israel by the agency of angels and through the hands of a mediator, the revelation of the LORD that comes through the Torah is not separable from his being, but is indeed the divine word. Why the Torah? Because it is the revelation of God's singular being, his essence, until the end that the promised seed comes, his blessed Son, who "is the radiance of the glory of God and the exact imprint of his nature" (Hebrews 1:3). In other words, Paul was simply saying, "The Torah is the revelation of God and godliness."

The Torah is Not for Eternal Life

Having explained why God gave the Torah, Paul hastened to clarify that the Torah does not contradict the Abrahamic promise of salvation through faith/faithfulness and the blessing of all nations in Messiah. He rhetorically asked, "Is the law contrary to the promises of God?" (Galatians 3:21). Then he answered his own question, "Certainly not! For if a law had been given that could give life, then righteousness would indeed be by the law." If it were possible that observing certain ceremonies and becoming Jewish could provide legal justification before God and eternal life, then salvation would indeed be by the Torah. It is not. "Scripture imprisoned everything under sin, so that the promise by faith in Jesus Christ might be given to those who believe" (Galatians 3:22).

Paul said that "Scripture (that is, the Written Torah) imprisoned everything under sin." "Imprisoned" is not the best choice of words. The Greek text means "to shut in, enclose, or confine," but not necessarily to imprison, and certainly not to incarcerate. The King James Version translates it as "The scripture hath concluded all under sin." I would put it this way: "The Torah has included everyone under sin." There is none righteous, and when Paul said "everything (or everyone) under sin," he meant both Jews and Gentiles. The revelation of God's righteous standard has identified all human beings as sinners, not just Jews.

Faithing

The Written Torah included both Jews and Gentiles under sin "so that the promise [given to Abraham] by the faithfulness of Yeshua the Messiah might be given to those who believe." The word "believe" here is just a participle form of the word "faith." The promise that came by the faithfulness of Yeshua is given to those who are "faith-ing."

"Faithing" is not a static faith, not assent to a creed or doctrine or a one-time confession. Faithing is the active, ongoing, trusting, relational, obedient, confident exercise of faith in God's promises. To those who have such faith and live the faith of Abraham, God is pleased to deliver the promises he made to Abraham. Not by the merit of *your* faith, but by the merit of the faithfulness of Yeshua the Messiah.

An Unfortunate Translation

In Galatians 3:23, Paul left the universal scope of all humanity to speak in the first person plural form about Israel's unique relationship with the Torah. He said "we" to speak specifically of the Jewish people (and converts), those under the law."

> Now before faith came, we [i.e., the Jewish people] were held captive under the law, imprisoned until the coming faith would be revealed. So then, the law was our guardian until Christ came, in order that we might be justified by faith. But now that faith has come, we are no longer under a guardian, for in Christ Jesus you are all sons of God, through faith. (Galatians 3:23–26)

This is an unfortunate translation. Being "held captive under the law, imprisoned" sounds like a dreadful prison sentence. It seems that the Apostle Paul depicted the Torah as a cruel prison guard. It sounds like the Torah was keeping people away from faith.

The English translators have depicted the Torah as something that holds people captive like prisoners and bars them from faith.

The Paidagogos

Paul drew upon a familiar illustration from the ancient Greco-Roman world of which he was a part. Well-to-do families often hired someone or assigned a household slave to serve as a warden for their children. This warden was called a *paidagogos*. The English word "pedagogue" (which means tutor) is derived from *paidagogos*, but the terms are not synonymous. The word *paidagogos* is actually a compound consisting of two Greek words. It could most literally be translated as "child-conductor" or "someone responsible for the conduct of a child."

This is confusing to us because in English a pedagogue is a teacher. In Paul's words, the *paidagogos* is not a teacher. Instead, the *paidagogos* was a type of caretaker entrusted with supervising and directing a child's conduct and moral behavior. He was responsible for overseeing the child's activities, particularly as the child became a teen and young adult. He ensured that the child was safe, stayed out of trouble, attended to his responsibilities, and did not fall in with the wrong crowd. The *paidagogos* taught the child social skills and manners. Moreover, the *paidagogos* was responsible for coordinating and overseeing the child's education by arranging tutors, lesson schedules, and courses of study. The *paidagogos*' job was "to conduct the boy or youth to and from school and to superintend his conduct ... he was not a 'teacher.'"[20] In that regard, he served as a type of bodyguard, high school principal, and school guidance counselor all rolled into one, with the responsibility of ensuring the student's safety and good behavior on the way to school and back.

I have sometimes encountered the word *paidagogos* as a loan word in rabbinic Hebrew. The *paidagogos* sometimes appears as a character in rabbinic parables, usually a servant whom a king appoints over the education and protection of a young prince. A few parables depict Moses as Israel's pedagogue.

---

[20] William Arndt and J. Wilbur Gingrich, *A Greek-English Lexicon of the New Testament and Other Early Christian Literature* (Chicago: University of Chicago Press, 1979), 603.

Classical Greek literature contains several descriptions of the *paidagogos.*[21]

In *The Republic,* Plato describes the *paidagogos* as a member of the retinue of household slaves in a typical wealthy Greek family. He characterizes *paidagogoi* as "men who by age and experience are qualified to serve as both leaders and custodians of children."

Consider the following conversation between Socrates and a boy (*Lysis* 4):

> Socrates: "Do your parents let you control yourself, or will they not trust you in that either?
>
> Boy: "Of course they do not."
>
> Socrates: "But someone is in control of you?"
>
> Boy: "Yes. My *paidagogos* here."
>
> Socrates: "Is he a slave?"
>
> Boy: "Why certainly, he belongs to us."
>
> Socrates: "What a strange thing! A free man controlled by a slave. But how does this *paidagogos* exert his control over you?'
>
> Boy: "By taking me to the teacher."

Likewise, Plato writes as follows in *Laws:*

> Just as no sheep or other witless creature ought to exist without a herdsman, so children cannot live without *paidagogoi,* nor slaves without masters. And of all wild creatures, the child is the most intractable, for insofar as it, above all others, possesses a fount of reason that is yet uncurbed, it is a treacherous, sly and most insolent creature. Wherefore the child must be strapped up, as it were, with many bridles—first, when he leaves the care of nurse and mother, with *paidagogoi* to guide his childish ignorance, and after that with teachers of all sorts of subjects and lessons, treating him as becomes a freeborn child.

---

[21] The examples listed are collected in Longenecker, *Galatians.*

Xenophon writes, "When a boy ceases to be a child and begins to be a lad others release him from his *paidagogos* and from his teacher; he is then no longer under them, but is allowed to go his own way."

Retranslating

This understanding of the function of the *paidagogos* clears up Galatians 3:23, where Paul says, "Now before faith came, we were held captive under the law, imprisoned until the coming faith would be revealed." The *paidagogos* was the child's guardian, not his jailer. When we understand that the *paidagogos* was responsible for protecting, supervising, and directing a child, then we have a better understanding of how the Greek text of Galatians 3:23 should be rendered into English. The Greek word which the English Standard Version translates as "held captive" has a different connotation. It can also be rendered as "protected," "kept safe," or "guarded." The word should be understood as speaking about how a pedagogue kept a child safe and out of trouble. Similarly, the Greek word which the ESV translates as "imprisoned" (the same word appears in 3:22) can be rendered as "kept in" or "enclosed" in a positive sense. The word should be understood as speaking about how a pedagogue kept a child inside for his school lessons. He did not allow the child to run off and follow his friends into trouble. He kept him shut up inside for the purpose of education and protection.

This is the background to Paul's pedagogue parable. The *paidagogos* represents Jewish status under the Torah, and Messiah is the teacher to whom the *paidagogos* brings the Jewish person. Based upon that information, we can retranslate the passage. I have placed my retranslations and clarifications in square brackets [like this]:

> Now before faith came, we [the Jewish people] were [protected] under the law, [kept inside for] the coming faith [that] would be revealed. So then, the [Torah] was our guardian until Christ came, in order that we might be justified [i.e., exonerated] by faith. (Galatians 3:23–24)

Those "under the law" were protected and kept inside by the Torah, preserved for the coming of the Messiah. Remember, the term "under the law" refers specifically to legal Jewish halachic status, whether by birth or conversion. Paul says that the Jewish people were protected under the law, by means of national Jewish identity, for the coming faith that would be revealed—that is the Messiah. The purpose of Jewishness is the revelation of Messiah.

Allow me to illustrate Paul's illustration with a parable:

> To what may the Torah be compared? It can be compared to a pedagogue who escorted a child to the schoolteacher, but once the child was under the care of the school-teacher, the pedagogue relinquished his care over the child. So, too, the Torah escorted the Jewish people to the Messiah, but once the people enter the care of the Messiah, the Torah relinquishes them to him.

This retranslation of Galatians 3:23–24 makes much better sense in the context from which Paul was writing. In Paul's metaphor, the Torah is the guardian appointed to watch over and protect the people of Israel and to arrange for their education by taking them to the teacher, the Messiah. The Torah did this by creating moral boundaries which kept Israel inside the parameters of ethical monotheism until the fullness of faith in Messiah was revealed. The revelation of Torah was the only place from which the people of Israel could draw hope for salvation, relationship with God, and the expectation of eternal life.

Prior to the revelation of Messiah, it made good sense for Gentiles to join themselves to Israel by means of conversion. That was the only way to get under the protection of the *paidagogos* and to be preserved for Messiah.

No Longer under a Paidagogos

Paul went on to explain, "But now that faith has come, we are no longer under a guardian" (Galatians 3:25). Just as the *paidagogos* brought the student to the teacher, the Torah brought the Jewish people to the Messiah. But the *paidagogos* is not the teacher; neither is the Torah the means to earn salvation. When Paul said, "We are no longer under a guardian," he did not mean that the Torah is done away with or cancelled. He meant that we should not look to Torah or legal conversion to Judaism as a means of earning salvation. Salvation is (and always was) through the grace of God in Yeshua the Messiah for Jews and Gentiles both.

Does this mean that Jewishness no longer has any value? Is Jewishness "then contrary to the promises of God? Certainly not!" (Galatians 3:21). It means that subsequent to Messiah, there is no salvation-related reason for Gentiles to undergo conversion and become Jewish, under the law. As he explained in Galatians 3:26, "For in Christ Jesus you are all sons of God, through faith."

The Gentile believers to whom Paul was writing had already been led to the teacher of righteousness. They were already sons through faith; they had already come to the teacher. In previous generations, prior to the revelation of Yeshua, there were valid reasons for Gentiles to become Jewish and thus under the law. Doing so brought them and their children inside, protected, and preserved by the Torah along with the rest of the Jewish people until the coming faith would be revealed. Now that it has been revealed, conversion "under the law" no longer serves that purpose. The Messiah is already revealed.

A Problem with a Metaphor

The problem with any metaphor, analogy, or parable is that the symbolism can always be pushed too far. In rabbinic literature and in the parables of Yeshua, a metaphor or parable like this ordinarily makes only a single point. After the point has been made, the parable is set aside. One does not attempt to draw further applications from a rabbinic parable. For example, one should not spend time puzzling about where the good shepherd in the parable of the lost sheep left the other ninety-nine while he sought the lost one. That's not the point of the parable.

So, too, here in Galatians 3, one might push the parable further and say, "The Jewish people are no longer under a guardian. Therefore, the Jewish people no longer need to obey the commandments of Torah."

That sounds like a logical inference, but that was not the point that Paul was trying to make. Whether or not the Jewish people have a covenantal obligation to keep the whole Torah was never a question for Paul, and it is never a question in the entire New Testament. That is not what Paul was speaking about in his *paidagogos* parable.

He was talking about the purpose of becoming Jewish in the first place. "Why then the Torah?" he asked. He demonstrated that, for Gentiles, coming under the law once had meaning and value because it was the only way to come under the protection of the guardian that would preserve them and their posterity within the people until the revelation of Messiah. Now that Messiah has come, that particular function of Jewishness is completed already for believers.

Again: One of the roles of the Torah (of Jewishness) was to preserve the people and bring them to Messiah. If you are already a believer in Messiah, becoming Jewish is not going to accomplish that for you. You're already there.

Paul was not saying more than that. We stray from his intention when we try to read more into it. He did not mean the Torah is obsolete, that Jewish people are no longer under the Torah, nor did he mean that Gentile believers can ignore the commandments in the Torah that apply to them. Instead, Paul was perfectly comfortable admitting that the commandments of the Torah continue to protect us, to instruct us, to guide us through life, to preserve us, and to escort us to the Messiah through whom we have eternal life.

A Brief Recapitulation of a Difficult Passage

1. God made promises to Abraham, saying that all nations would be blessed in his seed.

2. The Torah was added to define and condemn sin.

3. God gave the Torah to Israel through the hands of intermediaries, but it is still the essential revelation of the one God, for God is One.

4. The Torah does not contradict the promises that God made to Abraham.

5. The Written Torah includes both Jews and Gentiles
    in its condemnation of sin, so that the universal
    Abrahamic promise can be fulfilled only through
    the faithfulness of the Messiah.

6. Before the revelation of Messiah, the Torah
    preserved both the Jewish people and the Gentiles
    who joined them by conversion.

7. After a person becomes a believer, the Torah no
    longer performs that specific role of escorting him
    to Messiah.

NEITHER JEW NOR GREEK

(GALATIANS 3:26–29)

> When Paul declares that there is no
> difference between Jew and Gentile in
> Messiah, he does not mean to imply that
> Jews and Gentiles forfeit their unique
> identities and roles.

Have you ever heard it said that there is no longer Jew or Gentile because we are one in Messiah? If you have ever been around the Messianic Jewish movement, you have heard that said. What do people mean when they say that? From where do they get that notion?

It comes from the end of the third chapter of the book of Galatians:

> For in Christ Jesus you are all sons of God, through faith. For as many of you as were baptized into Christ have put on Christ. There is neither Jew nor Greek, there is neither slave nor free, there is no male and female, for you are all one in Christ Jesus. And if you are Christ's, then you are Abraham's offspring, heirs according to promise. (Galatians 3:26–29)

Neither Jew nor Greek

Paul expressed a similar concept in the third chapter of the book of Colossians:

> Put on the new self, which is being renewed in knowledge after the image of its creator. Here there is not Greek and Jew, circumcised and uncircumcised, barbarian, Scythian, slave, free; but Christ is all, and in all. (Colossians 3:10–11)

In addition, Paul said something similar in the second chapter of Ephesians, where he spoke of Jewish and Gentile believers combined into "one new man in place of the two, so making peace," that Messiah "might reconcile us both to God in one body" (Ephesians 2:15–16).

In summary, Paul taught that there is neither Jew nor Greek, slave nor free, male nor female, circumcised or uncircumcised, barbarian or Scythian; instead, we are one in Messiah as one new man. These sentiments run at the heart of Paul's theology; they express the heart of his unique gospel of Gentile inclusion.

(Some scholars suggest that Galatians 3:26–29 is not an original Pauline text and that he was quoting from an earlier baptismal creed of the early believers. I doubt very much that this is the case, unless it was a creed that Paul and Barnabas coined. At the time of the writing of Galatians, the rest of the Jewish believers did not yet concede a theology of "one new man." Instead, Paul's gospel of the Gentile inclusion was unique to him and his followers.)

In the church and in the Messianic Jewish movement, one often hears Paul's sentiment echoed: "There is no longer Jew nor Gentile, for we are all one in Messiah!" This is certainly a precious truth, and it is at the heart of who we are in the Messianic Jewish movement. That truth forms a critical and essential piece of our theology. Before we unpack it, I would like to look at a few ways in which this truth is misapplied in the body of Messiah today.

One New Christian

In the broader Christian community, this text proves that Jewish people, after coming to faith, are no longer really Jewish. Instead, they have become a new thing: a Christian. Therefore, they need no longer practice Jewish rituals or matters of Torah like circumcision, dietary laws, Sabbath, calendar, and so forth. They may do so if they like in order to retain a cultural connection with their people, just as a Norwegian may continue to eat Lutefisk and Lefse after becoming a Christian and just as people of any culture can and do retain their own particular music, distinctive dress, and local customs after becoming Christians. In no way, however, is the Jewish Christian obligated to keep the Torah or to marry within the Jewish people or to raise Jewish children because, after all, there is no difference between Jews and Gentiles in Christ.

> There is neither Jew nor Greek, there is neither slave nor free, there is no male and female, for you are all one in Christ Jesus. (Galatians 3:28)

We can call this "One New Man Theology." The one who espouses One New Man Theology actually implies that there are no Jews in Messiah whatsoever. Jewishness is erased by Christ. The Messiah obliterates the identity of the distinctive people of Israel, the heirs of the forefathers, the people of the covenant.

For most of the last two thousand years, this is what happened to every Jewish person who became a believer. The Jewish person who becomes a Christian marries a Christian; she marries a Christian, or their children do, and within a generation or two, they are lost from the Jewish people completely.

This is ironic because Christianity always bemoans the fact that the Jewish people are so hard to reach with the gospel. Christians wonder why there are so few Jewish believers. "Where are the Jewish believers?" the Christian asks. Moreover, Christian missions to the Jewish people continue to focus on Jewish evangelism, yet it seems that Jewish believers are so rare. Generation after generation of Jewish missions talk about when the great harvest of Jewish souls will happen.

Does no one notice the irony here?

Hundreds, thousands, tens of thousands, and hundreds of thousands of Jewish people have come to faith in Messiah and become Christians over the last century and a half, but they are almost all gone—vanished. Over the last two thousand years, a steady stream of Jewish people has confessed Messiah, beginning with the generation of the apostles, but they are gone, too, like chaff in the wind. They have left no enduring legacy. There is no Jewish form of Christianity or ongoing Jewish legacy of faith in Yeshua because, as soon as the Jewish people become believers, they are taught, "Now that you are a Christian, there is no difference between you and us, and you may marry our children, and our children may marry yours, and you no longer need to be Jewish or keep kosher, or keep Sabbath, or do anything that would preserve your identity as a Jew. You are no longer under the law."

For that reason, Jewish Christians are doomed to be swallowed by the church, stripped of their Jewish identity, absorbed into "Gentileness," and made into Gentiles. When Christians say, "There is no difference between Jew and Gentile in Messiah," they are really saying, "There is no Jew in Messiah." The "one new man" is always a Gentile.

Basic Darwinism

The result is Darwinian. It is basically natural selection, the survival of the fittest. Although natural selection probably cannot account for the origin of species as Darwin suggested, no one argues that natural selection determines basic outcomes of survival and extinction in nature.

Imagine that a certain species of toad once thrived, and among these toads, there were two types. One type of toad was afraid of snakes, and the other type of toad had no fear of snakes. This was just a genetic variable. A mother toad might give birth to a litter of toadlets, and half had a fear of snakes and half did not, just as some of your siblings have a different eye color than you.

For thousands of years, the toads that did not have a natural, built-in, instinctual fear of snakes kept getting eaten by snakes, and because they were eaten by snakes they rarely got the chance to pass their genetic data on to the next generation of toads. After several generations, no toads remained who did not have a fear of snakes. All the toads were all afraid of snakes because those who did not have a fear of snakes were eaten by the snakes. That process is called survival of the fittest—natural selection.

Now imagine the snakes bemoaning the fact that there are no longer any toads without a fear of snakes. Of course there aren't. The snakes ate them all.

A similar spiritual process of natural selection has been going on between Judaism and Christianity for two thousand years. Christianity is saying, "Why are the Jewish people so resistant to the gospel?" But not all Jewish people resist the gospel; it's just that Christianity swallows the ones who do not. *The only ones who have survived and are still identifiable as Jewish are those who have internalized a resistance to the gospel.* If their ancestors had not rejected Christ, they, too, would have been swallowed by the great Gentile collective called Christianity, and the family would no longer be Jewish.

This is a real problem with the One New Man theology. According to One New Man Theology, it's not that there is no longer Jew nor Greek, it's that in Messiah, everyone is Greek; there is no Jew.

One Law for Messianic Gentiles

In Messianic Judaism, we do not think that way, right?

Suppose that we simply reverse the values. In Messiah, there is neither Jew nor Greek because Gentiles are grafted into Israel. We are all one new man. Some Gentiles in Messianic Judaism interpret this to mean that, for all practical purposes, Gentile believers in Messiah are exactly the same as Jewish people. Both Jews and Gentiles have the same covenantal responsibilities, the same duties, and the same obligations. As one new man, both Jews and Gentiles are obligated to keep the whole Torah. Because of that, a Gentile is not really distinguishable from a Jew. This theology is popularly called "One Law Theology." It is based on passages such as Exodus 12:49: "There shall be one law for the native and for the stranger who sojourns among you."

I know about One Law Theology because I used to be one of its loud proponents and ardent practitioners. One Law Theology is the belief that Jewish people should keep the whole Torah, just as the Bible teaches, but Gentiles fall into the same category as Jewish people, so they should, too. In fact, the Gentile believers are obligated to do so because there is neither Jew nor Gentile in

Messiah. We are all the same. Rather than Jews assimilating into the Gentile Christian identity, under One Law, Gentiles assimilate into Messianic Jewish identity.

This theology is similar to that of Paul's theological opponents in Galatia, except that the One Law Messianic Gentile never makes a legal conversion. He adopts the identity and obligations of a convert, but does not do so through the Jewish community.

One Law Theology has not had an eighteen-hundred-year run like One New Man Theology, but we can predict the results just the same. By making all Gentiles the same as Jewish believers but without becoming Jewish, we effectively accomplish the same results as the Christian One New Man Theology. One Law Theology neutralizes Jewish identity, dilutes it, and eliminates it. The Gentile believer has the same legal status as a Jewish person, and this opens the possibility for and probability of intermarriage. It erases any definable borders which could be used to define who is Jewish and who is not Jewish.

This sociological problem always bothered me about One Law Theology, even when I accepted those theological premises and espoused the view. Sociologically speaking, One Law is the end of Jewish identity for Jewish believers. In its place comes a new pseudo-Jewish/Gentile identity in which differentiation between the two vanishes. As a One Law Messianic Gentile, for all practical purposes, I would be the same as a Jewish person. This spells extinction of a distinct Jewish identity for Jewish believers as surely as the other.

The "One Law" interpretation of "one new man" is exactly the same as the Christian interpretation, except for one difference:

> One New Man Theology says, "Since we are the same in Messiah, Jewish believers need not keep the Jewish aspects of Torah anymore."

> One Law Theology says, "Since we are the same in Messiah, we all need to keep the Jewish aspects of Torah."

Paul's Rule for All the Churches

A moment's reflection should be enough to realize that this is an impossible interpretation of Paul. The holy apostle expends a great deal of his energy arguing that Gentiles do not need to take on the commandments which identify a person as Jewish (such as circumcision) and that Gentiles do not need to be Jewish in order to be reckoned as part of the people of God. Obviously, Paul himself made a clear line of distinction between Jewish and Gentile believers. In his worldview, Jewish believers are obligated to the covenant responsibilities incumbent upon them. Gentiles are also obligated to God's Torah, but not to those particular aspects of it which define a person as Jewish (such as circumcision). Paul drew that line of division in all his writings, especially in Galatians. Messianic Jewish scholar David Rudolph refers to this as "Paul's rule for all the churches."[22]

> **Paul's Rule for All the Churches**: Only let each person lead the life that the Lord has assigned to him, and to which God has called him. *This is my rule in all the churches.* Was anyone at the time of his call already circumcised? Let him not seek to remove the marks of circumcision. Was anyone at the time of his call uncircumcised? Let him not seek circumcision. (1 Corinthians 7:17–18)

Paul told Jewish disciples of Yeshua not to "remove the marks of circumcision." He was not speaking literally about some kind of surgical reversal (epispasm) as some have suggested in the past. The "marks of circumcision" simply mean the marks of being Jewish: circumcision of sons, Torah observance, the Sabbath, the biblical calendar, Levitical functions, the dietary laws, *tzitzit, tefillin, mezuzah,* and the practice of Judaism (albeit, "Messianic" Judaism). In other words, Paul told Jews not to assimilate into a Gentile identity or forsake Torah.

---

[22] David Rudolph, "Paul's Rule for all the Churches," *Studies in Christian-Jewish Relations* 5:1 (2010).

Oneness Is Not Sameness

Consider the "neither slave nor free" part. Paul said that in Messiah there is neither slave nor free, but in his epistles Paul instructed slaves to serve their masters faithfully, diligently, not begrudgingly. He told slave owners to treat their slaves honorably, and he told freemen not to become enslaved to another. Clearly, there is a difference. Even "in the Messiah," the slaves are still slaves, the freemen are still free, and they have different roles and responsibilities.

Consider the "male and female" part. Paul said that in Messiah there is no male or female. If that is the case, why do conservative Christians object to the prospect of same sex marriages? If there is no difference, what difference does it make? Clearly, men are still men and women are still women, even in Messiah.

Paul was alluding to the holy marriage of the first man and the first woman, Adam and Eve, of whom it says that "they shall be one flesh." Oneness is not sameness. Adam and Eve are one new man, so to speak, because the man shall leave his mother and father, cleave to his wife, and they shall be one flesh. Every marriage, spiritually and metaphorically speaking, results in one new man, yet within that "one flesh," distinct roles and identities still exist.

In Messiah, Jew and Gentile are one but not the same. As regards salvation and our standing in the Messiah, there is no difference between Jew and Gentile. As the Apostle Peter declared, "He made no distinction between us and them, having cleansed their hearts by faith" (Acts 15:9). Jews, Gentiles, men, women, slaves, and freemen have the same access to salvation through the same Messiah, but that does not eliminate our distinct identities and roles.

The Way It Might Have Been

Things might be different today if eighteen hundred years ago, instead of absorbing and assimilating Jewish believers into a homogenized Gentile Christian identity, the Christian church had insisted that Jewish believers maintain their Jewish identity, as the Scripture says. Imagine if Christianity had done this one small thing. Forget about Constantine, seven ecumenical councils, and all the rest of Christian history. Make this one small change, the only necessary change to the theological equation.

If Christianity had honored Jewishness, upheld it, reinforced it, and protected it in the midst of Christianity, everything would have evolved differently. The church would have always had a Jewish core. Imagine how things might look today if Christians had protected the Jewish identity of Jewish believers in their midst and encouraged Jewish families to remain Jewish. Suppose Christians had encouraged Jewish people to observe their covenant obligations and encouraged Jewish believers to remain Sabbath keepers. What if Christians had encouraged Jewish believers to remain Torah-observant within Jewish synagogues, Messianic synagogues, or otherwise. Imagine how things would be different. With that strong Jewish core, Christianity would look completely different today.

Eighteen hundred years of Jewish believers maintaining strong Jewish identity would have resulted in a large believing Jewish constituency. They might not constitute the majority of the Jewish community, but I think it is fair to say that the Jewish community would have just as many followers of Yeshua as non-followers. The entire Jewish community would have been forced to interface with the teachings of Rabbi Yeshua. At the very least, Jewish believers would be an integral part of both Christianity and Judaism.

Instead, because of the Christian theological insistence on sameness, Jewish believers are an endangered species. Ironically, the Christian insistence on sameness between Jews and Gentiles has actually put up a dividing wall between the Christian and Jewish community. Our insistence on sameness has been the greatest theological impediment of all to the advance of the gospel in the Jewish community. Jewish believers today are few and fading, as always, because we want to believe that oneness is sameness.

Jewish identity is precious. It is slipping away. Secular and liberal Jews are not preserving it. Messianic Jews are not preserving it. Hitler tried to exterminate the Jewish race. Where he left off, intermarriage and religious attrition work to finish the job.

Heirs of the Promise

Is it not time for believers to turn this thing around? Jewish believers should be proud of being Jewish and hold on to that identity. Gentile believers need to set aside their jealousy, and let the Jewish people be Jewish. We are one body, many parts. We all have roles to play.

> For as many of you as were baptized into Christ have put on Christ. There is neither Jew nor Greek, there is neither slave nor free, there is no male and female, for you are all one in Christ Jesus. And if you are Christ's, then you are Abraham's offspring, heirs according to promise. (Galatians 3:26–29)

We have put on the identity of Messiah. In respect to our standing in Messiah, we are all one. And if we belong to the Messiah, then we are Abraham's seed, heirs of the Abrahamic promise, according to the promise.

The promise which Abraham's seed inherits is this: "In your seed all nations will be blessed." The seed of Abraham is the nation of Israel, but according to Paul, the "seed" of Abraham is the Messiah. Paul says that if we are in this seed, then we are heirs according to the promise that all nations will be blessed in Abraham's seed. Even the Gentile believers become Abraham's spiritual seed, and Abraham is the father of both Jews and Gentile believers in faith; as it says, "I will make you a father of many nations."

Therefore, Gentile believers have a place at the table of Abraham through the Messiah. This is what Paul means when he speaks of Gentiles grafted in to the nation of Israel and joined into one new man with the Jewish people.

Galatians
CHAPTER FOUR

SERMON TWENTY:
ELEMENTARY PRINCIPLES
(GALATIANS 4:1–12)

Paul warns the God-Fearers not to be
enslaved again by the pagan elementary
principles of the world through
observing days, months, seasons, and
years.

Have you ever heard that Christ redeemed us from the law?
"God sent forth his Son, born of woman, born under the law,
to redeem those who were under the law" (Galatians 4:4–5). Since
Christ redeemed us from the law, why would we want to become
enslaved all over again?

In Galatians 4, Paul seems to rebuke the Gentile Galatians for
keeping the biblical festivals. An honest, impartial reading sounds
like he rebuked them for observing "days and months and seasons
and years" and warned them not to become "enslaved" again (Galatians 4:10). This leads us to believe that Paul viewed the celebration of the Sabbath and festivals as a step backwards for Gentile
believers—a form of enslavement.

He said, "You observe days," meaning the Sabbath and festivals.
He said, "You observe months," meaning the new moons and the
biblical calendar. He said, "You observe seasons," meaning festival
seasons like the counting of the omer, the days of repentance, and
the days of awe. He said, "you observe years," meaning the sabbatical year of release.

Traditional Christian interpretation teaches that it is un-Christian to keep the biblical calendar or honor the Bible's holy days such as the Sabbath. (Christian tradition sees no conflict between Galatians 4:10 and the celebration of "days," so long as they are Sundays; "months;" so long as they are not the biblical months, "seasons;" so long as they are Lent, Advent, Christmas, or Easter, and so forth.) From this perspective, Galatians 4:10 is a rebuke of exactly what we are doing in the Messianic Jewish movement, a complete show-stopper. In fact, Galatians 4:10 could be understood to mean that God-fearing Gentile believers are not allowed to have any holy days. They can watch the Jewish community do so, but they themselves are barred from participation in the Sabbath and the calendar.

Before reassessing this traditional Christian interpretation of Galatians 4:10, the passage should be placed in its broader context by studying from the beginning of the chapter.

Recap and Review: Father of Many Nations

At the conclusion of the third chapter of the Holy Epistle to the Galatians, the Apostle Paul told the God-fearing Gentile believers in the congregations and communities of Galatia: "If you are Christ's, then you are Abraham's [seed], heirs according to promise" (Galatians 3:29). That is, if you belong to Messiah, who is himself the promised seed of Abraham, then you, too, may be reckoned as the seed of Abraham, i.e., the spiritual children of Abraham and the fulfillment of God's promises to Abraham.

Abraham is a father of many nations. The believers from the nations become the spiritual seed of Abraham and attain a fellow citizenship with the Jewish people in the greater commonwealth of Israel. Nevertheless, the Gentile believer does not and need not become Jewish, but instead he retains his distinct nationality. The Greek is still a Greek and not a Jew, and the Jew is still a Jew and not a Greek. Though they are one in Messiah, yet they are not the same. Therefore, Abraham is called "the father of many nations," not "the father of one nation."

The God-fearing Gentile believers in Yeshua, then, are "heirs according to the promise."

The Slave and the Heir

In what manner did Paul consider the Gentiles as heirs of the Abrahamic promises? Were they not actually all polytheistic pagans? Paul introduced a new analogy to explain how the Gentiles can be considered heirs of Abraham.

> I mean that the heir, as long as he is a child, is no different from a slave, though he is the owner of everything, but he is under guardians and managers until the date set by his father. (Galatians 4:1–2)

Paul spoke of a Roman household in which the father of the house has both slaves and children. The father's son is the heir to the entire estate, slaves included, but he will not come into his inheritance until he has reached the age predetermined by his father. Paul would have us imagine a situation where the father has died and left his estate to his son, but with the provision that, so long as his son is a minor, he remains a ward of the estate. As a minor, the son is not free to dispose of the estate or even free on his own volition. Instead, he is entrusted to legal guardians and managers until a certain age when he will receive the inheritance.

For the sake of illustration, imagine the son will not receive sovereignty over the estate until the age of eighteen. When the son becomes eighteen, then he may assume the privileges of an adult. Until then, however, he remains under the custodianship of guardians and managers. Although he is the estate's heir, his status is not different than a slave of the estate until he comes of age. In that regard, his rights over the property are no better and no different than those of a slave who belongs to him.

In the parable, Abraham is the father of many nations. He has bequeathed the promises of God to all nations, his spiritual heirs. The heirs, however, did not receive those blessings immediately. They were not yet of the age to inherit. Therefore, they remained subject to a custodianship in the interim.

Likewise, the Jewish people were also heirs to the same promise. Paul said, "In the same way we [the Jewish people] also, when we were children, were enslaved to the elementary principles of the world" (Galatians 4:3).

Elementary Principles

Paul explained that the Jewish people were once enslaved to "the elementary principles of the world." Likewise, the Gentiles were once slaves to "the weak and worthless elementary principles of the world" (Galatians 4:9).

No one is sure what Paul meant when he used this term: "elementary principles (*stoicheia*) of the world." Scholars bring a variety of opinions, but no one knows exactly what he meant. He used the same term in Colossians 2 regarding ascetic practices, and he used it twice in Galatians 4.

The Greek word *stoicheion* has to do with elements that comprise a series, essential parts, or members of a row. The term originally denoted a row, rank, or line in military formations. In Paul's day, the term was used of the degrees on a sundial by which time was calculated; of letters, syllables, or words in a sentence; of the basic elements of the cosmos (fire, earth, air, water); or even simply of the rudimentary fundamentals of a subject of study, like the three Rs: reading, writing, and arithmetic. No one is sure exactly what sense Paul intended. The analogy is notoriously cryptic. Two main theories seem possible: The elementary principles refer to Torah and Judaism or the elementary principles refer to paganism and idolatry.

Elementary Principles = Torah

Paul criticized the God-fearing Galatian Gentiles for observing "days and months and seasons and years" (Galatians 4:10). In the larger context of the epistle, it seems reasonable to assume that he meant Sabbath days, new moon observances, festival seasons (like Passover and the high holidays), and Sabbatical years—all components of the Torah calendar. The thought seemed to distress him. He wondered if he has labored in vain for the Gentiles of Galatia. He did not understand why they would want to "turn back again to the weak and worthless elementary principles of the world" and become enslaved by them again (Galatians 4:9).

If this interpretation is correct, then the elementary principles of the world must be Paul's way of referring to Torah and Judaism in general. If so, Galatians 4:3–5 can mean that the Messiah came to redeem the Jewish people from the keeping the law:

> In the same way we also, when we were children, we were enslaved to the elementary principles of the world [i.e., the Torah]. But when the fullness of time had come, God sent forth his Son, born of woman, born under the law, to redeem those who were under the law, so that we might receive adoption as sons. (Galatians 4:3–5)

According to this interpretation, Messiah was born under the Torah to rescue "those who were under the law" from further obligation to the Torah. The Jewish believer need no longer keep the Torah because the Messiah redeemed him from its jurisdiction. This is why Paul speaks of the Jewish people as those "who were under the law," using the past tense form of the verb and implying that they are no longer under the law.

This interpretation has several problems. A literal translation of Galatians 4:5 does not have a past-tense form of the verb. It literally says "that those under law he may redeem" (Galatians 4:5). They are still under the law. To be under the law is just Paul's way of saying "legally Jewish" and obligated to observe the Torah. The Messiah did not redeem the Jewish people from the Torah; he redeemed them from sin and exile. He rescues from condemnation, but not from obligation to obedience.

Moreover, this interpretation has Paul speaking of the Torah as something "weak and worthless" (Galatians 4:9), something he considers on the same level as "those that by nature are not gods (Galatians 4:8). If we accept that Paul was indeed speaking about the Sabbath, the festivals, and the Torah's ceremonies, then we must admit that he puts God's holy commandments into a category that he considers no different than idolatry. He refers to the holiness of the Sabbath, the holiness of the festivals, and the holiness of the Torah as "weak and worthless elementary principles of the world." In other words, Paul considers the Torah as the equivalent of a pagan idol, and he considers Torah observance and Judaism as the same as idol worship.

This explanation does not work unless we see Paul as a blasphemer. It contradicts the Bible, the other apostles, the Master's clear teaching about the Torah, and Paul's own life as an observant Jew.

Elementary Principles = Paganism

Alternatively, the "elementary principles" of which Paul spoke refer only to paganism and idolatry and not to Torah or Judaism at all. This definition can be derived from Galatians 4:8:

> Formerly, when you [Gentile believers] did not know God,
> you were enslaved to those that by nature are not gods.
> (Galatians 4:8)

In this verse, Paul obviously speaks about idolatry. The Gentiles in the Roman world were polytheistic idolaters, required by law to participate in the Roman cult and the worship of the emperor. They needed to be part of an approved religious affiliation, all of which were idolatrous and polytheistic except for Judaism. Paul contrasted the Gentile believers' former state with their current state. In their former state, they were enslaved to the idols they worshipped. In their current state, they know the one true God:

> But now that you have come to know God, or rather to be
> known by God, how can you turn back again to the weak
> and worthless elementary principles of the world, whose
> slaves you want to be once more? You observe days and
> months and seasons and years! (Galatians 4:9–10)

In this context, the "weak and worthless elementary principles of the world" are the idolatrous rituals and religion from which the God-fearing Gentiles had recently come. In that case, the "days and months and seasons and years" which the Gentiles observed and became enslaved by once more must be pagan holidays and celebrations.

In an article called "A Torah Observant Paul," Mark Nanos argues that Paul is not speaking about the Jewish calendar at all but rather about the pagan calendar.[23] Likewise, Justin Hardin makes the same argument in *Galatians and the Imperial Cult.*[24]

The God-fearing Galatian believers were, of course, ex-pagans who participated in the imperial cult, worshipping the gods and the emperors as required by law. This was a critically important part of their previous life, as much a center to their society as getting a driver's license and a Social Security number is to ours. Observing the calendar of the imperial cult was a required civic duty. To abstain from participation in these civic religious functions disrupted relationships with family, friends, business associates, and civic authorities. It also placed a person in jeopardy of persecution, arrest, and possibly execution for the crime of atheism. Roman law exempted only Jews from participation. The Galatian Gentile believers were not legally recognized converts to Judaism. They were God-Fearers, guests in the synagogue, so to speak. Though the Jewish community might have granted them the honorary guest status in the synagogue as God-Fearers, that was not official legal status or religion. Claiming, "I'm a God-Fearer" would not exempt them from the duty of observing the imperial cult. This left the God-fearing believers in a state of social limbo: not fully accepted by Judaism and, at the same time, in conflict with the authorities, their extended families, and all of society around them. The solution was to go the full distance and convert to Judaism. As Jews, they would be free from the pressure to conform to paganism or to observe the imperial-cult calendar. The Galatian Gentile believers felt forced to choose between two options:

(a) convert to Judaism and become legally Jewish

(b) at least nominally observe the calendar of the imperial cult

Apparently, Paul was concerned that most of his readers were considering the former route. It may be that many others had

---

[23] Mark Nanos, "A Torah Observant Paul?: What Difference Could it Make for Christian/Jewish Relations Today?" *Christian Scholars Group on Christian-Jewish Relations* (June 2005), n.p. [Cited 21 March 2011]. Online: http://www.marknanos.com/Boston-Torah-Obs-5-9-05.pdf.

[24] Justin Hardin, *Galatians and the Imperial Cult: A Critical Analysis of the First Century* (Tübingen, Germany: Mohr Siebeck, 2008).

already gone back to observing the events of the imperial cult and its calendar of days, months, seasons, and years and their appropriate observances, alongside their faith in Messiah. They were effectively trying to live in both worlds. It's an easy thing for the polytheistic mind to do: worship these gods one day and this God another day.

If this is the case, then it is possible that we should read the Epistle to the Galatians as an address to both groups, arguing against both options, and calling for a third option. Paul's third option calls for an identity in Messiah that completely breaks with "those that by nature are not gods" to which they were formerly enslaved, but it also maintains a distinct Gentile identity by not becoming Jewish.

If so, Paul warned the Galatian Gentiles not to return to observing the days of the imperial cult. This, he argues, would be a return to enslavement under those who are by nature not gods (i.e., the emperor-seen-as-a-deity). "Do you want to be their slaves all over again?" he asked.

The Fullness of Time

In that case, Galatians 4:3 speaks of Israel's enslavement to the same elementary principles of the world—not as a reference to Torah at all, but rather as a reference to the nation's own previous history of enslavement in Egypt and its periods of apostasy with idolatry. Might Paul be speaking of the exile, of which it says in the Torah, "And the LORD will scatter you among all peoples, from one end of the earth to the other, and there you shall serve other gods of wood and stone, which neither you nor your fathers have known" (Deuteronomy 28:64)?

The Messianic Redemption brings the end of the exile. Paul says, "But when the fullness of time had come, God sent forth his Son, born of woman, born under the law, to redeem those who were under the law, so that we might receive adoption as sons" (Galatians 4:4–5).

This requires a radical rereading of Galatians 4, but it provides a more satisfactory explanation of the passage. Consider the following paraphrase with my substitutions and insertions placed in square brackets [like this]:

> I mean that the heir, as long as he is a child, is no different from a slave, though he is the owner of everything, but he is under guardians and managers until the date set by his father [i.e., the Messianic Redemption]. In the same way we also, when we were children, were enslaved to the elementary principles of the world [to pagan nations and their gods, to the Roman power, and the authority of the emperor]. But when the fullness of time had come, God sent forth his Son, [the Messiah] born of woman, born under the law, [i.e., born Jewish] to redeem those who [are] under the law [i.e., those who are Jewish], so that we might receive adoption as sons [in the final redemption]. And because you [Gentile believers also] are sons, God has sent the Spirit of his Son into our hearts, crying, "Abba! Father!" So you are no longer a slave [to idols either], but a son, and if a son, then an heir through God. Formerly, when you did not know God, you were enslaved to those that by nature are not gods. But now that you have come to know God, or rather to be known by God, how can you turn back again to the weak and worthless elementary principles of the world, whose slaves you want to be once more? You observe days and months and seasons and years [of the Roman imperial cult]! I am afraid I may have labored over you in vain. Brothers, I entreat you, become as I am, [Torah-keeping] for I also have become as you are. (Galatians 4:1–12)

Abba!

Paul taught that believers, both Jewish and Gentile believers, have received the adoption as sons, not just sons of Abraham, but as sons of God. And how did this happen? When we placed faith in Yeshua of Nazareth and bound ourselves to him and his faithfulness, then "God has sent forth the Spirit of his Son into our hearts, crying, 'Abba! Father!'" (Galatians 4:6).

This is the source of the concept of having Jesus in your heart. In Paul's Hebraic idiom, the "heart" is not the organ that pumps the blood, but the seat of one's intellect, the mind, the brain, the seat of will and reason. It is the same concept communicated in the *Shema:* "You shall love the LORD with all your heart ... these words that I command you today shall be on your heart" (Deuteronomy 6:5–6). That is to say that the commandments are to be in a person's mind, in his memory, his thoughts, meditated upon and mentally rehearsed.

Paul said that the Spirit of Messiah is sent forth into the heart of the believer—that is the mind, the intellect, the will and reason of the believer—and that the Spirit of Messiah cries out from within the inner being of the believer, "Abba! Father!"

The Greek text actually says, "Abba," *alpha-beta-beta-alpha*, a transliteration of the Aramaic word for "father" used in Hebrew much like the English word "Papa." *Abba* serves as an emphatic form of the Hebrew *av* ("father"). It appears here as an apostolic-age memory, passed on to Paul and the early believers. They remembered that this is how the Master addressed God when he prayed. He spoke to God as "Abba." That explains why Paul brought it into the Greek text as a transliteration. The apostles remembered the sound of Yeshua's voice as he prayed, "Abba!"

The apostles remembered how he prayed. "In the days of his flesh, Jesus offered up prayers and supplications, with loud cries and tears, to him who was able to save him from death, and he was heard because of his reverence" (Hebrews 5:7). He continues to cry out now in our hearts, "Abba!" Because of that Spirit of sonship within us, Abba has adopted us as sons and daughters.

ALL THINGS TO ALL PEOPLE

(GALATIANS 4:12–20)

> What does Paul mean when he claims to
> become all things to all people, that by
> all means he might save some? Does this
> imply hypocrisy or a disingenuous type
> of evangelism?

In his epistle to the Galatians, the Apostle Paul told the God-fearing Galatian believers, "Brothers, I entreat you, become as I am, for I also have become as you are" (Galatians 4:12). In what way had Paul become like the God-fearing Gentiles, and in what way did he want them to become like him?

Some scholars, even the eminent Rabbi Yechiel Lichtenstein, suggest that this means that Paul chose to live as a Gentile, abandoning some matters of Torah (such as high dietary standards perhaps) in order to live, function, and reach out among the Gentiles. This may be the case. If so, Paul beseeched the Galatians to join him in his in-between status, neither at the highest Torah standard nor as a pagan participating in idolatry.

All Things to All People

Although we can only speculate as to what he means when he says, "I also have become as you are," it certainly relates to another key Pauline passage:

For though I am free from all, I have made myself a servant to all, that I might win more of them. To the Jews I became as a Jew, in order to win Jews. To those under the law I became as one under the law (though not being myself under the law) that I might win those under the law. To those outside the law I became as one outside the law (not being outside the law of God but under the law of Christ) that I might win those outside the law. To the weak I became weak, that I might win the weak. I have become all things to all people, that by all means I might save some. I do it all for the sake of the gospel, that I may share with them in its blessings. (1 Corinthians 9:19–23)

This passage presents several problems. It seems to imply that Paul adopted hypocritical pretenses in order to win people to the gospel. When around Jews, he acted Jewish; when around Torah-observant people he pretended to be Torah-observant; when around non-observant people he acted non-observant, and so forth. In fact, when Paul does make strong statements about his faithfulness to Torah, many New Testament teachers point to this passage to explain that Paul was only pretending to be Torah-observant, but in fact he no longer kept the law. For example, many New Testament teachers explain that when Paul paid for the sacrifices of four believing Nazirites and underwent the completion of his own Nazirite vow in Acts 21, he did so only for the sake of appearing to be Torah-observant so that he might "win those under the law."

That explanation paints a troubling portrait of Paul as disingenuous, deceitful, and hypocritical. This method of evangelism has often been attempted in Messianic Jewish circles. Jewish Christians used to pretend to be Torah-observant to hopefully win Jewish people to Messiah, but in fact they did not believe in the ongoing authority of the Torah. Their observance was only a pretense to lure Jews closer.

I do not believe that was Paul's mode of operation, nor do I believe it should be ours. The 1 Corinthians 9 passage employs terminology that we have previously learned in our study of Galatians. Having worked halfway through the Epistle to the Galatians, we stand in a position to understand 1 Corinthians 9:19–23 better.

To the Jews as a Jew

Paul says, "To the Jews I became as a Jew, in order to win Jews." In fact, Paul was Jewish. He never quit being Jewish. He only means that, when among Jewish people, he employed that common ground to his advantage. He shared with them a common cultural and historical heritage. He used that common ground in order to present the gospel. For example, when in the synagogue of Pisidian Antioch, he offered a teaching steeped in Jewish terminology and prophetic expectation to argue for Yeshua as the Messiah.

To Those Under the Law

Paul says, "To those under the law I became as one under the law (though not being myself under the law) that I might win those under the law." Why does he differentiate between "the Jews" and "those under the law"?

Previously, we have observed that Paul sometimes uses the term "under the law" to refer to the Jewish people in general (e.g., Galatians 4:4–5), but more often he uses it to refer to converts to Judaism, Gentiles who place themselves "under the law" in the same manner as the Jewish people by taking on "the works of the law" that identify a person as Jewish.

Because of that, I read this as referring to those Gentiles who have already converted. If so, the phrase should be understood, "To those who have gone through conversion and become Jewish, I became as one who had gone through conversion to become Jewish (though not myself having undergone conversion to become Jewish)." In other words, he accepted the proselytes' status as converts, reached out to them at their level, and presented the gospel as relevant to them in their new status as proselytes to Judaism, even though he was Jewish and not a proselyte to Judaism.

To Those Outside the Law

Paul says, "To those outside the law I became as one outside the law (not being outside the law of God but under the law of Christ) that I might win those outside the law" (1 Corinthians 9:21).

In this context, "outside the law" does not refer to lawlessness or paganism. It refers to Gentiles who have not undergone conversion and are not undergoing conversion, i.e., Gentile God-Fearers. Paul becomes as they are. For example, Paul set aside his high halachic dietary standards for the sake of table fellowship in Antioch. That is not to say he ate forbidden foods or unclean meats, but where there was room to budge, he did so. (The God-fearing Gentiles were probably, for the most part, eating according to the biblical dietary laws as well. At the very least, they did so when eating with Jews.)

Paul explains that he himself is not "outside of the law," that is to say, he himself is not a Gentile God-Fearer. Instead, he is under the "Torah of Messiah." He remains legally Jewish in Messiah, but he bends where he can bend and he flexes what can be flexed in order to win those who are not Jewish.

I Have Become as You

Perhaps this is how we should understand Galatians 4:12 as well: "Brothers, I entreat you, become as I am, for I also have become as you are. You did me no wrong." Paul entreated the Galatian Gentiles to make social sacrifices just as he did for them. In order to eat with them and fellowship with them, he had to bend his halachic standards. Now he begged them to join him in that place of social tension. Just as his loyalty to the non-Jews cost him prestige and status within the Jewish community, loyalty to Yeshua cost the God-Fearers social status in the Gentile world. The Gentile Roman world shunned them because they adopted aspects of Judaism and no longer participated in the Roman cult. The Jewish community looked askance at them because they did not elect to undergo full conversion.

Paul's First Arrival in Galatia

When Paul and Barnabas first arrived in the province of Galatia, Paul was sick and in need of rest. In another place, he described his typical experience: "On frequent journeys, in danger from rivers, danger from robbers, danger from my own people, danger from Gentiles, danger in the city, danger in the wilderness, danger at sea, danger from false brothers; in toil and hardship, through many a sleepless night, in hunger and thirst, often without food, in cold and exposure" (2 Corinthians 11:26–27).

Paul apparently arrived in need of convalescence and spent extended time in the community while he recovered. The God-fearing Gentiles of Galatia nursed him back to health while he shared the gospel message with them. He recalled, "It was because of a bodily ailment that I preached the gospel to you at first" (Galatians 4:13). He said that they received him as a messenger of God and as the Messiah Yeshua himself, a direct allusion to the Master's words to the apostles: "Whoever receives you receives me" (Matthew 10:40).

Recalling that first visit with some nostalgia, Paul asked, "What then has become of the blessing you felt? For I testify to you that, if possible, you would have gouged out your eyes and given them to me" (Galatians 4:15).

Readers sometimes speculate that Paul suffered some sort of eye trouble, perhaps a result of his Damascus-road blinding, but that cannot be proven from this verse. This may simply be an idiom like, "You would have given your right arm for me" or "You would have given me the shirt off your back."

Paul the Enemy

Paul asked, "Have I then become your enemy by telling you the truth?" (Galatians 4:16). The answer is yes, that is the case. All through the Bible, every teacher and prophet who speaks the truth of the word of God experiences enmity from those to whom he speaks it. Sadly, that seems to be the biblical pattern, and Paul experienced it with the Galatians. By telling the Galatians that they should not consider conversion as an option, he earned the enmity of those who were already inclined to go down that path.

The Influencers

Paul spoke directly of his conflict with the influencers, his opponents in the theological battle for the allegiance of the God-fearing Gentiles in Galatia. He said, "They make much of you, but for no good purpose. They want to shut you out, that you may make much of them" (Galatians 4:17).

"They" are believers in Messiah, possibly proselytes who do not accept Paul's unique gospel of Gentile inclusion. We have been referring to them as "the influencers" because they were *influencing* the believing Gentiles to undergo conversion to become Jewish, but they did not refer to themselves by that name.

Paul said, "They make much of you, but for no good purpose." They made much of the Galatian Gentiles; they made much over them because they were trying to persuade them that their Gentile status in the synagogue and in Judaism was inappropriate. They applied all forms of persuasion: taking up the cause of the Gentile believers, showing sympathy for their plight, all in an attempt to bring them into the fold. As believing proselytes themselves, they were motivated to do so because the God-fearing Gentile believers did not share their own status. The God-Fearers had upset the established social boundaries, and that probably made it difficult for Jewish believers and proselytes who were trying to have a positive, normal relationship with the rest of the Jewish community. Moreover, they probably truly believed that, without full conversion, the Gentile believers were shut out of the kingdom. Paul said, "They want to shut you out, that you may make much of them." The influencers wanted to shut the God-fearing Gentile believers out of the synagogue and theologically out of the kingdom unless they agreed to undergo circumcision and conversion.

Paul's Big Concern

Paul expressed his anguish for the believers. He truly believed that the conversion of the God-fearing Gentiles was a mistake. He declared that he was "again in the anguish of childbirth until Christ is formed in you!" (Galatians 4:19). That is to say that he felt like a woman going through labor a second time, giving birth to the same baby. Nevertheless, he was willing and able to go through it all again for a single goal: "Until Messiah is formed in you."

How does Messiah form inside of someone or inside of a body of believers? Paul mentions the concept here offhandedly, but the entire epistle looks toward that goal. He was worried about them until Messiah was formed within them.

In first-century Judaism, a disciple sought to emulate his teacher. Yeshua himself said: "A disciple is not above his teacher, but everyone when he is fully trained will be like his teacher" (Luke 6:40).

What is your goal in life? Job, career, status, spouse? If you are a disciple of Yeshua, your goal is supposed to be imitation of the Messiah. Paul referred to that goal when he used the phrase "until Messiah is formed in you." It is a simple principle to grasp, but not such a simple principle to implement.

Perhaps Paul feared that the Galatian Gentiles were trading their identity in Messiah for identity in Judaism, so he was afraid that they were abandoning that high calling of discipleship. That does not mean that Judaism and discipleship to Messiah are incompatible; not at all. For Jewish believers, they are not only compatible; they are inseparable. For a Jewish believer to abandon Judaism is an abandonment of discipleship. Paul was speaking to Gentile believers, and in his mind if the Gentile believers were to become Jewish, they would forfeit their central identity in Messiah alone. They would become Messianic Jews so long as they retained their faith through the conversion, but they no longer needed to rely solely upon Yeshua for their sense of attachment to God, the kingdom, and the people of Israel.

The great danger was that Messiah might not be fully formed in them. Their Jewish identity might become fully formed, but Messiah might be set aside—set on the shelf, so to speak, put into the "maybe-he-is, maybe-he-isn't-the-Messiah" category, or placed into the "I think he was a good man and a good teacher" category because Messiah will no longer matter. Yeshua will no longer be the Gentile believer's center of identity. This was a big concern for Paul.

Christianity

This is also a big concern for me—not because of Judaism, though, but because of Christianity. Unlike in Paul's world, where being a Christian required an all-or-nothing commitment of radical devotion and discipleship to Yeshua, being a Christian in today's world can mean a taking-for-granted, lukewarm, casual, religious affiliation in any number of institutions which requires no social discomfort whatsoever. Being a nominal Christian requires no separation from the world—nothing, really. The average believer today has no compulsion to become like the Teacher.

Do we even know his teachings? In speaking with people, I find that, on the whole, we do not. Based on our behavior, one would think that most Christians, most believers, most Messianics have never even read the Sermon on the Mount. Where is longsuffering? Where is forgiveness? Where is the man who turns the other cheek? Where is the man who repays evil with good? Where is the man who removes the log from his eye before pronouncing judgment on the speck in his neighbor's eye? Where is the man who walks the straight and narrow, who asks, seeks, and knocks?

If we were serious about the business of seeing Messiah formed within us, we would be serious about the business of heeding his words and obeying them, lest we be like the foolish man who heard his words but did not heed them, and so built his house upon the sand.

Most believers are not serious about the business of seeing Messiah formed. Most of us are not even aware that the goal of discipleship is to be like the Master.

We see ourselves and other professing believers behaving in the same worldly ways as the rest of the world, as if it is completely normal for a Christian to do that. We have the same entertainments, the same low standards and values, the same rates of promiscuity, the same types of materialism, the same rates of marriage failure, and the same types of petty quarrels, rivalries, and hatreds—as if it means nothing at all to be a disciple or to be a believer.

Why is this? Because we do not have this goal: to be like Messiah. We do not have this purpose: Messiah formed within us. Even if it is our goal, it is too easily forgotten, abandoned, set aside, and left to wither.

Consider the Apostle Paul's words; empathize with his anguish; internalize his pain. He felt like a woman in labor for the same child, as it says in the prophet Hosea 13:13: "The pangs of childbirth come for him, but he is an unwise son, for at the right time he does not present himself at the opening of the womb." It is like the opposite of being born again. Our Master says, "Amen, Amen,

I say to you, unless one is born again he cannot see the kingdom of God" (John 3:3).

Remember the holy apostle's philosophy of life: "I have been crucified with Christ. It is no longer I who live, but Christ who lives in me. And the life I now live in the flesh I live by faith in the Son of God, who loved me and gave himself for me" (Galatians 2:20). May the Holy One, blessed be he, be pleased to grant us success, that his son Yeshua may be fully formed within us, "until we all attain to the unity of the faith and of the knowledge of the Son of God, to mature manhood, to the measure of the stature of the fullness of Messiah" (Ephesians 4:13).

SARAH, HAGAR, ISAAC, AND ISHMAEL
(GALATIANS 4:21–31)

> Paul develops a parable (midrash)
> based upon the story of Hagar and
> Sarah, Ishmael and Isaac, to point out
> the difference between God-Fearers and
> proselytes.

In Galatians 4, Paul offers us a parable in which he briefly retells the story of Sarah and Hagar and their children, Isaac and Ishmael. He uses that story to illustrate his argument against the influencers in Galatia who were encouraging the Gentile believers to undergo circumcision and become Jewish.

In traditional Christian interpretation, this passage is fairly straightforward and is interpreted by Paul himself. He wrote, "These women are two covenants. One is from Mount Sinai ... she corresponds to the present Jerusalem, for she is in slavery with her children. But the Jerusalem above is free, and she is our mother" (Galatians 4:24–26). Hagar represents the Old Covenant, i.e., Torah and Judaism. Sarah represents the New Covenant, i.e., the gospel and Christianity.

Hagar's children, the Jews, are slaves. Sarah's children, the Christians, are free. "What does the Scripture say? 'Cast out the slave woman and her son, for the son of the slave woman shall not inherit with the son of the free woman'" (Galatians 4:30).

This interpretation of the passage is prevalent and has been around since the early centuries of Christian interpretation. The message is simple: Judaism, bad; Christianity, good. Torah = slavery; gospel = freedom. Jews are slaves; Christians are free.

Judaism = Hagar/Jerusalem Below

Ishmael = Jews (in slavery)

Christianity = Sarah/Jerusalem Above

Isaac = Christians (free)

Under this interpretation, if a Jewish or Gentile believer observes the Torah, he is considered to be taking on a yoke of slavery and ignoring Paul's admonishment to "cast out the slave woman" (the Torah) and her son (the Jews). For the son of the bondwoman (Jews) shall not be an heir with the son of the free woman (Christians). This is how early Christianity understood the passage.

We will work through the passage verse by verse to arrive at a better understanding of the parable.

Desiring to Be Under the Law

Paul prefaced his midrash with the provocative, "Tell me, you who desire to be under the law, do you not listen to the law?" (Galatians 4:21). Paul used the term "under the law" to refer to someone who is Jewish or to a Gentile who has become legally (halachically) Jewish through conversion. When Paul said, "You who want to be under law," he referred to the Gentile God-Fearers of Galatia who were planning on undergoing ritual conversion to become Jewish. Paul challenged them: "Tell me, you people who want to become Jewish under the Torah, don't you know what it says in the Torah?" Then he briefly retold the story of Abraham's two wives (Sarah and Hagar) and his two sons (Isaac and Ishmael).

Benei Avraham

"For it is written that Abraham had two sons" (Galatians 4:22). Paul regarded the story of Isaac and Ishmael relevant to the subject of conversion because both Isaac and Ishmael were *benei Avraham* (sons of Abraham). When a Gentile converts and becomes Jewish, he takes the last name "*ben Avraham* (son of Abraham)." When a Gentile woman undergoes a conversion to become Jewish, she receives the last name "*bat Avraham* (daughter of Abraham)." The Galatians were trying to achieve that "*ben Avraham*" status by becoming Jewish. They wanted to join the legal family of Abraham.

In the synagogue world, a *ben Avraham* is a convert. Paul used the story of Isaac and Ishmael to illustrate two different types of *benei Avraham*, in other words, two different types of Gentile proselytes. He was not contrasting Jews against Christians, nor was he contrasting Jews against Gentiles. He was not talking about Jews at all. Instead, he used the Isaac and Ishmael analogy to contrast two different types of Gentiles: "For it is written that Abraham had two sons, one by the slave woman and one by a free woman" (Galatians 4:22).

Flesh versus Promise

Hagar was a slave woman. She was Sarah's maidservant. Sarah was a freewoman. Paul explained, "But the son of the slave was born according to the flesh, while the son of the free woman was born through promise" (Galatians 4:23). "According to the flesh" means physically. It does not mean sinful or bad; it means physically or bodily. Abraham and Hagar conceived Ishmael by natural, physical means: "according to the flesh."

Abraham and Sarah conceived Isaac, however, through a supernatural miracle. Isaac was "born through promise." What was the promise? Paul has brought up "the promise" four or five times in the epistle already. He dedicated most of the third chapter to the subject and equated it with the whole gospel message: "And the Scripture, foreseeing that God would justify the Gentiles by faith, preached the gospel beforehand to Abraham, saying, "In you shall all the nations be blessed'" (Galatians 3:8). Again, in Galatians 3:16:

> "Now the promises were made to Abraham and to his offspring. It does not say, 'And to offsprings [seeds],' referring to many, but referring to one, 'And to your offspring [seed],' who is the Messiah."

The Promise: All nations will be blessed in Abraham's seed, the Messiah.

Abraham's wife Sarah conceived and gave birth to Isaac according to God's promise to give Abraham seed. Abraham believed, and God credited it to him as righteousness. Isaac was born through the miraculous promise, but Ishmael was born as a result of Abraham going to Hagar, attempting to fulfill God's promise himself. Ishmael was born in the normal, physical way a son is born: by human, physical efforts.

These Women Are Two Covenants

Paul explained, "Now this may be interpreted allegorically: these women are two covenants." Most traditional church interpretations explain the two covenants as the Old Covenant and the New Covenant. In the context of Paul's epistle to the Galatians, however, the two covenants under discussion are the Old Covenant (from Sinai) and the even older covenant, the covenant God made with Abraham. The parable of the two mothers/two covenants illustrates Paul's discussion about two covenants in Galatians 3:

> Now the promises were made to Abraham and to his [seed]. It does not say, "And to [seeds]," referring to many, but referring to one, "And to your offspring," who is Christ. This is what I mean: the law, which came 430 years afterward, does not annul a covenant previously ratified by God, so as to make the promise void. For if the inheritance comes by the law, it no longer comes by promise; but God gave it to Abraham by a promise. (Galatians 3:16–18)

Sarah and Hagar are two covenants. Hagar represents the covenant at Sinai. Sarah represents the covenant with Abraham, which is older and cannot be replaced by a covenant made 430 years later, just like Hagar cannot replace Sarah. This totally changes the conventional, replacement-theology interpretation of the passage.

Hagar and Ishmael

Paul explained:

> Now this may be interpreted allegorically: these women are two covenants. One is from Mount Sinai, bearing children for slavery; she is Hagar. Now Hagar is Mount Sinai in Arabia; she corresponds to the present Jerusalem, for she is in slavery with her children. (Galatians 4:24–25)

Hagar represents Mount Sinai, which represents Torah. She bears children for slavery. The children born for slavery are not Jewish people or those who keep Torah. The discussion contrasts two different types of *benei Avraham*, i.e., two different types of proselytes. The parable, it turns out, is actually about two different types of Gentile believers. The children to whom Hagar gives birth by natural means (Sinai and present Jerusalem) are Gentile believers undergoing legal conversion in order to become Jewish. They are proselytes going through a physical (fleshly) conversion.

Paul compared those converts to Ishmael, the son of Hagar, because there was nothing miraculous about the way that they entered the family of Abraham. They became sons of Abraham by physical means. In another passage, he called it the circumcision of the flesh and the circumcision made with hands, according to the flesh. The proselytes became "sons of Abraham," just as Ishmael was a real son of Abraham. Converting, going under the law, and becoming legally Jewish makes a person a legitimate son of Abraham, just as Ishmael really was born as Abraham's son. Ishmael's status, even as a son of Abraham, was that of a slave, so to speak. He was the son of a slave girl, second behind Isaac. His is a second-class status.

Paul said that "Hagar is Mount Sinai in Arabia; she corresponds to the present Jerusalem, for she is in slavery with her children." Her children are proselytes. When a Gentile became Jewish, he became legally accountable to the legal authority of the sages, the Sanhedrin in Jerusalem which adjudicated Jewish law—he placed himself under the authority of the Jewish courts. Paul saw this as problematic for Gentile believers, perhaps because in Paul's day (as in our own) the religious authorities were not always friendly toward believers.

Sarah and Jerusalem

Sarah, on the other hand, represented the promises of the Abrahamic covenant, corresponding to the heavenly New Jerusalem of the Messianic Age and the world to come: "The Jerusalem above is free, and she is our mother" (Galatians 4:26). Note that Paul said, "She is our mother," not "your mother," because the New Jerusalem is the future city of both Jewish and Gentile believers.

To establish the analogy, Paul quoted a proof text from Isaiah 54, a prophecy addressed to the city of Jerusalem which predicts the final Messianic Redemption, the ingathering, the building of Messianic Jerusalem, and the advent of New Jerusalem of the world to come. In that oracle, the prophet depicts ruined Jerusalem as a barren woman because her children have gone into exile. At the time of the redemption, she realizes she has more children than she thought possible. The Jewish people return to her, and many Gentiles come as well. The rabbis homiletically interpreted the barren woman of Isaiah 54 as Sarah, the barren one who became the mother of a nation. Paul followed that traditional interpretation, making Sarah symbolic for New Jerusalem, and he proved it by quoting the first verse of Isaiah 54.

> "Sing, O barren one, who did not bear; break forth into singing and cry aloud, you who have not been in labor! For the children of the desolate one will be more than the children of her who is married," says the LORD. "Enlarge the place of your tent, and let the curtains of your habitations be stretched out; do not hold back; lengthen your cords and strengthen your stakes. For you will spread abroad to the right and to the left, and your offspring will possess the nations and will people the desolate cities." (Isaiah 54:1–3)

To Paul and the apostles, the prophecy of Isaiah 54 was especially relevant because it came right after Isaiah 53, the prophecy of the Suffering Servant, which described the sufferings of the Messiah. The result of the Messiah's death and resurrection, described in Isaiah 53, is the redemption of Jerusalem described in Isaiah 54. Paul quoted that proof text in his analogy:

But the Jerusalem above is free, and she is our mother. For it is written, "Rejoice, O barren one who does not bear; break forth and cry aloud, you who are not in labor! For the children of the desolate one will be more than those of the one who has a husband." Now you, brothers, like Isaac, are children of promise. (Galatians 4:26–28)

Children of the Promise

Paul told the Gentile God-Fearers of Galatia, "You brothers, like Isaac, are children of the promise." Paul contrasted them against those Gentile believers who had undergone legal, halachic conversion. To Paul, the God-fearing Gentile who remained a Gentile was a child of the promise that God made to Abraham: All nations will be blessed in your seed. Paul likened the God-fearing Gentile believer to Isaac, who was also a child of the same covenant promise.

On the other hand, the Gentile believers who underwent circumcision and went "under the law" to become Jewish he likened to Ishmael. They set aside the promise that God made to Abraham about all nations being blessed in his seed. The proselyte forfeits that promise by becoming a child of the natural children. The proselyte adopted the natural means, according to the flesh—literally, the removal of some flesh—the normal way of becoming part of Abraham's family.

Ishmael Taunts Isaac

Paul took the analogy a step further and said, "Just as at that time he who was born according to the flesh persecuted him who was born according to the Spirit, so also it is now" (Galatians 4:29). When did "he who was born according to the flesh" (Ishmael) persecute "him who was born according to the Spirit" (Isaac)? The story is in the Torah:

And the child (Isaac) grew and was weaned. And Abraham made a great feast on the day that Isaac was weaned. But Sarah saw the son of Hagar the Egyptian, whom she had borne to Abraham, laughing. So she said to Abraham,

"Cast out this slave woman with her son, for the son of this slave woman shall not be heir with my son Isaac." (Genesis 21:8–10)

Have you ever wondered what Ishmael was mocking Isaac about? Paul knew because the story was well entrenched in Jewish legend. It appears in the midrash and in the *targumim*. Ishmael mocked Isaac regarding the commandment of circumcision:

> Ishmael said to Isaac, "I am more beloved than you because I was circumcised at the age of thirteen." Isaac retorted, "I am more beloved than you because I was circumcised at eight days." Ishmael taunted, "That makes me more beloved. At the age of thirteen, I could have protested the procedure, but I did not … I am more beloved than you because I was circumcised at the age of thirteen, but you were circumcised as a baby and had no choice in the matter."[25]

Ishmael can one-up Isaac because, unlike Isaac, he underwent circumcision at the age of thirteen, i.e., as an adult. Paul said, "Just as at that time he who was born according to the flesh persecuted him who was born according to the Spirit, so also it is now." Those "born according to the flesh" are Gentile believers in Galatia who, like Ishmael, went through circumcision as adults and became legally Jewish. They were criticizing those Gentile believers who had not taken that step. Like Ishmael taunting Isaac, the proselytes taunt the God-Fearers and encourage them to convert. *These are the influencers.* The influencers are Gentile believers who had already converted. Like Ishmael, they underwent circumcision as adults. They can claim to be more beloved because they willingly took upon themselves a commandment which the God-fearing Gentiles had not undertaken.

The Point of the Analogy

Just as Sarah had Abraham send Hagar and Ishmael away, Paul urged the Gentile God-Fearers to reject the pressure and persua-

---

[25] Genesis *Rabbah* 55:4.

sion of those who had gone through a conversion. He preached, "What does the Scripture say? 'Cast out the slave woman and her son, for the son of the slave woman shall not inherit with the son of the free woman'" (Galatians 4:30).

"The son of the slave woman," that is, those who became proselytes, "shall not inherit with the son of the free woman," that is, those who remained Gentiles but became sons of Abraham by faith. Paul did not mean that those who underwent conversion lost their salvation, but he broke with their doctrine and dogma. "So, brothers, we are not children of the slave but of the free woman," he insisted (Galatians 4:31). Therefore, Paul identified the Gentile God-Fearers as *benei Avraham,* sons of Abraham. They were spiritual proselytes.

It's an analogy, a midrash. Do not take it too literally. It was an illustration, and usually a midrash only attempted to illustrate a single point. Paul's point was that there are two different ways for a Gentile to enter Abraham's family. One is the normal way: according to the flesh, through circumcision and conversion. This is Ishmael. The other is a matter of faith in the promise that God is going to bless all nations (not just one nation) in the seed of Abraham, the Messiah. Through those who chose the latter route, Abraham became the father of many nations. Isaac represents those Gentiles who remain Gentiles yet enter the family of Abraham spiritually by means of faith in Messiah alone. This is the same point he made at the end of the previous chapter: "And if you are in Messiah, then you are Abraham's [seed], heirs according to promise" (Galatians 3:29).

Summary of the Parable

The passage contrasts two types of proselytes: the legal proselyte and the spiritual proselyte. The one becomes part of Abraham's family by conventional conversion, the other through faith in Messiah, the promised seed of Abraham, in whom all nations find blessing. The passage does not contrast the Old Testament against New Testament or the Old Covenant against the New Covenant. It does not equate Judaism and Torah with slavery, nor does it pit Christians against Jews.

It means that if you are a Jewish believer, you should be proud of being Jewish because you are a child of Abraham, legally, physically, and spiritually. It means that if you are a Gentile believer, you, too, are part of the people, a spiritual son of Abraham, and that is remarkable—miraculous even. You are a child of the promise that God made to Abraham so long ago.

Galatians

CHAPTER FIVE

CIRCUMCISION AND UNCIRCUMCISION
(GALATIANS 5:1–6)

Paul warns Gentiles about relying on Jewish status for salvation and declares circumcision irrelevant with regard to salvation.

I gnatius of Antioch was a Christian bishop in the city of Antioch, the same Antioch where the believers were first called by the Greek name *Christianoi,* where Paul and Barnabas ministered. Paul probably wrote his epistle to the Galatians from that city.

Ignatius lived early enough that he might possibly have known some of the last of the apostolic generation. Born before the destruction of the Temple, he served in Antioch at the beginning of the second century. Some say he had heard John teach. We do not know if this is true, but we do know that he was a great fan of the Apostle Paul.

Ignatius Reads Paul

Pauline language permeates the epistles of Ignatius. For example, consider the following passage from Ignatius' epistle to the Magnesians:

It is absurd to speak of Jesus Christ with the tongue, and to cherish in the mind a Judaism which has now come to an end. For where there is Christianity there cannot be Judaism. For Christ is one, in whom every nation that believes, and every tongue that confesses, is gathered unto God. And those that were of a stony heart have become the children of Abraham, the friend of God; and in his seed all those have been blessed who were ordained to eternal life in Christ. (*Magnesians* 10:3–4)

Ignatius wanted to convince the Magnesian believers to desist from the practice of Judaism because he believed that Judaism was incompatible with the Christianity that Paul espoused. To Ignatius of Antioch, Judaism and Christianity were separate entities and stood in antithesis to one another. He seems to have drawn this conclusion from the writings of Paul.

Gentile Christians like Ignatius misunderstood Paul because they misunderstood Judaism, and Christian-thought leaders like Ignatius worked hard to tear the Jewishness out of Christianity. Consider how Ignatius of Antioch would have read and understood the first four verses of the fifth chapter of Galatians:

For freedom Christ has set us free; stand firm therefore, and do not submit again to a yoke of slavery. Look: I, Paul, say to you that if you accept circumcision, Christ will be of no advantage to you. I testify again to every man who accepts circumcision that he is obligated to keep the whole law. You are severed from Christ, you who would be justified by the law; you have fallen away from grace. (Galatians 5:1–4)

What did Ignatius of Antioch hear when he read those verses? Here's how I imagine he interpreted them: Christianity is freedom; Judaism and the Torah is slavery. The Christian who observes the Jewish law renders Messiah of no advantage because the Messiah came to cancel the Jewish Torah and set men free from those rituals. In Messiah, Judaism has now come to an end. In fact, if a Christian keeps the Old Testament law, he severs himself from Messiah, falls from grace, and is in danger of damnation.

Observance of the the commandments that Paul elsewhere calls "holy, righteous and good" can get a person sent to hell. This might explain why Ignatius was so passionate in his efforts to sever the relationship between Judaism and Christianity.

Apologies to Ignatius

My apologies to Ignatius, but that's not exactly what Paul meant to say in Galatians 5:1–4. Ignatius may have responded, "Who are you to say that you have a better interpretation of Paul's writings? You live nineteen hundred years further removed from Paul than I, and half a world away!"

I hope Ignatius will pardon my chutzpah, but a few things need to be clarified. Paul was speaking only to Gentile believers, not Jews. To Paul, it goes without saying that Jewish believers are keeping the whole Torah and should be keeping the whole Torah. Paul was not speaking against Torah or Judaism; rather, as we have learned, he was addressing Gentiles who were considering undergoing a legal conversion to become Jewish.

Paul said, "For freedom Christ has set us free; stand firm therefore, and do not submit again to a yoke of slavery" (Galatians 5:1). The Messiah has set us free. We are indeed free, if the Son has set us free, but from what are we freed? Ignatius may have responded, "You see, Christ has set us free from the law. In Christ, we are no longer under the law!"

Free from What?

Again, my apologies to Ignatius, but as a fellow Gentile, Ignatius was also never "under the law." How can a Gentile who was never "under the law" be set free from something to which he was never yoked in the first place? As we learned in the previous chapter of Galatians, believers in Messiah are sons of the free woman, Sarah, who represents heavenly Jerusalem. Paul urged his Gentile disciples, therefore, not to undergo circumcision for conversion to become legally Jewish, a transition which he equated with taking on another yoke of slavery. Those words were not for the Jewish person who was already Jewish but for the Gentile believer. Why would Paul consider conversion to Judaism a yoke of slavery? From Paul's perspective, the God-fearing Gentile believer is already a son of Abraham by faith. Therefore, conversion to become a *ben Avraham* ("son of Abraham," the synagogue term for a proselyte) is something like campaigning for an office to which one has already been elected. It is like taking out a mortgage for a house you already own. In that regard, Paul saw it as a type of slavery: working to achieve a status that is yours already. Not that the Gentile believers already had Jewish status—not at all. They were not Jewish, but they were sons of Abraham by faith and part of the greater people of God.

Christ of No Advantage

Paul stated emphatically in Galatians 5:2: "Look: I, Paul, say to you that if you accept circumcision, Christ will be of no advantage to you." Faith in Messiah gave the God-fearing Gentile believers the advantage of a new identity as sons of Abraham. The Messiah brought them into the Abrahamic promise and gave them a position within the people of God. Ordinarily, outside of Messiah, that status could only be achieved by going through a halachic conversion and becoming Jewish. Therefore, Paul reasoned, if the Gentile believer converted in order to achieve that status, he denied what Messiah had already done for him. He underwent conversion in order to achieve that status on his own. That rendered Messiah of no advantage to him. One can go through a conversion without faith in the Messiah; one need not have faith in Yeshua to become Jewish. Many Gentiles in the first century did just that. They were not followers of Yeshua. They just became Jewish because Judaism was a popular option.

Let me explain this by way of a parable.

It can be compared to a man who was married to a woman for several years. After several years of marriage, however, he began to wonder if his original marriage to her was legitimate. Some people (certain influencers) began to tell him, "You did not get the proper type of marriage license. Your marriage is illegitimate in the eyes of the state; therefore, you are not really married." He decided that the thing to do was to get remarried with the proper license. He went to his wife and explained the situation: They were not really married and actually never had been. What they needed to do was go through a new wedding with the proper license. First, he had to ask her for her hand. "Will you marry me?" he asked. The wife, who had several children by this man, felt deeply offended that her husband considered their marriage illegitimate. "Whose children are these? Who have I been living with all these years if you are not my husband?" she asked.

In a similar way, the God-fearing Gentiles entered the family of Abraham and the people of God through faith in Messiah. They took a position within the greater commonwealth of Israel, i.e., the kingdom of heaven. Under the instigation of the influencers, they had begun to doubt the legitimacy of their participation in Abraham's family, and they doubted their citizenship in the kingdom. They sought another way to achieve that same status. In so doing, they devalued and discredited what Messiah had already done for them. They dismissed Messiah's work on their behalf to bring them into the kingdom.

That was how Paul saw it. He said, "If you accept circumcision, Christ will be of no advantage to you." Instead, the proselyte enters the family of Abraham through the natural route, like Ishmael, rather than relying on the promise, like Isaac. Undergoing a circumcision of the flesh, he opted for a physical status through the flesh rather than a spiritual status through the promise that all nations will be blessed in Abraham's seed. After conversion, he will no longer be a member of all nations. He must leave the promise given to Abraham behind.

One Simple Verse

Paul warned Gentiles that, if they underwent conversion, they would be liable for keeping the whole Torah, not just circumcision. As Paul attempted to dissuade the God-fearing Gentiles of Galatia from undergoing circumcision, he emphatically warned, "I testify again to every man who accepts circumcision that he is obligated to keep the whole Torah" (Galatians 5:3).

Actually, he was warning the women, too, not just the men. The word "man" in the Greek text of Galatians 5:3 is a gender-neutral term. It should be translated as "every person." Did Paul imagine that women wanted to be circumcised, too? Of course not. He was speaking of circumcision as equivalent to a legal conversion to Judaism. So to put it plainly, the verse says, "I testify again to every person who becomes Jewish that he (or she) is obligated to keep the whole Torah."

Galatians 5:3 is irrefutably simple to understand. Pauline scholar Richard Longenecker says, "Paul here points out that circumcision obligates one to keep all of the prescriptions of the Mosaic law."[26] Jewish Roots scholar Brad Young says, "[Paul] also maintained that if one is circumcised, he is required to keep all the law ... all the commandments of the covenant made at Sinai with the children of Israel."[27] New Testament scholar Pinchas Lapide, an Orthodox Jew, writes: "Of course, all of this [exemption from Torah] applies only to Gentile Christians. For Jews and for Jewish proselytes the Mosaic law, as Paul sees it, retains its full and unaltered validity."[28] In his commentary on Galatians, Messianic Jewish scholar Reb Yosef Shulam says, "Those seeking circumcision are binding themselves to the observance of [the whole Torah]."[29] Jewish New Testament scholar Mark Nanos observes, "Paul's own comment in Galatians 5:3 bears witness to the concern for full Torah observance that obtains for Jewish people and extends to those who complete proselyte conversion."[30] He also notes that Gentiles who become proselytes to Judaism and take on halachic (legal) Jewish identity "will then be obliged to observe the whole Law."[31]

---

[26] Longenecker, *Galatians*, 226. To my knowledge, no credible scholar within mainstream Christianity, Judaism, Messianic Judaism, New Testament academia, or higher biblical criticism has ever interpreted the verse to support a One Law theology that says Jewish and Gentile believers have the exact same obligations to the Torah.

[27] Brad Young, *Paul the Jewish Theologian: A Pharisee among Christians, Jews, and Gentiles* (Peabody, MA: Hendrickson, 2002), 90.

[28] Pinchas Lapide and Peter Stuhlmacher, *Paul: Rabbi and Apostle* (trans. Lawrence Denef; Minneapolis: Augsburg Publishing House, 1984), 42.

[29] Hilary Le Cornu and Joseph Shulam, *A Commentary on the Jewish Roots of Galatians* (Jerusalem, Israel: Akademon, 2005), 327.

[30] Nanos, *The Irony of Galatians*, 253.

[31] Ibid., 142.

If the plain meaning of the text is true, then obviously the inverse is also true: every person who is not Jewish is not obligated to keep the whole Torah. This teaches us three important things:

1. There is a difference between being Jewish and being Gentile.

2. Jewish believers are obligated to keep the whole Torah.

3. Non-Jewish believers are not liable for the whole Torah in the same way as Jewish believers.

The Oral Torah?

Some Messianic Gentiles espousing a One Law Theology explain that Galatians 5:3 refers not to the Torah, but to the Oral Law. Is it possible that Paul meant to refer to the Oral Torah instead of the Written Torah? Perhaps he meant, "If you become Jewish, you will be obligated to keep both the Oral Law and the Written Law." Gentiles, on the other hand, were only required to keep the Written Torah.

That explanation does not work. Paul did not refer to Jewish tradition as Torah. Neither he nor the apostles spoke of an Oral Law. The Oral Law, as a formal body, was not yet compiled or codified. Instead, Paul speaks of the "customs of the fathers" and the "traditions," but he never equates those customs and traditions with the Torah. None of the apostles did. Paul would not refer to the "customs of the fathers" as the law.

Moreover, contrary to One Law Theology, this interpretation purports that Jewish believers do have a different obligation to Torah than Gentile believers: Jewish believers must keep the Written and Oral Torah, but Gentiles must keep only the Written Torah.

Two Different Standards

Galatians 5:3 raises the question that seems to vex Gentile Christians the most. Would God have two different standards for his people? Would God require one thing of Jews and something else of Gentiles?

Yes, and Galatians 5:3 proves it. The Torah itself differentiates when it offers laws for distinct groupings of people such as men, women, widows, children, judges, kings, priests, Levites, strangers, natural born, and so on. Each group is held to a different standard. For example, it is not a sin for a Levite to attend the funeral of his best friend, but according to Leviticus 21, it would be a sin for a priest to do so. That represents different standards.

It also raises this question: Which parts of the Torah did Paul imagine that non-Jews did not have to keep? Did he think that God-fearing Gentiles could commit adultery or charge one another interest on loans?

He did not enumerate a list of the specific commandments that would suddenly become incumbent upon the proselyte to Judaism but not upon a God-Fearer because those things were already well understood within the synagogue and the Torah culture to which the Gentile believers belonged. However, notice that Paul does provide the God-Fearers with a list of prohibitions and a list of positive commandments just a few verses further into the chapter—Galatians 5:14–23. To Paul, those standards of behavior "are self-evident" (Galatians 5:19).

One thing not required of Gentiles, but certainly a commandment to Jewish believers and proselytes to Judaism, was circumcision itself. Circumcision is definitely a commandment in the Torah. If Gentile believers are not required to be circumcised, then the idea of "One Law," with identical obligation for both Jewish and Gentile believers, is flawed.

Beyond circumcision, Paul could have listed the specific signs given to Israel over and against the freedom granted to humanity as a whole: in general, the Levitical, Temple-based, and priestly commandments; the requirement to rest from production and creation on the Sabbath; the requirement to keep the festivals; and the requirement to keep the dietary laws given to Israel, not to mention specific ritual elements such as *tzitzit* and *tefillin* which identify as person as Jewish. In another passage, Paul singled out those same items as commandments for which Gentiles are not to be judged:

> Therefore let no one pass judgment on you in questions
> of food and drink, or with regard to a festival or a new
> moon or a Sabbath. (Colossians 2:16)

That is not to say that Gentiles should not be keeping the dietary laws, the festivals, the new moons, or the Sabbaths. It simply means that no one could judge Gentiles regarding those things because those aspects of Torah were not legally required of the Gentiles.

Beyond those specific Jewish responsibilities, Paul and the apostles believed that the rest of the Torah (with only a few exceptions such as priestly and sacrificial functions or signs given specifically to the Jewish people) was certainly incumbent upon Gentile believers.

The Torah itself makes such distinctions between Jews and Gentiles. For example, consider the conflicting dietary laws in Genesis 9:3 and Leviticus 11 or the law of the Passover sacrifice in Exodus 12:42–51.

Forfeiting Salvation?

Did Paul teach that proselytes will lose their salvation? Paul did seem to indicate that if a person denies the efficacy of Messiah's work for him and looks instead to becoming Jewish as the means by which he will merit the world to come, he places his soul in jeopardy. He said in Galatians 5:4, "You are severed from Christ, you who would be justified by the law; you have fallen away from grace."

Please do not misunderstand me or Paul. I am not suggesting that a conversion to Judaism means forfeiting salvation and neither is Paul. Halachic conversion certainly does not mean forfeiting salvation, and there are good reasons why a believer should undergo a conversion, such as intermarriage. Preferably, such a conversion should take place under Messianic Jewish auspices. So long as the person undergoing conversion holds fast to Yeshua, his salvation is secure with the Master.

On the other hand, if the believer undergoes conversion because he does not believe that Messiah is adequate for salvation, but instead that legal status as a Jew is adequate, then he has rejected Messiah's work. This may be why Paul considered it "a different gospel." If a person rejects the Master's work on his behalf, he has severed himself from Messiah in order to be justified by being a part of Israel: "You who would be justified by the law."

Paul said this person has fallen away from grace. Messiah is no longer of any advantage to him.

Neither Circumcision nor Uncircumcision

Paul was concerned about God-fearing Gentile believers taking on Jewish status (the works of the Torah) in order to earn salvation. He said, "For through the Spirit, by faith, we ourselves eagerly wait for the hope of righteousness" (Galatians 5:5). The "we ourselves" of whom he speaks are the Jewish believers of which he is one. In other words, "We Jews are trusting Messiah for righteousness. We are not relying on our status as Jews for exoneration and salvation."

Paul went on to state, "For in Christ Jesus neither circumcision nor uncircumcision counts for anything, but only faith working through love" (Galatians 5:6). He used the terms "circumcision" and "uncircumcision" to mean "Jewish" and "Gentile," respectively. Neither being Jewish nor being a Gentile is relevant to the issue of exoneration before God and salvation. In the Messiah Yeshua, the only thing that matters is the faithfulness of Messiah working through love, transforming us, and bringing us into the kingdom. Within this love, being Jewish and being Gentile loses relevance.

When Paul said neither circumcision nor uncircumcision count for anything, Christians often mistakenly assume that he completely dismissed the value of Jewish identity. We read this to mean that being Jewish no longer has any relevance. That mistaken reading has led to a smug, anti-Jewish arrogance on the part of Gentile Christians.

On the contrary, Paul did believe that being Jewish was important. He clarified that in two important passages from the Epistle to the Romans:

> Then what advantage has the Jew? Or what is the value of circumcision? Much in every way. To begin with, the Jews were entrusted with the oracles of God. (Romans 3:1–2)

> They are Israelites, and to them belong the adoption, the glory, the covenants, the giving of the law, the worship, and the promises. To them belong the patriarchs, and

from their race, according to the flesh, is the Messiah. (Romans 9:4–5)

Paul did not dismiss Jewishness at all. He only meant to say that the question of Jewishness is irrelevant in regard to salvation. To paraphrase his sentiments, he says, "We Jewish believers rely on Messiah, not our Jewishness, for salvation, so why would you God-fearing Gentiles decide that Messiah is inadequate for salvation and that you must become Jewish in order to merit it? Don't you realize that as far as salvation in the Messiah is concerned, the question of whether you are Jewish or Gentile is irrelevant?"

1 Corinthians 7:19

Galatians 5:6 sounds similar to another important passage from 1 Corinthians. When writing to the mixed community of Jews and Gentiles in the city of Corinth, Paul said:

> Neither circumcision counts for anything nor uncircumcision, but keeping the commandments of God. (1 Corinthians 7:19)

It sounds like the same thing that he wrote in Galatians 5:6. Yet some Messianic Gentiles have understood this to mean that a Gentile is obligated to all the commandments whether he is Jewish or not. In other words, being Jewish or not being Jewish is irrelevant. What counts is keeping the whole Torah. Is that what he is saying?

The passage comes in the context of Paul's rule for all the churches. According to that rule, Paul urged the Corinthian Gentiles not to become Jewish—the same message he gave the Galatians. At the same time, he told the Jewish believers of Corinth not to forsake the distinctive Jewish identity and live like Gentiles.

In other words, the uncircumcised Gentile believer should keep the commandments that apply to him; the circumcised Jewish believer should keep the commandments that apply to him. In his book *Paul and the Jewish Law*, Peter Tomson writes:

> Paul can only mean that gentiles should obey commandments also, although evidently not the same ones as Jews. He views Gentiles as included in the perspective of the

Creator which involves commandments for all ... The saying would then imply that whether or not one is a Jew does not matter before God, but whether one performs the commandments incumbent upon one does.[32]

Moreover, the Greek word translated as "commandments" in 1 Corinthians 7:19 is a word that Paul ordinarily uses to refer to the individual commandments, "where the individual commandment is distinguished from the whole law."[33] We can understand it to mean, "Keeping the commandments of God that apply to you is what counts." Certain commandments (such as circumcision) are not incumbent upon Gentiles.

All of God's laws are moral laws, but no one is morally obligated to every one of them. Men cannot keep the law of purification after childbirth. Women cannot be circumcised. Numerous commandments are incumbent upon men but not upon women. Some laws are only for the king of Israel. Others are only for the priesthood. Still others apply to judges, military officers, and so forth. Some laws apply only to "the native born" of Israel; others apply also to the proselyte.

Messianic Jewish scholar Dr. Mark Kinzer points out that by saying "circumcision is nothing and uncircumcision is nothing," Paul simply means that Jewish identity does not elevate the Jew above his Gentile brother in Messiah:

> [Paul] does not mean that one's identity, whether Jewish or Gentile, is thus irrelevant to one's relationship with God. If there are different commandments for Jews and Gentiles, different roles and responsibilities assigned by God, then circumcision or uncircumcision make a great difference in one's relationship with God. What Paul

---

32 Peter Tomson, *Paul and the Jewish Law* (Minneapolis, MN: Fortress Press, 1990), 271–272, cited in Mark Kinzer, *Post-Missionary Messianic Judaism* (Grand Rapids, MI: Brazos Press, 2005), 74.

33 Gordon D. Lee, *The New International Commentary on the New Testament: The First Epistle to the Corinthians* (Grand Rapids, MI: Eerdmans, 1987), 313 n30.

means is that circumcision and Jewish identity do not elevate the Jew above the Gentile before God.[34]

Keeping the commandments that the Bible has assigned to you is what counts before God—not your halachic, legal status in the eyes of men.

Why Keep the Jewish Commandments?

I am a Messianic Gentile, a modern-day God-Fearer practicing Messianic Judaism. Generally speaking, God-fearing Gentiles in the Messianic Jewish movement are Sabbatarian and Torah-observant, more or less. We have not fallen from grace, nor has the Torah severed us from Messiah.

We encourage all of God's people to join together and bear as many of the LORD's commandments as they are able. The Sabbath, the dietary laws, the festivals, are good, godly, and filled with blessing. Observing them is the natural path of biblical life. Gentile believers can find great blessing keeping even the commandments to which they are not obligated when they do so out of a heart of love for God, respect for his holy day, imitation of his holy Son, and identification with his people Israel.

The Torah is not a yoke of slavery for us, nor does it render Messiah of no advantage to us because we are not keeping the Torah or practicing Messianic Judaism in order to achieve status as sons of Abraham or in order to merit the kingdom of heaven. We rely on Messiah's faithfulness to bring the kingdom and to bring us into it. Concerns about losing one's salvation by keeping Torah are misplaced.

A more pertinent question would be, "If Gentiles are not obligated to do the same commandments as Jewish believers, then why would a Gentile elect to adopt commandments specifically incumbent upon Jewish people?" That is a fair question. It is not a question of salvation; it is a question of "why bother?" The answer to that has nothing to do with being saved or not. It has nothing to do with "is it a sin?" or not. It is about restoring something that was lost.

---

[34] Kinzer, *Post-Missionary Messianic Judaism*, 74.

The God-fearing Gentile believers in Galatia to whom Paul wrote, just like the Gentile believers in Magnesia to whom Ignatius wrote, were already part of a synagogue environment. They were already Sabbatarian. They were already living, for all practical purposes, a Jewish lifestyle. God-fearing Gentiles lived Torah lifestyles, not to the same extent as their Jewish co-religionists, but to a far greater extent than we do. Biblical Christianity was a sect of Judaism that included both Jewish believers and Gentile God-Fearers, both with their respective roles, but it was not a separate religion from the rest of Judaism.

Ignatius might have had a problem with it, but Paul had no problem with Gentile believers keeping the Sabbath, the festivals, and the dietary laws.

Contrary to what Ignatius of Antioch says, it is not absurd to speak of Jesus Christ with the tongue and to cherish Judaism at the same time. Where there is true biblical Christianity such as existed in the days of the apostles, there must also be Judaism. For Messiah is one, in whom every nation that believes, and every tongue that confesses is gathered unto God.

SERMON TWENTY-FOUR:
LED BY THE SPIRIT
(GALATIANS 5:7–26)

Paul argues that Gentile believers are not
"under the Torah," but neither are they
free from obligation to the Torah. They
are to walk according to the Spirit by
keeping the Torah's commandments.

In the Epistle to the Galatians, the Apostle Paul says, "If you are led by the Spirit, you are not under the law" (Galatians 5:18).

The meaning seems obvious. If you have become a Christian, you don't need to keep the Torah, the Old Testament laws, because now you are led by the Holy Spirit. On this basis, the majority of professing Christian teachers would argue that it is not necessary for Jewish believers to observe the Sabbath or the biblical dietary laws because, as Christians with the Holy Spirit, they are no longer under the Torah.

If a person has the Holy Spirit, he gets his directions straight from God, so he no longer needs the Torah. Each Christian becomes the new Moses of his own life, hearing straight from God.

That explanation, however, does not work for Messianic Judaism. Yeshua claimed that he did not come to cancel the Torah. The apostles and earliest Yeshua-believers were Jewish, "under the law," zealous for the Torah, *and* Spirit-led.

To discover what it means to be "led by the Spirit," we will work through the remainder of the fifth chapter of Paul's Holy Epistle to the Galatians.

A Little Leaven

Paul originally introduced the God-Fearers of Galatia to his gospel. The Gentiles in Galatia began with that message still burning in their hearts. They laid hold of the good news of forgiveness for sins, peace with God, inner transformation, and the anointing of the Holy Spirit. On fire for the Messiah, they ran like runners in a race. Paul said, "You were running well. Who hindered you from obeying the truth?" (Galatians 5:7).

The image is that of a runner in a race thrown off course and sent in the wrong direction when someone cuts in on him. The runner is still moving fast, but he is swerving in the wrong direction.

According to Paul, the Galatians no longer obeyed the truth because they accepted another gospel that said that only people legally Jewish qualified for salvation. He said, "This persuasion is not from him who calls you. A little leaven leavens the whole lump" (Galatians 5:8–9). In this case, the leavening agent was the false teaching of the influencers. The false teaching from just a few people spread through the whole community.

Having stated his case—his arguments, his proof texts, his analogies, and so forth—Paul concluded his argument against conversion:

> I have confidence in the Lord that you will take no other view than mine, and the one who is troubling you will bear the penalty, whoever he is. (Galatians 5:10)

Sympathy for the Influencers

Paul identified the influencers as "the one who is troubling you." Based upon what we have already learned, the influencers seem to have been proselytes themselves, Gentile believers who had undergone conversion to become legally Jewish, perhaps because they believed that salvation and the kingdom of heaven are reserved only for Jewish people. They underwent circumcision and conversion in order to achieve salvation. They believed that one cannot be a true disciple of Yeshua of Nazareth unless he takes on Jewish identity, and they spread that message in Galatia.

I have often thought about these influencers and how it would be easy to recreate their argument from Scripture. A person can assemble compelling proof texts from the Torah to defend the influencers' theological position. In Paul's day, a large contingency of the Jewish believers sided with the theology of the influencers. The influencers were not evil people. They were just wrong. They had a strong biblical argument based upon several seemingly logical conclusions. Their opinion was still vogue when it later showed up in Paul's own home-base community of Antioch. To settle the matter at that time, Paul had to bring the question before the apostles in Jerusalem for a final ruling (Acts 15).

Preaching Circumcision

Paul asked the Galatians, "If I, brothers, still preach circumcision, why am I still being persecuted? In that case the offense of the cross has been removed" (Galatians 5:11).

Paul admitted that he used to "preach circumcision." He used to believe and teach that only Jews are eligible for salvation, the resurrection, the kingdom of heaven, and the world to come. He used to teach that righteousness and Messiah are only for the Jewish people. He admits that this used to be his assumption and that he used to preach this message.

When did he "preach circumcision"? Before he was a believer? Not likely. Paul was not doing Gentile outreach before he was a believer. He must have taught circumcision in the early days of his faith. When he presented the gospel to Gentiles, he taught it along with the obligation of conversion. He was not the only one to "preach circumcision." All the apostles and all the believers taught that message. They taught salvation by faith in Messiah but only for Jewish people. The opinion did not begin to change until Peter's encounter with the sheet from heaven and Cornelius the Gentile (Acts 10). Since then, Paul became the champion of the new position regarding Gentiles, so much so that he referred to it as, "my gospel." In Galatians 5:11, he identified his message to Gentiles as the reason he endured persecution.

The Offense of the Cross

Paul's persecutors came from the rest of the Jewish community, the non-Messianic Jews, so to speak. They did not persecute him because he taught about faith in the suffering Messiah. That was a tolerable opinion, one to be argued, discussed, dismissed, or entertained, but not the main source of Paul's trouble with them. Paul's trouble with the Jewish community resulted from his radical, controversial message of Gentile inclusion.

Paul's controversial gospel brought Gentiles crowding into Jewish space. The influx of Gentiles brought a lot of problems, I am sure, and it was theologically offensive to the exclusivist, theological particularity of Judaism: "We are the chosen people! How can you tell all these Gentiles that they are also the sons of Abraham?" To most Jewish ears, Paul's gospel sounded absurd and offensive.

The offense of the cross in Paul's gospel was not the cross itself. Judaism did have room for a suffering Messiah within its theology. Today the cross is highly offensive to Judaism, but not so much in those days. The offense of the cross was the offensive notion that Gentiles could be reckoned as part of the people of God merely by the merit of the one who suffered on the cross. That message kept getting Paul kicked out, chased around, occasionally flogged, and at least once pelted with stones.[35]

This explains what he meant when he asked, "[If I] still preach circumcision, why am I still being persecuted? In that case the offense of the cross has been removed." In other words, "If I were to agree with the influencers and return to the position that says that, after becoming a believer, a Gentile needs to undergo circumcision and become Jewish, my message would no longer be controversial in the Jewish community."

---

[35] 2 Corinthians 11:25.

One Final Thought

Paul closes the whole argument with one last final thought on the subject. He says, "I wish those who unsettle you would emasculate themselves!" (Galatians 5:12).

He did not literally mean it; he was being sarcastic. It was a caustic poke at the influencers preaching circumcision. Paul said to the influencers, "Why don't you just go 'circumcise' yourself!" He was a little irritated.

A New Question

Paul's cynical emasculation comment concludes his whole argument about whether or not Gentiles need to become Jewish to be saved. His resolution to that question, however, raises a second question. If the God-fearing Gentile believers are not required to become Jewish, what are they required to do?

The Gentile believers might come to the conclusion that, since they do not need to be Jewish and "under the law," they do not need to obey the Torah at all. They might misuse this freedom. Freedom from the requirement to become Jewish is not freedom to sin.

Paul anticipated the problem. He answered, "For you were called to freedom, brothers. Only do not use your freedom as an opportunity for the flesh" (Galatians 5:13).

The problem that he faced amounted to a halachic (legal) question: "Being Jewish means being under the law. If Gentile believers are not Jewish and therefore not required to keep Torah by the same standard and with the same obligations as Jewish people, then what is the required Torah standard for Gentile believers?"

What is the Gentile believer's obligation to Torah and what is his relationship to Torah?

Start with the Basics

Paul established that a different standard of Torah applies to the God-fearing Gentile believers. He started to define that standard with the most fundamental teaching of Yeshua:

Only do not use your freedom as an opportunity for the flesh, but through love serve one another. For the whole law is fulfilled in one word: "You shall love your neighbor as yourself." (Galatians 5:13–14)

The Master taught that all the commandments hang on these two greatest commandments: Love God with all your heart, and love your neighbor as yourself. Love for one's neighbor is expressed in deeds of service: "Through love serve one another."

Neither Paul nor Yeshua dismissed the rest of the Torah. Paul did not say, "You don't have to worry about keeping any specific laws in the Torah just so long as you love one another." The point is that love is the fulfillment of the commandments, and keeping the Torah while hating one's neighbor is not keeping the Torah.

By citing this commandment first, Paul pointed his Gentile readers to a whole sphere of moral, ethical, interpersonal commandments of the Torah. In essence, he bound all of the "do-unto-others" commandments upon the God-fearing Gentiles. All those commandments hang upon the command to love one's neighbor, whether honoring one's parents, not charging a brother interest on a loan, giving to the poor, leaving the corner of the field, caring for orphans and widows, matters of tort law, justice, mercy, fairness—the vast majority of the Torah's commandments hang upon this one command to love your neighbor.

Paul laid a foundation of love as the fundamental commandment. He warned, "If you bite and devour one another, watch out that you are not consumed by one another" (Galatians 5:15). A community of faith is a difficult testing ground of love. More often than not, human beings turn against one another. They harbor malice and bitterness toward one another. They store up unforgiveness, and finally they emotionally consume one another. Paul told the Galatians to concern themselves, first and foremost, with overcoming that natural tendency and committing to one another in love.

Walk in the Spirit

Paul instructed the God-fearing Gentiles to "walk by the Spirit" so that they would not "gratify the desires of the flesh" (Galatians 5:16). He was giving the Gentile believers *halachah*, so to speak.

The word *halachah* means "walk." The rabbis used the term to refer to the legal way to "walk" out the commandments of the Torah. Invoking the same semantics, Paul instructed the God-Fearers to walk by the Spirit rather than gratifying the desires of the body. He alluded to a prophecy from the prophet Ezekiel about the Messianic Era:

> And I will give you a new heart, and a new spirit I will put within you. And I will remove the heart of stone from your flesh and give you a heart of flesh. And I will put my Spirit within you, and cause you to walk in my statutes and be careful to obey my rules. (Ezekiel 36:26–27)

The one who walks according to the Spirit will walk in God's statutes and obey his rules. Even though the Messianic Era has not yet arrived, Paul believed that disciples of Yeshua have already entered the kingdom, in part, and received a portion of the Holy Spirit as a down payment. Therefore, believers can begin to take advantage of this prophecy right now. They can opt to walk by God's Spirit and keep his laws.

Desires of the Flesh

Paul did not pit the Spirit against the Torah, as the usual Christian interpretation does. To Paul, the Holy Spirit and the Torah fit hand and glove. He did, however, contrast our human, physical inclination against the leading of God's Spirit.

> For the desires of the flesh are against the Spirit, and the desires of the Spirit are against the flesh, for these are opposed to each other, to keep you from doing the things you want to do. (Galatians 5:17)

Our normal, mortal human inclination is errant. In other words, human beings are naughty. From the days of Noah, "the LORD saw that the wickedness of man was great in the earth, and that every intention of the thoughts of his heart was only evil continually." Even when we do not want to sin, we still sometimes do sin. Our human bodies and minds rebel against God's authority. The believer who is trying to follow God has a war within his heart—a war within his mind, for his thoughts, for his speech, and for his behaviors.

Judaism refers to this warfare as the evil inclination struggling with the good inclination. Every human being has a desire to do good and a desire to do evil. Paul went further than that. In Paul's view, both the evil inclination and the good inclination are part of "the flesh," i.e., the human being. Paul taught that the whole human being is opposed to God. All the desires of the human being are in opposition to the desires of the Holy Spirit. And that is what confounds us in our attempts to grow, in our attempts to be better disciples, to improve ourselves, and to earnestly repent.

Led by the Spirit

Paul told the Gentiles to be "led by the Spirit." In other words, he told them to submit to God's desires: "But if you are led by the Spirit, you are not under the law" (Galatians 5:18). That is to say, if you obey God's desires for your life and for your behavior, you are not "under the law." It does not mean, "You are not under the authority of God's commandments." That's not how Paul uses the term "under the law." He used it to mean "halachically Jewish." But this reading does not make sense either:

> If you are led by the Spirit, you are not Jewish.

Yeshua, Paul, and all the apostles were "under the law" in that they were all Jewish. Paul was not saying that Jewish people and proselytes cannot be Spirit-led.

"Under the law" implies being obligated to the whole Torah as a Jew, but Paul was talking to Gentiles who were not "under the law." So he was saying, "Yes, it is true you are not under the law, but you are still led by the Spirit." In other words, he used the term "led by the Spirit" to mean that a Gentile has obligations to Torah, despite the fact that he is not "under the law."

The "Duh ... Obvious"

Which commandments of the Torah apply to Gentile believers? Paul answered, so to speak, with self-obvious examples. He says,

"It is self-evident." He felt that the answer to that question should be "duh ... obvious." Keeping Torah, led by the Spirit, meant rejecting the works of the flesh, and "the works of the flesh are evident" (Galatians 5:19). He provides a list with several examples. It is not an exhaustive list, but it contains some basic categories:

> Now the works of the flesh are evident: sexual immorality, impurity, sensuality, idolatry, sorcery, enmity, strife, jealousy, fits of anger, rivalries, dissensions, divisions, envy, drunkenness, orgies, and things like these.(Galatians 5:19–21)

Sexual Immorality: Paul censures "sexual immorality, impurity, sensuality." That invokes a lot of Torah. Those prohibitions invoke Leviticus 18, Leviticus 20, lots of laws from Deuteronomy—the Torah's prohibitions on adultery, fornication, prostitution, and promiscuity. That these prohibitions also apply to Gentiles was, in Paul's opinion, self-evident.

Idolatry: A generous amount of the Torah's prohibitions are concerned with idolatry. With that one word, Paul invoked many passages and commandments. In his opinion, it should be self-evident that those prohibitions apply equally to both Jews and to Gentile believers.

Sorcery: The Torah contains prohibitions on sorcery and occult arts in Leviticus 19, Deuteronomy 18, and elsewhere. In Paul's mind, it was self-evident that those prohibitions apply to the God-fearing Gentiles.

Enmity: Paul believed that Torah's prohibitions on "enmity, strife, jealousy, fits of anger, rivalries, dissensions, divisions, envy" apply equally to Jews and Gentiles, and he felt that much should be obvious to everyone. For example, the Torah prohibits hating one's brother, despising a stranger, striking one's mother or father, coveting a neighbor's possessions, carrying a grudge, and so forth. This is all Torah.

Drunkenness and orgies: In Roman culture, drunkenness and orgies were part of the nightlife options, much like going out to the clubs. Paul thought that it should be obvious that the debauchery of the pagan world is not acceptable for God-fearing Gentiles led by the Spirit. He pairs drunkenness with orgies because that was the reality of the Gentile world in which the Galatians were living. According to the rabbis, the Torah juxtaposes the laws about the test of the wayward wife (Numbers 5) next to the laws of the Nazirite (Numbers 6) to warn about the relationship between inebriation and sexual immorality.

The "works of the flesh" are all prohibitions that may be derived from the Torah. It is not an exhaustive list. Paul punctuated the list with the words "things like these." He used the short litany of sins as a way of saying, "It is not difficult to figure out what laws of Torah apply to the Spirit-led, God-fearing Gentile believer." The God-Fearer is not "under the law" as a Jewish person, but that doesn't mean he has no obligation to Torah. Most commandments that Paul considered as self-evident have a universal, moral, ethical core. The sages say something similar in the Talmud:

> The Torah states in Leviticus 18:4, "You shall fulfill my judgments." This refers to matters that, even if they had not been written down in the Torah, common sense would dictate that they should be written. They are idolatry, adultery, murder, robbery, and blasphemy." (b.*Yoma* 67b)

Fruit of the Spirit

When Paul spoke of walking by the Spirit, he was not referring to following after mystical visions and revelations. Instead, he provided a list of attributes that describe a Spirit-led person. The Gentile believer is not "under the law" in the same sense as a Jewish believer, but Paul thinks it obvious that the Gentile believer is beholden to all the moral character qualities derived from the Torah:

> But the fruit of the Spirit is love, joy, peace, patience, kindness, goodness, faithfulness, gentleness, self-control; against such things there is no law. (Galatians 5:22–23)

The term "fruit of the Spirit" can be understood as "evidence of the Spirit of God in one's life." Paul pointed out that the Torah has no prohibitions against the fruit of the Spirit.

Envying One Another

Having concluded his argument against conversion and having made his case that the Gentile believer remains beholden to the general principles and prohibitions of the Torah's universal morality, he reminded his readers that followers of Yeshua are to have "crucified the flesh with its passions and desires" (Galatians 5:24). If we have crucified the flesh with its passions and desires, we will naturally walk according to the Torah's morality. He said, "If we [Jewish and Gentile followers of Yeshua] live by the Spirit, let us also walk by the Spirit" (Galatians 5:25). If we have been spiritually reborn, then our lives should reflect that.

Finally, he warned against the petty nature of human jealousy and covetousness. The root of the problem, he deduced, is envy. He criticized those Gentile believers who had undergone a conversion to attain Jewish status. He said, "Let us not become conceited, provoking one another" (Galatians 5:26), which is what the influencers were doing. Taking pride in their Jewish status, they provoked the God-fearing Gentiles and pressured them to undergo the same conversion. Paul warned his readers not to be "envying one another," which is what the God-fearing Gentiles were doing as they envied the status of the Jewish believers and proselytes in the community.

Galatians

CHAPTER SIX

SERMON TWENTY-FIVE:

TORAH OF MESSIAH
(GALATIANS 6:1–10)

God-fearing Gentile believers are not
lawless free agents, but rather they are
held to a standard of Torah under the
Torah of Messiah: You shall love your
neighbor as yourself.

In the fifth chapter of Galatians, Paul addresses the inevitable
question which must arise from his gospel of Gentile inclusion.
If the Gentiles are not obligated to keep the Torah as Jews—that
is to say, not obligated to convert and take on the specific aspects
of Torah incumbent upon Jewish people—then what are they
obligated to do? What kind of obligation to Torah do God-fearing
Gentiles have?

Recap and Review: Torah for God-fearing Gentiles

In the fifth chapter of Galatians, Paul answered this question by
first pointing to the mitzvah, "You shall love your neighbor as
yourself" (Leviticus 19:18).

> For the whole law is fulfilled in one word: "You shall love
> your neighbor as yourself." (Galatians 5:14)

Our Master considered this to be the greatest commandment,
second only to the commandment to love God with all your heart,

soul, and mind" (Matthew 22:37). Yeshua taught that all of the Torah hung upon those two commandments. By citing this commandment first, Paul pointed his Gentile readers to a whole sphere of moral, ethical, interpersonal commandments of the Torah. In essence, he bound all of the "do-unto-others" commandments upon the God-fearing Gentiles. All those commandments hang upon the command to love one's neighbor, whether honoring one's parents, not charging a brother interest on a loan, giving to the poor, leaving the corner of the field, caring for orphans and widows, matters of tort law, justice, mercy, fairness—the vast majority of the Torah's commandments hang upon this one command to love your neighbor. Do unto others as you would have them do unto you, and that which is hateful to you do not do unto others.

Paul went on to say that the prohibitions binding upon the God-fearing Gentiles are duh … obvious: the acts of the flesh. He provided a sample list:

> "Sexual immorality, impurity, sensuality, idolatry, sorcery, enmity, strife, jealousy, fits of anger, rivalries, dissensions, divisions, envy, drunkenness, orgies, and things like these. I warn you, as I warned you before, that those who do such things will not inherit the kingdom of God." (Galatians 5:19–21)

He told the God-fearing Gentiles of Galatia to live by the Spirit, bearing the fruit of the Spirit, in keeping with what it says in Ezekiel: "I will put my Spirit within you, and cause you to walk in my statutes and be careful to obey my rules" (Ezekiel 36:27). Likewise, he said that the Torah never prohibits the fruit of the Spirit: "Love, joy, peace, patience, kindness, goodness, faithfulness, gentleness, self-control; against such things there is no law" (Galatians 5:22–23).

The Brother Who Transgresses

In Galatians 6:1, Paul continued to work toward answering the question, "What is the God-fearing Gentile's obligation to Torah?" He said, "Brothers, if anyone is caught in any transgression, you who are spiritual should restore him in a spirit of gentleness. Keep watch on yourself, lest you, too, be tempted" (Galatians 6:1).

When Paul spoke of those "who are spiritual," he meant those who were walking out the Torah in the leading of the Holy Spirit, as he has just finished explaining. In other words, "You who are leading godly lives with the fruit of the Spirit in your life (one of which is gentleness) shall restore him and correct him." This is a commandment directly from the Torah:

> You shall not hate your brother in your heart, but you shall reason frankly with your neighbor, lest you incur sin because of him. (Leviticus 19:17)

Just as the Torah says, the Gentile God-Fearer is not to hate his brother. He should correct him if he sins, but he should beware lest he incur sin because of him—"lest you, too, be tempted," Paul says.

Both Leviticus 19:17 and Galatians 6:1 rely upon a sense of community accountability to an established set of norms. Neither the Torah nor Paul envision a community in which each man defines what is permissible and what is not permissible. If Paul intended to tell the Gentiles, "Do not worry about the laws in the Torah. Just do whatever the Spirit leads you to do," then he had absolutely no basis to say, "If anyone is caught in any transgression, you who are spiritual should restore him." Under a "Spirit-led" economy of personal revelation, who could say whether a particular act constituted a transgression or not?

Moreover, if it were the case that the Gentile believers had no obligation to Torah, how could any of them be said to transgress at all? Transgress what? And how could those "who are spiritual" judge it as a transgression?

Galatians 6:1 assumes a community norm based upon the broad ethical principles Paul has already laid out.

Correcting a Brother

Rebuking and restoring the brother who has stumbled into some transgression is a dangerous thing to attempt. A few warnings are appropriate. The commandment applies only to serious moral failings. The only such example we have from Paul's congregations was a man who began a relationship with a woman who had been married to his father. It was a public matter, and one that was a clear violation of Torah's standards. That is the type of thing we are talking about here, not the nickel-and-dime sins of personality and personal shortcomings that everyone has all the time. If we were to rebuke one another for the latter, the fellowship of faith would be constantly rebuking one another. Everyone can see everyone's faults.

Paul's admonition does not call for pointing out faults; it calls for bringing correction when some serious transgression surfaces.

The commandment to correct a brother applies on a community level, and this is where Paul's concern was. The Master spells out the procedure for bringing such a rebuke in Matthew 18. It began with a private meeting, a private conversation, and progressed from there, bringing a second witness, and from there, bringing the matter to the elders. Again, this is only in the case of egregious, willful transgression. The commandment to rebuke a brother is not about hurt feelings. Lest we get the wrong idea, Paul said, "Bear one another's burdens, and so fulfill the law of Christ" (Galatians 6:2).

The Torah of Messiah

What did Paul mean by the term "law of Christ?" What was the "Torah of Messiah?" Christians sometimes teach that Yeshua replaced the Torah of Moses with the Torah of Christ. On the contrary, the "Torah of Messiah" is not a different Torah or a replacement of the Torah. Rather, it presented a re-prioritizing of the Torah under the Master's principle that all the commandments hang upon the two greatest commandments: love of God and love of neighbor.

> **The Torah of Messiah:** You shall love the Lord your God with all your heart and with all your soul and with all your mind. This is the great and first commandment. And a second is like it: You shall love your neighbor as yourself. On these two commandments depend all the [Torah] and the Prophets. (Matthew 22:37–40)

Love is the defining, fundamental principle of Yeshua's approach to Torah. The Torah of Messiah begins with love for God and love for neighbor. The rest of the commandments of the Torah hang upon those two loves. James the brother of the Master refers to it as "royal Torah."

> **The Royal Torah**: If you really fulfill the royal law according to the Scripture, "You shall love your neighbor as yourself," you are doing well. (James 2:8)

Carry Your Own Load

When we have to rebuke a brother or sister who has stumbled into some sin, the way to do so is in gentleness and love, bearing that person's burden like Messiah who took the chastisement for our sins upon himself. Paul warned his readers against regarding themselves as righteous. He warns us against comparing ourselves to others and thinking, "I am more spiritual than that guy. I'm more righteous than that person." Instead, he said, test yourself against yourself, not by comparing yourself with others:

> For if anyone thinks he is something, when he is nothing, he deceives himself. But let each one test his own work, and then his reason to boast will be in himself alone and not in his neighbor. (Galatians 6:3–4)

If after soberly measuring one's own spiritual progress, it turns out that a man really does walk in spiritual growth and obedience, then he has something to be happy about. He should not congratulate himself for being more godly or righteous than his neighbor, "for each will have to bear his own load" (Galatians 6:5).

This seems to contradict what he said about carrying one another's burdens. On the one hand, Paul said, "Carry each other's burdens;" on the other hand, he said, "Each will have to bear his own load." Do we carry each other burdens, or does everyone have to bear his own load? When it comes to loving one's neighbor and offering correction, carry his burdens. When it comes to measuring one's own personal righteousness and spirituality, do not compare yourself to others because each will have to bear his own load.

For example, you might look at your brother and you see that he is an ill-tempered, angry person. You might think, "I am glad that I am patient and kind, unlike this fellow who is always crabby and rude." That assessment is unfair because you are not him. If you were him, you would be wired just like him with the same genetic propensities, chemistry, neurological balance, social circumstances, nature, and nurture. Perhaps he has a natural, God-given predisposition to be cantankerous that you do not have. What you do not realize is that because he is naturally ill-natured, he actually has to work much harder at being kind than you do. For you it might be natural, and there is no real merit in doing what comes naturally. Even though everyone thinks of you as kinder, gentler, and nicer than him, he is actually the one who is making an effort to be nice, not you. His Father who sees what is done in secret will reward him for that effort, but for you there will be no reward because for you there was no commensurate effort. In the end, it turns out that your nasty friend was spiritually far ahead of you.

That is an example of what it means, "Each will have to bear his own load." You cannot compare yourself with others because everyone is different—apples and oranges, no two are the same. Adages like "give the benefit of the doubt" and "don't criticize a man until you've walked a mile in his shoes" apply.

Paul instructed us to carry each other's burdens. If I see my brother in sin, I must realize, first and foremost, that he carries a burden. Before I try to offer rebuke or criticism, I must first realize that I, too, have shortcomings. If I were him, I would have the same shortcomings he does. This is a basic principle of empathy and a paraphrase of the fundamental teaching of the Torah of Messiah: Love your neighbor as yourself; do unto others as you would have them do unto you.

Empathy is the ability to project oneself consciously into another's place and to see the world through another person's eyes—or at least attempt to do so.

Rebuke Yourself

Restoring a brother who sins is a delicate process because the Torah also forbids shaming and embarrassing others. The Master equated insulting someone with the sin of murder. The Talmud puts it just as succinctly: "He who publicly shames his neighbor is as though he shed blood" (b.*Bava Metzia* 58b).

In the Hebrew text of Leviticus 19:17, the verb "rebuke" is repeated for emphasis: *hocheach tochiach*. The Baal Shem Tov taught that the double expression teaches how one should approach the difficult commandment of criticizing others. First, a man should rebuke himself and recognize his own shortcomings so that he will feel empathy with the sinner. Only then is he ready to reprove his neighbor. This particular teaching of the Baal Shem Tov is in line with that of the Master: "First, take the log out of your own eye, and then you will see clearly to take the speck out of your brother's eye" (Matthew 7:5).

Love Bears All Things

Although it is a commandment to rebuke one's neighbor in order to restore them if they are caught in a transgression, real love also covers sin. For example, when Noah was drunk and naked, one son pointed it out to the others, but the other two sons covered their father's nakedness, walking backwards, not even looking on their father's shame. The Apostle Peter says, "Above all, keep fervent in your love for one another, because [as it says in Proverbs 10:12] 'Love covers a multitude of sins'" (1 Peter 4:8).

This is also a principle of love: Love looks the other way. Paul says, "Love bears all things" (1 Corinthians 13:7).

Reaping What We Sow

Paul reminded the Galatians of their obligation to support their Bible teachers: "One who is taught the word must share all good things with the one who teaches" (Galatians 6:6). "The workman is worth his hire," Yeshua says. This is a principle derived from the Torah, which called upon the people to collect a tithe to support the Levitical class. Likewise, the prophets received community support. Moreover, the Torah requires us to compensate a laborer fairly.

God Is Not Mocked

Paul knew that the ignorant and unstable would twist his words to their own destruction. He knew that some would take his declarations about Gentiles "not under the law" as a license for sin. Therefore, he warned his readers, "Do not be deceived: God is not mocked, for whatever one sows, that will he also reap" (Galatians 6:7).

To claim that we can sin and sin freely without consequence is to mock God, who judges the world in fairness and repays each man according to what he has done. Paul contrasted two types of sowing. One man "sows to his own flesh," and one man "sows to the Spirit."

The one who sows to the flesh does so by satisfying the desires of the flesh, committing the acts of flesh: immorality, impurity, sensuality, idolatry, sorcery, enmity, strife, jealousy, fits of anger, rivalries, dissensions, divisions, envy, drunkenness, orgies, and things like these. Because he has sown the deeds of the flesh, he will reap the corruption of the flesh, i.e., he will not attain the kingdom and the world to come. "I warn you, as I warned you before, that those who do such things will not inherit the kingdom of God" (Galatians 5:21).

The one who sows to the Spirit does so by planting the fruit of the Spirit: "love, joy, peace, patience, kindness, goodness, faithfulness, gentleness, self-control" (Galatians 5:22–23). "The one who sows to the Spirit will from the Spirit reap eternal life" (Galatians 6:8).

The one who truly belongs to the Master crucifies "the flesh with its passions and desires," lives "by the Spirit," and walks by the Spirit (Galatians 5:24–25). The one who does not will reap corruption. He will forfeit the resurrection of the righteous, and he will face the final judgment.

Paul offered this dire warning at the end of the epistle lest anyone be tempted to interpret his words as freedom from obligation to Torah. Although he had argued against the obligation for Gentile believers to undergo circumcision, to convert, and to take on the "works of the law" unique to Jewish people, he in no way exempted the God-Fearers from obedience to the universal statutes and principles of God's Torah.

He encouraged the Gentile believers, saying, "Let us not grow weary of doing good, for in due season we will reap, if we do not give up" (Galatians 6:9). The "due season" is the resurrection of the dead which he has promised they will share in along with Israel.

> So then, as we have opportunity, let us do good to everyone, and especially to those who are of the household of faith. (Galatians 6:10)

THE AUTOGRAPH
(GALATIANS 6:11–18)

Paul's closes the letter with a subscription in his own hand, in which he addresses the underlying motivations of the influencers and establishes a halachic ruling for his disciples.

All of Paul's letters come with a salutation at the beginning and a subscription at the end. In the subscriptions to his epistles, Paul ordinarily closes with a few concluding comments, a few greetings to people he knows, maybe a doxology or word of thanksgiving, maybe a request for prayer, and then a closing blessing of grace and peace.

A common feature in Paul's subscriptions is what scholars call his autograph. That is, at the end of each of his letters, he writes the subscription himself, in his own handwriting. Up until that point, a scribe has been writing on his behalf while he dictates, but he always closes his letters in his own handwriting. For example, consider the following subscriptions:

> I, Paul, write this greeting with my own hand. If anyone has no love for the Lord, let him be accursed. Our Lord, come! The grace of the Lord Jesus be with you. My love be with you all in Christ Jesus. Amen. (1 Corinthians 16:21–24)

I, Paul, write this greeting with my own hand. Remember my chains. Grace be with you. (Colossians 4:18)

I, Paul, write this with my own hand. (Philemon 1:19)

I, Paul, write this greeting with my own hand. This is the sign of genuineness in every letter of mine; it is the way I write. The grace of our Lord Jesus Christ be with you all. (2 Thessalonians 3:17–18)

Paul used his "autograph" as his sign of authenticity in every letter he sent. People could know that the letter came from Paul and was not a forgery of some type (as mentioned in 2 Thessalonians 2:2) if the subscription was written in his own hand.

The Autograph of Galatians

In Galatians 6:11, we find that Paul's autograph has begun. He writes, "See with what large letters I am writing to you with my own hand." Many have speculated about why Paul wrote with such large letters. Some have suggested that Paul had poor eyesight, perhaps a result of his Damascus-road blinding, so he wrote in large letters, but that is merely speculation. Far more likely, Paul closed his letter to the Galatians with large letters to draw attention to these last words and to emphasize their importance.

Perhaps if the book of Galatians had been an e-mail or a post on an internet forum, Paul would have unleashed the power of the Caps lock button, writing in all capitals, bold, and underlined as he entered the subscription. Paul says: "See with what large letters I am writing to you with my own hand. I HAVE THE CAPS LOCK BUTTON ON."

Paul's large letters call for careful attention to his closing remarks. He did not want the Galatians to miss what he had to say next.

A Good Showing in the Flesh

It is those who want to make a good showing in the flesh who would force you to be circumcised, and only in order that they may not be persecuted for the cross of Christ. (Galatians 6:12)

Paul dug at the motivation behind the influencers. He asked himself, "Why are they so eager to convince these God-fearing Gentiles to undergo circumcision and become Jews?"

What was driving the influencers to be so influential? What was behind their agenda?

Paul made a judgment about their motivations. He suggested that the influencers were only trying to "make a good showing in the flesh," that is physically in the eyes of men. Their concern was primarily a matter of prestige. They were concerned about how things looked in the eyes of the larger community. They wanted to influence the Gentile God-Fearers to go through full conversion in order to make themselves look good, "in order that they might not be persecuted for the sake of the cross of Christ."

In previous sermons, we have discussed the identity of the influencers and have come to certain, albeit, tentative conclusions. I understand the influencers to have been believers in Yeshua, and I think this verse proves that. If they were not believers, why would they have any concerns about being persecuted for the sake of the cross of Messiah? I have argued that they themselves were most probably Gentiles who, either prior to becoming disciples of Yeshua or after becoming disciples, went through full conversion themselves, and are now proselytes.

This explains their motivation for trying to influence other Gentile believers to also go through the same process. They were believers, and because they were Gentile proselytes, their relationship with the believing God-Fearers compromised their standing in the Jewish community. The rest of the Jewish community to which they belong viewed them with suspicion because of their close association with non-Jews. They were under enormous social pressure within the synagogue because of their faith in Messiah, and they were in danger of being persecuted for the cross of Messiah.

I have seen this happen a lot in Messianic Judaism. Suddenly the opinion of the non-Yeshua-following Jewish community becomes more important to a person than the fellowship of other believers. Ordinarily, it does not take long after that until the brother or sister renounces Yeshua as Messiah altogether. They did not want to suffer social stigmatization for the sake of the Master.

Recap and Review: Persecuted for the Cross

When we hear about people being persecuted for the cross, we assume that they were being persecuted because of their faith in Messiah. If that were the case, how would influencing the God-Fearers to also take on circumcision and Jewish status relieve that at all? The influencers were not renouncing faith in Messiah, nor were they asking the God-fearing Gentiles to do so. They were only pressuring them to undergo full conversion. Paul has already defined what he means by being persecuted for the cross in Galatians 5:11. In Paul's day, the primary stumbling block of the cross was not the cross itself. It was not the idea that the Messiah had to suffer and die. That was an acceptable, albeit, radical, interpretation of the suffering-servant passages in Isaiah 53 and several other prophecies. The cross had not yet come to be associated with an antithetical religion called Christianity.

In Paul's day and in his terminology, the offense of the cross was the offensive idea of Gentile inclusion. That is the message that always got Paul in trouble with the synagogue.

Paul recounted how he suffered, "with countless beatings, and often near death. Five times I received at the hands of the Jews the forty lashes less one. Three times I was beaten with rods. Once I was stoned" (2 Corinthians 11:23–25), not for preaching Yeshua as the Messiah but for preaching the opportunity of universal salvation for all who would believe, to the Jew first, but also to the Gentile. He was bringing Gentiles into the synagogues and giving them a place at the table as theological co-heirs with Israel, fellow citizens, and sons and daughters of Abraham by faith. That unpopular message invited heavy persecution.

The influencers sought to avoid persecution by washing their hands of Paul's gospel and by persuading the God-fearing Gentiles to undergo conversion. Paul explained, "They desire to have you circumcised that they may boast in your flesh" (Galatians 6:13).

If the believing proselyte could get the other Gentiles to also undergo full conversion, many social tensions and uncomfortable dynamics within the Jewish community would vanish. It would look good to the synagogue leaders and the whole community. It would uphold the theology of particularity and eliminate the awkward sense of dual relationship.

They Do Not Keep Torah

Paul remarked that the influencers did not keep the Torah themselves: "For even those who are circumcised do not themselves keep the Torah, but they desire to have you circumcised that they may boast in your flesh" (Galatians 6:13). Surely the proselytes were Torah-observant. As he said in Galatians 5:3, "Every man who accepts circumcision … is obligated to keep the whole Torah." That was Paul's view, and it's the Torah view, but it was not always the proselyte's view.

Paul was taking a shot at the "once-saved-always-saved," "once-baptized-always-saved," cheap-grace, "all-Israel-has-a-share-in-the-world-to-come" theology. We discussed this earlier in our studies in Galatians, but to review, consider Romans 2, where Paul wrote directly to what may have been believing Gentile proselytes in Rome. He could have addressed the same words directly to the influencers in Galatia:

> If you call yourself a Jew and rely on the law and boast in God, and know his will and approve what is excellent, because you are instructed from the law; and if you are sure that you yourself are a guide to the blind [i.e., the Gentiles], a light to those who are in darkness …You who boast in the Torah dishonor God by breaking the Torah … For circumcision [being Jewish] indeed is of value if you obey the Torah, but if you break the Torah, your circumcision [Jewishness] becomes uncircumcision [Gentile-ness]. (Romans 2:17–25)

People tend to trade institutional status for actual obedience and relationship with God. The Christian says to himself, "I'm a Christian, I've been baptized, so I have nothing to worry about." The same thing seems to have been happening among the proselytes in Rome and Galatia. After becoming Jewish, the proselyte slipped into a spiritual lethargy, as if to say, "I have already arrived at the goal."

New Creation

> For even those who are circumcised do not themselves keep the Torah, but they desire to have you circumcised that they may boast in your flesh. But far be it from me to boast except in the cross of our Lord Jesus Christ, by which the world has been crucified to me, and I to the world. For neither circumcision counts for anything, nor uncircumcision, but a new creation. (Galatians 6:13–15)

In regard to who will enter the kingdom, who will inherit eternal life, and who will attain the resurrection of the dead, Paul said, "Neither circumcision counts for anything, nor uncircumcision, but a new creation."

He was not dismissing being Jewish, nor was he saying that there is no such thing as being Jewish, nor did he mean that distinctions between Jews and Gentiles do not matter, nor did he imply that Israel is irrelevant now. He was only speaking about this matter of salvation and relationship with God. God does not show favorites when it comes to judging our souls. The only thing that matters is being a new creation.

Paul used the phrase "new creation" to allude to our mother *Chavah* (Eve), the wife of Adam, the first female. *Chavah* is the only new creation that God formed after the completion of the heavens and the earth. He formed her from Adam's flesh and presented her to him as a new creation: the first woman. "This is flesh of my flesh and bone of my bones," Adam said. Paul hinted at that story when he said, "Neither circumcision counts for anything, nor uncircumcision, but a new creation." For a female, physical circumcision or uncircumcision actually counts for nothing because it is an irrelevant question. Spiritually speaking, believers are new creations, formed of the body of Messiah. Regarding our salvation and standing with God, circumcision should be similarly irrelevant.

A Halachic Ruling

Paul issued this halachic ruling for his disciples: They were not to regard one another's status in the kingdom on the basis of whether they are Jewish or Gentile. Instead, the important thing was whether or not they had entered into Messiah and become a new creation in Messiah. The new creature is not primarily defined as Jewish, nor as Gentile, nor as male, nor as female, nor as slave, nor as free. Although it might be any of those things, those categories are not the central identity of the new creature. Instead, the new creature's central identity is that of a child of God.

This ruling was supposed to be *halachah* for Paul's congregations: "And as for all who walk by this rule, peace and mercy be upon them, and upon the Israel of God" (Galatians 6:16).

The Israel of God

Our English Standard Version of the Bible punctuates Galatians 6:16 according to the theological assumption that Paul would never refer to Gentile believers as Israel. Therefore, the ESV punctuates it as if Paul said, "As for all you Gentiles who walk according to this rule, peace and mercy be upon you, and also upon the Jewish people, the Israel of God."

Many modern interpreters hurry to make the same distinction because, ever since the early church, this verse has been understood to mean that the Jewish people are no longer the Israel of God, but from now on, only Christians are the true Israel of God. It feeds replacement theology where Christianity is the new eschatological Israel. As Justin Martyr explained to Trypho the Jew in the early second century:

> For we who have been led to God through this crucified Christ are the true spiritual Israel, and descendants of Judah, Jacob, Isaac, and Abraham. (*Dialogue* 11)

In other words, according to church interpretations, the Jews are no longer the Israel of God; now the Church is the true Israel. That is not what Paul was saying. Paul did not suggest that Christians have replaced the Jews as the new Israel. Neither was he making a distinction between Jews and Gentiles in Galatians 6:16. Instead, in

Paul's theology, Gentile believers have come to be, through association with Messiah, part of a larger Israel, the Israel of God.

The entire thrust of Galatians so far has demonstrated that Gentile believers are sons of Abraham by faith and that their uncircumcised Gentile status should not be a basis for exclusion. In Romans 11, in Ephesians 2, and elsewhere, Paul speaks inclusively of the Gentile believers, envisioning them as grafted in to Israel, fellow heirs, and citizens of the greater commonwealth of Israel. He uses the same kind of terminology here. He never refers to the Gentile believers simply as Israel, nor does he call them Jews. He includes the Gentiles in what he refers to as "the commonwealth of Israel," but he does not call them Israelites. He considers the Gentiles as wild branches grafted in to the nation, but he does not call them natural branches. And in 1 Corinthians 10:18, he distinguishes between the Corinthian Gentiles and the entity which he calls "Israel according to the flesh," i.e., natural, physical Israel.

The "Israel of God" is Paul's broader, eschatological community of Israel. He regarded his God-fearing Gentile believers as spiritually part of that broader Israel. It was not a flesh relationship, nor was it a literal or legal identity. Rather, it belonged to the realm of faith, a matter of the Spirit, and a part of the inheritance in Messiah.

Stigmata

> From now on let no one cause me trouble, for I bear on
> my body the marks of Jesus. (Galatians 6:17)

Paul claimed to bear "the marks of Yeshua" on his body. The Greek word translated as "marks," *stigmata*, is the same word from which we derive the English word "stigma." *Stigmata* refers to branding marks such as those with which a slave might be branded—markings or a tattoo that showed to whom you belonged. Think of it in English. Certain associations carry a stigma. You don't want to be stigmatized because then you will be associated with that undesirable thing.

Paul says he carried in his body the stigmata, the marks of Messiah. Some have made the nonsensical suggestion that Paul and the early believers had some sort of tattoo that they took to mark themselves as believers. That would be a violation of a Torah law.

Paul's *stigmata* (marks) were the wounds of Messiah, the marks left on his body from countless beatings, five times lashed, three times beaten with rods, once pelted with stones.

With those closing words, Paul told the Galatian Gentile believers, "Unless the influencers are willing to lay down their bodies for you, like I have laid down my body for you, do not let them give me any trouble." In another passage, writing to the Gentiles in Colossae, he said, "Now I rejoice in my sufferings for your sake, and in my flesh I am filling up what is lacking in Christ's afflictions for the sake of his body, that is, the church" (Colossians 1:24).

He closed the epistle with the benediction of grace: "The grace of our Master Yeshua the Messiah be with your spirit, brothers. Amen."

So ends the Holy Epistle of the Apostle Paul to the Galatians.

In the merit of studying these words, may the grace of our Master Yeshua the Messiah also be with us.

BIBLIOGRAPHY

Abegg, Martin. "Paul, 'Works of the law' and MMT," *Biblical Archae-ology Review* 20:06 (November-December, 1994): 11–12.

Arndt, William and J. Wilbur Gingrich. *A Greek-English Lexicon of the New Testament and Other Early Christian Literature.* Chi-cago: University of Chicago Press, 1979.

Dunn, James. *The New Perspective on Paul: Revised Edition.* Pea-body, MA: Eerdmans, 2008.

Eisenbaum, Pamela. *Paul Was Not a Christian: The Original Message of a Misunderstood Apostle.* New York, NY: HarperOne, 2009.

Fee, Gordon D. *The New International Commentary on the New Testament: The First Epistle to the Corinthians.* Grand Rapids, MI: Eerdmans, 1987.

Gaston, Lloyd. *Paul and the Torah.* Vancouver: University of British Columbia Press, 1987.

Hardin, Justin. *Galatians and the Imperial Cult: A Critical Analysis of the First Century.* Tübingen, Germany: Mohr Siebeck, 2008.

Kinzer, Mark. *Post-Missionary Messianic Judaism.* Grand Rapids, MI: Brazos Press, 2005.

Lancaster, D. Thomas. *Grafted In: Israel, Gentiles, and the Mystery of the Gospel.* Marshfield, MO: First Fruits of Zion, 2009.

Lapide, Pinchas and Peter Stuhlmacher, *Paul: Rabbi and Apostle.* Translated by Lawrence Denef; Minneapolis, MN: Augsburg Publishing House, 1984.

Le Cornu, Hilary and Joseph Shulam, *A Commentary on the Jewish Roots of Romans.* Baltimore, MD: Messianic Jewish Publish-ers, 1997.

Le Cornu, Hilary and Joseph Shulam. *A Commentary on the Jewish Roots of Galatians*. Jerusalem, Israel: Akademon, 2005.

Longenecker, Richard, *Galatians*. Volume 41 of Word Biblical Commentary; Dallas, TX: Word Books, 1990.

Nanos, Mark. "A Torah Observant Paul?: What Difference Could it Make for Christian/Jewish Relations Today?" *Christian Scholars Group on Christian-Jewish Relations* (June 2005). No Pages. Cited 21 March 2011. Online: http://www.marknanos.com/Boston-Torah-Obs-5-9-05.pdf.

Nanos, Mark. *The Irony of Galatians: Paul's Letter in First Century Context*. Minneapolis, MN: Fortress Press, 2002.

Nanos, Mark. *The Mystery of Romans*. Minneapolis, MN: Fortress Press, 1996.

Pines, Shlomo. *The Iranian Name for Christians and the "God-fearers"*. Jerusalem, Israel: Israel Academy of Sciences and Humanities, 1967.

Rudolph, David. "Paul's Rule for all the Churches," *Studies in Christian-Jewish Relations* 5:1 (2010).

Sanders, E. P. *Paul and Palestinian Judaism*. Minneapolis, MN: Fortress Press, 1977.

Stern, David. *Messianic Judaism: A Modern Movement with an Ancient Past*. Clarksville, MD: Messianic Jewish Resources International, 2007.

Tomson, Peter. *Paul and the Jewish Law*. Minneapolis, MN: Fortress Press, 1990.

Young, Brad. *Paul the Jewish Theologian: A Pharisee among Christians, Jews, and Gentiles*. Peabody, MA: Hendrickson, 2002.

Zetterholm, Magnus. *Approaches to Paul: A Student's Guide to Recent Scholarship*. Minneapolis, MN: Fortress Press, 2009.

Zetterholm, Magnus. *The Formation of Christianity in Antioch: A Social-Scientific Approach to the Separation Between Judaism and Christianity*. London: Routledge Tayor & Francis Group, 2005.